LATE
PERENNIALS

Volume 2
LATE PERENNIALS

ROGER PHILLIPS & MARTYN RIX

Assisted by Peter Barnes, James Compton & Alison Rix
Layout Jill Bryan & Gill Stokoe

MACMILLAN

Acknowledgements

We would like to thank James Compton for his help with the *Labiatae* and *Kniphofia*, Peter Barnes for the ferns, Brian Mathew for photographs of *Iris* and *Acanthus*, Martin Gardiner for the photographs taken in Chile, and Jacqui Hurst for help with the studio photographs.

Most of the specimens photographed in the studio came from the following gardens, and we should like to acknowledge the help we had from them, and from their staff:

The Crown Estate Commissioners at the Savill Gardens, Windsor Great Park; The Royal Botanic Garden, Edinburgh; The Royal Botanic Gardens, Kew; The Royal Horticultural Society's Garden, Wisley; University Botanic Garden, Cambridge; The Chelsea Physic Garden; Eccleston Square, London SW1; Washfield Nurseries, Hawkhurst, Sussex; Beth Chatto Gardens, Elmstead Market, Essex; Middelton House, Enfield, Middlesex; David Austin Hardy Plants; Kelways, Langport, Somerset; Green Farm Plants, Bentley, Hants; Goldbrook Plants, Hoxne, Suffolk; Hopleys Plants, Much Hadham, Herts.; Sandling Park, Hythe, Kent.

We would also like to thank the following for their help, encouragement, and for growing the perennials we photographed: Crynan Alexander, John D'Arcy, Claire and David Austin, Bill Baker, David Barker, Igor Belolipov, Alan Bloom, John Bond, Sandra Bond, Roger Bowden, Chris Brickell, Patty Carr, Beth Chatto, Duncan Donald, John Drake, Alec Duguid, Pamela Egremont, Jack Elliott, George Fuller, Martin Furness, Jim Gardiner, Martin Gardiner, Geoffrey and Kathleen Goatcher, François Goffinet, Tony Hall, Brian Halliwell, Carolyn and Alan Hardy, Harry Hay, Diana Hewitt, Nigel Holman, Tinge Horsfall, Christopher Lloyd, John Lloyd, David McClintock, Keith MacDevette, Deborah Maclean, John and Marisa Main, Brian Mathew, Philip McMillan Browse, Michael Metianu, Bob Mitchell, Shirley Moorhead, Mikinori Ogisu, Andrew Paterson, Roger Poulett, Charles and Brigid Quest-Ritson, Richard Rix, Ted Rix, Tony Schilling, Bill Smalls, Gordon Smith, Geff Stebbings, Elizabeth Strangman, Greta Sturdza, Harriot Tennant, Ann Thatcher, Piers Trehane, Rosemary Verey, Peter Yeo.

We would also like to thank Brent Elliott and the staff of the Lindley Library for all their help and patience during the preparation of the text.

First published in hardback 1991 by Pan Books
This edition published 1996 by Macmillan
an imprint of Macmillan Publishers Ltd
25 Eccleston Place London SW1W 9NF and Basingstoke
Associated companies throughout the world
ISBN 0 330 32775 5
Text © Roger Phillips and Martyn Rix 1991
Illustrations © Roger Phillips and Martyn Rix 1991

The right of Roger Phillips and Martyn Rix to be identified as the authors of this work has been asserted by them in accordance with the Copyright, Designs and Patents Act 1988.

9 8 7

A CIP catalogue record for this book is available from the British Library.

Printed by Toppan Printing Co, (Singapore) Pte. Ltd

Contents

Early spring in the woodland at the Pepsi-Cola Garden, New York, with *Dicentra spectabilis*, *Ajuga* and ferns

Gardening with Perennials

All the plants shown in this work will grow happily outside somewhere in Europe or North America, but gardeners on the east coast of America and in the colder parts of Europe have particular problems to contend with, different from those encountered near the milder west coasts of either continent. The possibility of intense cold in winter and extreme heat and humidity in summer restrict the range of exotic perennials that can be grown. Fortunately the North American native flora is very rich in perennials which naturally tolerate these extremes, and similar climatic conditions in parts of eastern Asia, Siberia and eastern Europe enlarge the range of plants from which to make a choice.

California and other Mediterranean regions, with hot, dry summers and mild winters, can grow a completely different range of plants; again the native floras of these areas are very rich. Plants from parts of the world with a Mediterranean climate, such as the Cape region of South Africa and southern Europe, and western Asia are among the most beautiful and diverse of any in the temperate zone. The advantage of growing plants which are adapted to climates with a summer drought is that they require little or no water from June onwards; indeed too much water in summer will often kill the plants altogether.

Many gardens in North America are made in clearings in woodland, not the primaeval forest of giant oaks, hickories and chestnuts which the first settlers found, but the trees which have grown up on abandoned farmland, often less than a hundred years old. Black cherry, ash, maples and Robinia, the Black Locust, are common examples of trees of secondary forest, and they often have greedy surface roots. Ash and lime and wild cherry, and the roots of a hedge, often produce similar problems in Europe.

Although this work deals only with herbaceous perennials, gardeners should not expect to achieve good results with perennials only. Bulbs and shrubs are the necessary companions of perennials in permanent and informal plantings; annuals, biennials and bedding plants are invaluable for filling gaps in borders, either where some perennial has died or not grown as it should, or where something has grown too well and had to be removed. The following notes put forward some ideas for gardeners in harsh climates, such as the east coast of America and California, and suggest plants suitable for situations they may find in their own gardens. Further very stimulating ideas, most wittily presented, can be found in *The Perennial Gardener* by Frederick McGourty (Houghton Mifflin, Boston 1989), who has his own perennial garden in Norfolk, Connecticut, and has long been a professional garden designer.

1. **Planting for beds around the house** The plants in this area want to be neat and rather low, with good foliage and leaf contrasts. Sweet-smelling flowers are especially valuable, so the scent can come into the house on warm days. Suitable plants for the shady side of the house are violets, the smaller Hostas, ferns like *Adiantum pedatum* or small forms of *Polystichum*, *Ajuga reptans*, *Helleborus*, *Dicentra*, especially the forms of *D. formosa* and *D. eximea*, and dwarf and striped grasses and sedges like *Hakonechloa macra* 'Aureola'. Dwarf shrubs are also suitable in this sort of planting; those with scented flowers in early spring, such as *Daphne* or *Sarcococca* are especially valuable, and there are *Daphne* species suitable for every climatic zone. Patches of intense colour in summer can be produced by shade-tolerant annuals like *Impatiens* or *Begonia semperflorens*, and earlier by smaller spring-flowering perennials, such as *Pulmonaria*. Early flowering bulbs like snowdrops, aconites, and *Chionodoxa* are happy when grown in places which are covered, in summer, by the leaves of Hostas and similar perennials.

For sunny borders around the house, plants of similarly compact habit are needed, but they have to be tolerant of great heat. The shorter bearded irises, *Dianthus*, and low grey-leaved plants are suitable, as is lavender in areas where it will thrive. Sun-loving lilies will be happy in this area, as they appreciate the protection for their young shoots. All these plants require good drainage, so special preparation may be needed on heavy soils. No lily is more suitable here than the common *Lilium regale*, which will prove long-lived in poor, stony soil, and is wonderfully scented on summer evenings.

2. **Perennial borders in lawns and island beds, in full sunlight** This is the area of the garden in which cultivars of popular herbaceous genera are appropriate; the borders can either be composed of collections of one genus, such as day-lilies, or contain a mixture of plants to give a long and effective display of colour. Large-flowered *Phlox*, border delphiniums, *Gypsophila paniculata*, paeonies, lupins, and other strong-growing perennials can be grouped in colour schemes to give either a powerful or subdued effect. Soils will need to be rich and well-manured and the plants will mostly need staking against heavy rain and summer storms. The essential feature of an island bed is that it can be admired from any direction. When it is being planted, the height of the plants must be carefully checked, so that the tallest are in the middle of the bed, and there is a gradient to the shortest around the edges.

3. **Perennials on banks and rock outcrops** In many gardens among undulating areas of lawn or mown grass, are outcrops of rock or rocky banks which can be ugly if left bare. A large clump of a perennials alongside the rock will give it a sense of purpose, while the rock itself provides a good background for the perennial. If the surrounding soil is moist, a large clump of *Aruncus* makes a fine feature, while a tall bearded Iris will be suitable in a dry

position. The essential characteristic of a plant for this position is that it should be large and have a bold habit of growth. Irises are also suitable to clothe a rocky bank in the sun or even under slight shade of trees, as long as they get some direct sun during the day.

4. Borders along stone or brick walls and fences, hedges or shrubs These borders are best kept narrow, less than two metres wide, and they have the advantage of a definite background. I have seen attractive examples of this type of border planted entirely with one species or cultivar such as one of the smaller-flowered day-lilies, with a long flowering season, like 'Hyperion', or 'Golden Chimes'. Japanese anemones are suitable for a shady bed for late flowering; they can be mixed with early flowering bulbs and ferns, or with an early-summer flowering perennial such as *Aquilegia*. A low border on the north side of a wall can be planted with a combination of ferns and hostas; the golden and striped varieties will brighten what might otherwise be a dark area.

Where the border is backed by a hedge, or a bank of shrubs, it is advisable to leave a gap between hedge and border, both for weeding and so that the plants at the back of the border do not suffer from root competition. If tree roots are troublesome, it may be necessary to make a barrier to keep them at bay.

5. The woodland edge In this case the border forms the visual transition between the grass and the woodland. The bed should be rather narrow and sited so that its background is the shade under the trees; therefore it will often be on the north side of the wood, and the plants will be seen against the light. In this position plants with white, airy flowers create a beautiful effect from a distance, and dark reds and purples are lit up by the sun. White Astilbes, *Lysimachia clethroides*, *Thalictrum dipterocarpum*, *Physostegia virginiana* 'Alba', *Phlox carolina* 'Miss Lingard', *Campanula lactiflora*, *Papaver bracteatum* 'Goliath' and *Aquilegia atrata* are all striking in this sort of position.

6. Swamp gardens, lakeside beds, the edges of streams or creeks, and places with poorly-drained soil Soils which are wet and poorly drained are unsatisfactory for the majority of ordinary perennials, but there are numerous beautiful plants whose natural habitat is swampy, and which thrive in or even require such conditions. Many irises, *Lythrum*, *Caltha*, *Trollius*, *Rodgersia*, *Lobelia*, and many others need wet soils. Bog primulas, *Meconopsis* and other Himalayan plants are suitable in cooler climates.

Soils which are waterlogged in winter but dry out in summer pose a greater problem. *Iris spuria* grows naturally in this type of position, and a collection of its cultivars would be suitable, provided that the place is in full sun.

7. Perennials in woodland The native American flora is particularly rich in woodland perennials. Many of the most beautiful, such as the Virginian bluebell *Mertensia virginiana*, are spring flowering, and drifts of *Phlox stolonifera* in its various colour forms are equally lovely. There are, however several which flower later in the summer and will make a fine feature in a shady clearing; *Veratrum*, *Cimicifuga*, *Campanula*, and *Telekia* are all large perennials for this position in the garden, and they can be preceded by spring flowering bulbs such as snowdrops, *Scillia*, *Erythronium*, *Chionodoxa* and *Aenemone blanda*.

8. Meadow and prairie gardens The formation of a prairie or meadow garden may at first thought appear easy, but in practice it is often difficult to achieve the necessary degree of soil fertility, so that the ranker herbs and coarse grasses do not smother the more delicate flowers. The drier and poorer the site, the easier it is to establish an attractive meadow, and large numbers of one plant produce a fine effect. American *Asclepias tuberosa* and *Salvia campanulata* are lovely in drifts, and *Camassia* and *Fritillaria meleagris* can be planted in the wetter areas. European 'weeds' such as Queen Anne's Lace, Ox-eye Daisies and Chicory, with *Salvia pratensis* may prove easier to establish. Larger perennials such as Goldenrod, *Vernonia*, *Eupatorium* and Asters can make a fine show in the early autumn, and will do best in somewhat swampy ground.

9. Dry Mediterranean gardens The examples mentioned above apply mostly to gardens in northern Europe and on the east coast of America, or to areas which have rain in summer, and a freezing winter. As mentioned above, a different range of plants can be grown in California and southern Europe, and many are suited to parts of the garden which are not irrigated, or watered only occasionally in the summer. American shrubs such as *Ceanothus* are very good in these areas, and perennials such as *Romneya*, *Zauschneria*, *Yucca* and various *Penstemon* species will grow equally well and produce colour in summer. There are many attractive perennials from the European Mediterranean which grow as easily; *Acanthus*, *Phlomis*, *Origanum*, *Paeonia*, *Erigeron*, *Iris* and *Euphorbia* all contain good species tolerant of summer drought and heat.

Late summer in a woodland clearing in the Leonard J. Buck Garden, New Jersey with *Veronia novaboracensis* and Goldenrod (*Solidago*)

Melica
altissima

Carex
comans

Carex
muskinguemensis

Carex elata
'Aurea'

Phalaris
arundinacea
'Picta'

Milium
effusum

Grasses and sedges collected at Wisley, 15 May. ¼ life size

Melica altissima L. **'Purpurea'** (*Graminae*)
Native of E Europe from Czechoslovakia and
Russia southwards to E Turkey and C Asia,
growing in scrub and on rocks by streams,
flowering in May–August. Plant forming loose
clumps of stems to 2.5m. Leaves to 15mm wide,
flat. Flowering panicle 10–20cm, dense or open
at the base. Spikelets 7–10mm long. For
woodland soil and partial shade or sun. Hardy
to −20°C.

Milium effusum L. **'Aureum'** (*Graminae*)
Bowles' Golden Wood Millet Grass   Native
of Europe, from the British Isles south to Spain
and east to Siberia and the Himalayas, and of
North America from Maine to Ontario, south to
Massachusetts and Illinois, growing in damp
woods, flowering in June–July. Plant tufted
from a thin rootstock, short-lived. Leaves
5–10mm wide, golden yellow in 'Aureum',
which comes true from seed. Stems 50–120cm,
with the flowering part 10–25cm, pyramidal
with often deflexed branches. Spikelets 2–3mm.
An elegant and beautiful grass for a shady
position. The leaves of the golden form are
beautiful in mild winters. Hardy to −20°C or
less.

Panicum virgatum L. **'Rubrum'** (*Graminae*)
Switch Grass   Native of North America, from
Maine west to Saskatchewan, south to Florida,
Arizona and Costa Rica, and in the West Indies,
growing in both wet and dry places, flowering in
August–September. Plant with creeping
rhizomes and upright stems to 1.2m. Leaves
6–12mm wide, red in late summer in 'Rubrum'.
Spikelets 3–5mm long. For any good soil in full
sun. Hardy to −20°C or less.

Phalaris arundinacea L. var. **picta** **'Picta'**
(*Graminae*)   Native of Europe, including the
British Isles, where it is very common,
eastwards to Siberia, and North America, south
to New Jersey and to Colorado, growing in wet
places and shallow water, flowering in June–
July. Plant with creeping rhizomes. Stems
upright 60–200cm. Leaves *c.*10mm wide.
Spikelets *c.*5mm, crowded. A fine plant for any
large border, growing well in normal garden
soil. Hardy to −20°C or less.

Stipa gigantea Link (*Graminae*)   Native of
C & S Spain and Portugal, growing on dry,
rocky slopes at *c.*1500m, flowering in April–
May. Plant forming massive clumps of tough
but floppy leaves. Stems to 2.5m tall. Awns
2–12cm long, scabrid. For well-drained, dry,
sandy or chalky soil. Hardy to −15°C, but likely
to be damaged by colder winters, especially on
heavy soils. Also in danger from slugs, which
eat the soft bases of the shoots.

Stipa pulcherrima C. Koch   Native of most of
Europe, from C France and N Germany
eastwards to Sicily and S Russia, the Caucasus
and the Kopet Dağ, growing in steppes and dry,
rocky and stony meadows, flowering in June–
August. Plant forming small clumps. Leaves lax
but scabrid and tough, 1mm in diameter.
Flowering stems to 1m, with a short panicle
10–15cm long. Awns to 50cm with a short
corkscrew base and long seta with silky hairs to
7mm long. Hardy to −25°C, if dry. See also
p.170.

Panicum virgatum 'Rubrum'

Carex comans Berggren **'Pale-Green Form'**
(*Cyperaceae*)   Native of New Zealand, growing
in pastures, where it is a common weed, and in
damp places at up to 1300m. Plant forming
dense tufts of fine lax leaves to 1mm wide and
slender stems to 70cm long, usually green but
whitish in this form shown here, or brownish.
An unusual plant, like a mop of long, pale hair.
Hardy to −10°C.

Carex elata 'Aurea'   See p.10.

Carex muskinguemensis Schweinitz   Native
of E North America from Ohio to Manitoba
south to Missouri and E Kansas, growing in
moist woods and scrub, flowering June–August.
Plant with a creeping rhizome and upright
stems to 60–90cm. Leaves to 5mm wide. Spikes
16–26mm long. For any moist soil in sun or
partial shade. Hardy to −20°C.

Stipa gigantea with *Cotinus coggygria* 'Folii Purpureis' at Withersdane Hall, Wye, Kent

Phalaris arundinacea 'Picta' at Cedar Tree Cottage, Sussex

Milium effusum 'Aureum' (young leaves in spring)

Stipa pulcherrima

9

Carex elata 'Aurea' at Longstock Park Gardens, Hampshire

Carex elata 'Aurea'

Carex pendula

Cyperus longus by the Seven Acres Lake, Wisley

Carex elata All. **'Aurea'** syn. *C. stricta* Good. (*Cyperaceae*) **Bowles' Golden Sedge**   Native of most of the British Isles and Europe to North Africa and the Caucasus, growing in shallow, usually alkaline water and wet fens, flowering in April–June. Plant forming clumps about 1.5m across. Stems to 1.2m tall, slightly arching. Leaves 2–6mm across. Male spikes 1–2; female spikes 2–4, 30–70cm long, erect in fruit. The clone usually grown is 'Aurea', said to have been found by E. A. Bowles in the Norfolk Broads, or perhaps Wicken Fen, near Cambridge. The clumps are bright in spring, greener in late summer. *C. flava* L. with stems up to 50cm tall and short spikes of deflexed fruit is sometimes sold in place of *C. elata* 'Aurea'. It grows in similar habitats in N Europe and North America.

Carex pendula Hudson   Native of most of the British Isles and Europe, except the far north, south to North Africa and Turkey, growing in woods and damp shady places, usually on heavy soils, flowering in April–June, fruiting in July–August. Plant forming large clumps about 2m across. Flowering stems arching to 150cm. Leaves 15–20mm wide, deep green. Female spikes 4–5, pendulous, 7–16cm long, with numerous small fruits. Hardy to −25°C. An elegant, evergreen, large plant for a partially shaded position. The male spikes (shown here) are conspicuous in flower in spring; the female hanging spikes in fruit in summer.

Carex pseudocyperus L. **Cypress Sedge**
Native of most of Europe, including the British Isles, and across Europe and N Asia to Japan; of North America, from Nova Scotia west to Saskatchewan and south to Connecticut and Michigan and of New Zealand (South Island), growing on the edges of rivers, canals and lakes and in wet bogs, flowering in June–August. Stems upright to 1m tall; leaves 5–10mm wide, longer than stems. Male spikes 1; female spikes 3–5, nodding, 2–6cm long, 8–12mm in diameter, the fruits with a long, pointed beak. Beautiful for the edge of a pond or lake.

Cyperus longus L. (*Cyperaceae*) **Galingale**
Native of Europe, from England, where it is confined to the south from Cornwall and Pembrokeshire to Kent, to Hungary and southwards to Spain and Portugal and east to Turkey and SE Russia, growing in marshy places and shallow water by ponds, often under trees, flowering in July–September. Stems forming loose clumps to 150cm. Leaves 2–10mm wide. Spikelets 4–25mm × 1–2mm, dark brown or reddish. An elegant and graceful plant for the waterside.

Glyceria maxima (Hartm.) Holmberg **'Variegata'** (*Graminae*) **Reed Grass**   Native of Europe, from the British Isles, where it is common, to S France and east to the Caucasus, C Asia and NW China, growing in shallow water by ditches, canals and slow rivers, flowering in July–August. Plant with a creeping rhizome and erect stems to 2m. Leaves to 2cm wide. Spikelets 5–8mm long, narrowly ovate, dark brown, rather hard. Hardy to −20°C.

Helictotrichon sempervirens (Vill.) Bess. ex Pilg. (*Graminae*)   Native of SE France and NW Italy, in the SW Alps, growing on rocky and stony hillsides, flowering in June–July. Plant forming dense clumps of upright, blue-grey leaves to 60cm. Flowering stems to 1.2m, the branched inflorescence with 30–55 spikelets, each 10–14mm long. For a sunny position in well-drained soil. Hardy to −15°C.

Imperata cylindrica 'Rubra'

Scirpus lacustris subsp. *tabernaemontani* 'Zebrinus'

Lymus arenarius (L.) Hochst. **Lyme Grass**
Found wild on sand dunes in the south of
England and S Europe, it has broader, equally
blue leaves to 1cm or more wide, 150cm long,
but has a spreading invasive root system.

Imperata cylindrica (L.) Beauv. **'Rubra'**
(*Graminae*)   Native of China, Korea and Japan,
growing in waste places at low altitudes,
flowering in May–June. Plant forming a tuft of
flat upright leaves 20–50cm tall, 7–12mm wide,
a beautiful red in 'Rubra'. Inflorescence 30–
80cm, with hairy nodes, and silvery, spike-like,
erect panicles of spikelets 3.5–4.5cm long, with
a tuft of silvery hairs. One of the most distinct
and striking of all small ornamental grasses. For
sun or partial shade. Hardy to −15°C.

Miscanthus sinensis Anderss. **'Zebrinus'**
(*Graminae*)   This form of *Miscanthus sinensis*
(see p.229) has been long cultivated in Japan.
The unusual horizontal bands of variegation are
also seen in *Scirpus* 'Zebrinus'.

Scirpus lacustris L. subsp. **tabernaemontani**
(C.C. Gmel.) A. & D. Love **'Zebrinus'** syn.
Schoenoplectus tabernaemontani (C.C. Gmel.)
Pallas (*Cyperaceae*)   Native of Europe, from
the British Isles, south to Portugal and east to
Siberia and NW China, in Sinjiang, growing in
streams, canals, ditches, ponds and bogs,
especially near the sea, flowering in June–July.
Plant with a creeping rhizome. Stems rather
slender to 1.5m tall, glaucous and banded in
'Zebrinus'. Spikelets 5–6mm long. A striking
plant for shallow water. Hardy to −25°C or less.

Scirpus sylvaticus L. **Wood Club Rush**
Native of Europe, from the British Isles, east to
the Caucasus, Siberia, NW China and North
America, from Maine and Michigan south to
Georgia, growing in wet places by streams and
in open woods, flowering in June–July. Plant
with a creeping rhizome and arching stems to
1m. Leaves green, flat, 2cm wide. Spikelets
3–4mm long. A graceful plant for the waterside
or bog garden. Hardy to −20°C or less.

Helictotrichon sempervirens

Scirpus sylvaticus

Carex pseudocyperus

Glyceria maxima 'Variegata'

Miscanthus sinensis 'Zebrinus'

Eriophorum vaginatum near Aviemore

A moss garden at Ryoan-ji, Kyoto, Japan

Carex fraseri Andr. (*Cyperaceae*) Native of E North America, in SW Virginia, West Virginia, E Tennessee and North Carolina, growing in moist woods, flowering in May–July. Plant forming dense clumps. Stems 15–45cm long. Leaves 2.5–5cm wide, deep green, evergreen. Spike terminal, solitary, male at apex, with white female fruits below. For moist soil and shade. One of the most striking sedges with broad leaves and white fruits. Some other American sedges, such as *C. platyphylla* Carey, have equally broad leaves, but several spikes, the male and female usually separate.

Carex morrowii Boott **'Evergold'** Native of Japan in W Honshu, Shikoku and Kyushu, growing in woods at low altitudes, flowering in April–May. Plant forming dense clumps, to 1m across, of evergreen leaves, to 9mm wide, with a pale yellowish or white centre in 'Evergold' or a narrow white edge in 'Variegata'. Flowering stems 20–50cm, with 1 terminal male spikelet and 2–4 female spikelets to 2.5cm long. Fruits sparsely puberulent. For moist, leafy soil in shade or partial shade. Hardy to −10°C. 'Evergold' is sometimes listed under *C. oshimensis* Nakai.

Carex ornithopoda Willd. **'Variegata'** From Europe, is superficially similar to *C. morrowii*, but has narrower leaves to 4mm wide, and small female spikes 3–10mm long. It is suitable for dry, sunny places on sandy or chalky soils.

Eriophorum vaginatum L. (*Cyperaceae*) **Sheathing Cottongrass** Native of N Europe, from Scotland and Ireland, southwards to Spain, N Italy and Greece and eastwards to Siberia, and N Japan, growing in peaty wet bogs, mainly in the mountains, flowering in April–May, and fruiting (shown here) in May–June. Plant forming dense clumps. Stems 30–50cm. Leaves very narrow, to 1mm wide. Flower heads solitary, with white silky bristles *c.*2.5cm long. A beautiful plant for a moist peaty

Leucobryum glaucum

Hakonechloa macra 'Aureola'

Luzula nivea 'Schneehaschen'

Luzula sylvatica at the base of a beech hedge, Kildrummy Castle, Aberdeenshire

Carex ornithopoda 'Variegata'

Carex fraseri

Carex morrowii 'Evergold'

position, to associate with heathers. *E. scheuchzeri* Hoppe, from N Europe, North America and the Alps, is similar, but less densely tufted, and with bristles up to 3cm. *E. callithrix* Cham., from Newfoundland and Alaska, and south to Massachusetts and Wisconsin, has similar loosely sheathing stem leaves. *E. angustifolium* Honck., with several nodding flower heads, has long creeping rhizomes; it is the common cottongrass in N Europe.

Hakonechloa macra Mak. ex Honda **'Aureola'** (*Graminae*)   Native of Japan, in the Tokaido district of SE Honshu, growing on wet cliffs in the mountains, flowering in August–October. Plant with shortly-creeping rhizomes forming dense clumps. Stems arching, 40–70cm long. For moist, peaty soil in shade or partial shade. Hardy to −15°C. A beautiful grass for the front of a cool border.

Leucobryum glaucum (Hedw.) Schp. (*Dicranaceae*)   Native of Europe, including Britain, of Asia and of North America, growing

on open woodland, in bare acid woods, or even as an epiphyte on trees in wet areas. A moss, forming rounded hummocks to 20cm across, then becoming flattened, pale green when fresh, white when dry. Individual shoots 20cm long, *c*.6mm across, with crowded scale-like leaves. For damp or wet, very acid soil in shade or a cool position in the open. Mosses are rarely planted in European gardens, though they may be tolerated or even encouraged, and good examples of *Leucobryum* 'lawns' can be seen at Knightshayes Court in Devonshire, and at the Savill Gardens, Windsor. In Japan, however, moss culture is an important aspect of gardening. They are especially useful in forming neat, slow-growing, green ground-cover in places where it is too dark for grass to survive. The modern gardener has one great advantage when growing moss: it is not killed, and even seems positively to be encouraged, by paraquat, so it becomes easy to grow, requiring no mowing or fertilizer, and hardly increasing in height. Other mosses worth encouraging are *Mnium hornum* and various *Polytrichum* species.

Luzula nivea (L.) DC. **'Schneehaschen'** or **'Snow Leveret'** (*Juncaceae*)   Native of N France south to the Pyrenees, C Italy and N Yugoslavia, growing in subalpine woods, scrub, and shady slopes, flowering in June–July. Plant forming loose tufts to 60cm across, spreading by stolons. Flowering stems to 60cm. Leaves 3–4mm wide, with scattered white hairs. Flowers 5mm long. For a hardy, moist position, and leafy soil. Hardy to −20°C.

Luzula sylvatica (Huds.) Gand. syn. *L. maxima* (Reich.) DC.   Native of Europe, from the British Isles south to Spain and eastwards to Turkey and the Caucasus, growing in damp acid woods, and on rocky slopes in moorland, flowering in May–June. Plant forming dense clumps of soft, bright leaves *c*.12mm wide. Flowering stems 30–80cm, arching. Flowers in clusters of 3–4, dark brown, 3–3.5mm long. For a shady position, or a cool peaty place in full sun. Hardy to −20°C. 'Marginata' has a narrow white margin to the leaf, but is less beautiful than the wild type.

Clematis integrifolia at Harry Hay's, Surrey

Clematis integrifolia 'Hendersonii'

Clematis integrifolia f. *rosea*

Anemonopsis macrophylla Sieb. & Zucc.
(*Ranunculaceae*)   Native of Japan, in C
Honshu, growing in woods in the mountains,
flowering in July–September. Plant with a thick
rootstock and upright stems to 80cm. Leaves
much divided, 2- to 3-ternate, with leaflets
4–8cm long. Flowers with 7–10 sepals, and
about 10 petals, nodding, 3–3.5cm across. For a
very sheltered and shady position and leafy, acid
soil. Hot, dry wind soon causes the leaves to die,
although the root may survive. Hardy to −15°C.

Clematis addisonii Britton (*Ranunculaceae*)
Native of E North America, from S West
Virginia and North Carolina, possibly to
Tennessee, growing on scrubby slopes,
flowering in May–June, in July in cultivation.
Plant with several annual climbing stems to 2m.
Leaves obtuse, bluish green, ovate, sessile or
the uppermost stalked with a few tendrils,
5–10cm long. Flowers 1.8–3cm long with thick,
fleshy sepals. For any good soil in sun or partial
shade. Hardy to −15°C.

Clematis texensis at Harry Hay's, Surrey

Anemonopsis macrophylla

Clematis fremontii

Clematis recta f. *purpurea*

Clematis addisonii at Harry Hay's, Surrey

Clematis × *bonstedtii* 'Wyevale'

Clematis × *jouiniana* 'Praecox'

Clematis × **bonstedtii** hort. **'Wyevale'** syn. *C. davidiana* 'Wyevale' *C.* × *bonstedtii* is the hybrid between *C. heracleifolia* 'Davidiana' and *C. stans*; 'Wyevale' was formerly considered a selection of 'Davidiana' and is named after the nursery in Hereford. The flowers of 'Wyevale' are a good pale sky-blue, well scented, *c*.4cm across. Stems upright to 1m, requiring staking. Hardy to −20°C or less. Other varieties, and *C. stans* itself, have more tubular, paler flowers; see *Shrubs* p. 199.

Clematis fremontii S. Wats.   Native of North America, in Kansas, Nebraska and Missouri, growing on limestone hills, flowering in April–May. Plant with hairy stems 15–45cm tall, from a stout rootstock. Leaves sessile, glabrous except on the veins and edges; flowers *c*.2.5cm long. For well-drained soil in full sun. Hardy to −20°C or less.

Clematis integrifolia L.   Native of Europe, from Austria south to Bulgaria and east to C Asia and the Caucasus, growing in grassland and steppes, flowering in June–August. Plant with several upright or sprawling stems to 1m from a stout rootstock. Leaves to 9cm long, ovate. Flowers nodding, with 4 sepals to 5cm long. Forma *rosea* has pink flowers and was distributed by the Plantsmen in the 1960s. 'Hendersonii' has blue flowers, around 6cm long. 'Olgae' has scented flowers with wavy margins to the sepals. For good soil in full sun and exposure. Hardy to −20°C or less.

Clematis × **jouiniana** C. K. Schneid. **'Praecox'**   A hybrid between *C. heracleifolia* 'Davidiana' and *C. vitalba*, raised in *c*.1900 in Metz. Stems to 3m in a year, often from a woody base. Flowers each about 2cm long, produced in great quantity in July–September, scented. For sun or partial shade, either on a wall or scrambling through scrub. Hardy to −20°C or less.

Clematis recta L.   Native of Europe, from France and Spain, east to Poland, Bulgaria, Russia and the Caucasus, growing in scrub and sunny hills, flowering in June–July. Plant forming a clump of hollow stems to 1.5m. Leaves 1-pinnate, the leaflets to 9cm long. Flowers 1–4cm across. Forma *purpurea* (shown here) has purple leaves; the intensity of colour varies with the season and the clone. For any soil in full sun. Hardy to −25°C.

Clematis texensis Buckley   Native of E North America, in Texas, between Colorado and the Rio Grande, growing in rich soil on shady limestone ledges, often along streams, flowering in July–September. Stems often annual, sometimes persistent near the base in warm winters, to 3m from a stout rootstock. Leaves glaucous, simple or 3-foliate, apiculate, cordate. Flowers 2–3cm long, scarlet to reddish purple. For a warm position; hardy to −15°c.

Delphinium nudicaule at Axeltree Nursery, Kent

Delphinium barbeyi in the mountains above Flagstaff, Arizona

Delphinium × *belladonna* 'Lamartine'

Delphinium × *belladonna* 'Moerheimii'

Delphinium × *ruysii* 'Pink Sensation'

Delphinium cardinale

Delphinium tatsienense at Crathes Castle, Aberdeenshire

Delphinium elatum in the Order Beds at Kew

Delphinium barbeyi Huth (*Ranunculaceae*) Native of E Arizona, Wyoming, Colorado, Utah and New Mexico, growing in grassy subalpine 'parks', flowering in July–August. Plant with stems to 2.5m from a stout rootstock. Leaves with 5 divided lobes. Flowers with lanceolate-acuminate sepals, *c*.2cm across. Rhachis of the inflorescence glandular. For any good soil in a sunny position. Hardy to −20°C perhaps.

Delphinium × belladonna (Kelway) Bergmans   These more delicate branched *Delphiniums* are the result of crossing *D. elatum* hybrids and a branching species, such as *D. grandiflorum* L., from Siberia and N China, very similar to *D. tatsienense*. The early crosses were done by Kelways, Ruys and Lémoine in around 1900; a few of these are still grown today. Shown here are: 'Lamartine', raised by Lémoine in 1903, and 'Moerheimii', raised by Ruys in 1906.

Delphinium cardinale Hook. syn. *D. coccineum* Torr. **Scarlet Larkspur**   Native of S California from Monterey Co. to San Diego Co., and in Baja California, growing in open places in dry scrub and chaparral, and in open woods, flowering in May–July. Stems upright, to 2m, unbranched or with smaller racemes at the base of the inflorescence, from a thick, woody rootstock. Leaves appearing in autumn, 5-lobed to the base, the lobes each divided into 3. Flowers on short ascending pedicels 2–6cm long, scarlet, rarely yellowish, 2–3cm across; spur stout 1.5–2cm long. For well-drained soil in a warm position, dry in summer. Hardy to −10°C perhaps.

Delphinium elatum L.   Native of Europe, from the E Pyrenees and Provence east to the Caucasus, and in C Asia, Siberia and NW China, growing in grassy places and open woods, from 1500–1900m in the Alps, flowering in June–August. Plant with a stout, woody rootstock and numerous stout stems to 2m. Leaves 5-lobed and toothed; sepals to 1.6cm long; spurs *c*.1.7cm. For ordinary well-drained, rather moist soil in sun or partial shade. This is

the main species from which the garden delphiniums have been raised. It was introduced into cultivation in 1597, probably from Siberia via St Petersburg, but most of the early breeding work was done by Kelways at Langport from 1875 onwards, and more recently by Blackmore and Langdon of Pansford, near Bristol.

Delphinium nudicaule Torr. & A. Gray Native of California and S Oregon, from Monterey Co. northwards in the Coast Ranges and from Mariposa and Plumas Cos. northwards in the Sierra Nevada, growing in chaparral and in open woods and on rocky banks below 2200m, flowering in May–June. Plant with an elongated rootstock and swollen roots. Stems to 60cm, usually sparsely branched with few flowers. Flowers with long pedicels and spurs 2.5–3.2cm long, the sepals forming a cup, usually red, sometimes orange or yellowish. For well-drained soil in a warm position in sun or partial shade, dry in summer. Hardy to −15°C perhaps.

Delphinium × ruysii hort. ex Möllers **'Pink Sensation'** syn. 'Rosa Uberraschung'   A hybrid between a garden delphinium and *D. nudicaule*, raised by Ruys in the 1920s. Thousands of seedlings were raised, using *D. nudicaule* as the seed parent, but all appeared to be pure *nudicaule*, until, after the programme had been abandoned, one seedling was found which appeared to be a hybrid. In the second generation 'Pink Sensation' was raised, and it proved to be tetraploid and fertile. Stems branching to 90cm. Hardy to −15°C, perhaps less.

Delphinium tatsienense Franch.   Native of W China, in S Sichuan, growing on rocky and grassy slopes at *c*.4000m, flowering in June–July. Plant with a woody rootstock and several branched stems to 60cm. Flowers *c*.2.5cm across, bright blue, on slender ascending pedicels. Spur 3cm. For well-drained, sandy soil in sun or partial shade. Rather short-lived but easy to raise from seed. Hardy to −15°C or less.

Delphinium brunonianum by a stream near Gadsar, Kashmir

Delphinium brunonianum

Delphinium brunonianum Royle
(*Ranunculaceae*)   Native of the Pamirs and the
Himalayas from Afghanistan and N Pakistan to
E Nepal and SE Xizang, growing on cliffs,
screes and stony slopes, at 4300–5500m,
flowering in July–September. A glandular-hairy
plant, with few stems to 20cm from a stout
rootstock. Leaves rounded in outline, 3–8cm
across, lobed to ⅔. Flowers 3–5cm long,
purplish with a broad, blunt spur. For well-
drained soil in full sun, moist in summer. Hardy
to −20°C or less. Very similar to *D.
cashmerianum*, but usually dwarfer with larger
flowers and with glandular hairs, or hairs with
swollen yellow bases on the inflorescence.

Delphinium caeruleum Camb.   Native of
Sikkim and Bhutan, growing on cliff ledges and
grassy, rocky slopes at 4000–4500m, flowering
in August–October. Plant with widely

branching stems 5–15cm tall, to 30cm in
gardens. Flowers widely separated, on pedicels
2–8cm long. Petals and sepals *c*.15mm long;
spur 18–22mm. For well-drained soil in full
sun. Hardy to −20°C.

Delphinium cashmerianum Royle   Native of
the Himalayas, from Pakistan to N India,
growing on alpine slopes (and recorded on
irrigated land in Ladakh by O. Polunin), at
2700–4500m, flowering in July–September.
Plant not glandular-hairy, with flowers usually
2–3cm long with a more slender spur to 1.5cm
long. Stems to 30cm; leaves 3–5cm across,
deeply lobed. For well-drained soil in sun or
partial shade. Hardy to −20°C or less.

Delphinium glaucum Wats. syn. *D. scopulorum*
Gray var. *glaucum*   Native of California north
to Alaska, and in the Rockies, growing in wet
meadows near streams at 1500–3000m,
flowering in July–September. Plant with
upright stems to 2.5m, from a stout woody
rootstock. Leaves 8–15cm broad, much
divided. Flowers 16–24mm across; spur
8–10mm long. A tall, robust plant for any good
moist soil. Hardy to −20°C or less.

Delphinium patens Benth.   Native of
California, in the coast ranges and the W Sierra
Nevada, growing in open woods and scrub at up
to 1200m, flowering in March–May. Stems to
40cm, rather thick and fistulose, from a
tuberous rootstock. Inflorescence single or
branched, 6–15 flowered. Flowers to 3cm
across: spur 8–11mm long, rather stout. For
well-drained soil in full sun, dry in summer.
Hardy to −10°C.

Delphinium pyramidale Royle   Native of the
Himalayas, from Pakistan to C Nepal, and
common in Kashmir, growing on stony slopes
by streams and in scrub at 2000–3600m,
flowering in July–September. Plant with few
upright stems to 90cm from a stout rootstock.
Leaves with lobes not overlapping. Flowers
c.3cm long, hairy. For well-drained but moist
soil in sun or partial shade. Hardy to −20°C or
less.

Delphinium semibarbatum Bienert ex Boiss.
syn. *D. zalil* Aitch.   Native of NE Iran,
Afghanistan, and C Asia from the Kopet Dağ
and Badghis to the Dzungarian Ala Tau and
Tienshan in NW China, growing on grassy
steppes, flowering in April–July. Plant with
upright stems to 80cm from a thickened
rootstock. Leaves divided into threadlike
segments. Flowers *c*.1cm across; spur *c*.1cm.
This unusually coloured species should be
perfectly hardy to cold, but resents warm, damp
conditions in winter and summer. For a hot, dry
position, with water only in spring. Hardy to
−20°C or less.

Delphinium trolliifolium Gray   Native of NW
California and W Oregon, growing in moist,
shady places below 1200m in the evergreen
forest zone, flowering in April–July. Plant with
upright stems to 1.5m from a deep woody
rootstock. Lower leaves 10–15cm wide, much-
divided. Inflorescence lax, with divergent
pedicels to 5cm long. Flowers 3–5cm across;
spur 15–20mm. An attractive species for a cool,
semi-shaded position. Hardy to −15°C perhaps.

Delphinium semibarbatum

Delphinium trolliifolium in the University Botanic Garden, Cambridge

Delphinium cashmerianum

Delphinium glaucum in the Order Beds at Kew

Delphinium patens near Silver Lake

Delphinium pyramidale in Kashmir

Delphinium caeruleum

DELPHINIUM

Delphinium 'Guy Langdon'

Delphinium 'Lilian Bassett'

Delphinium 'Strawberry Fair'

Delphinium 'Fanfare' in the trials at Wisley

Delphinium 'Shasta'

Delphinium 'Blue Tit'

Delphinium 'Macaz'

Delphinium 'Spindrift'

Delphinium 'Leonora'

Delphiniums in Beryl Pye's garden at Eccleston Square, London

New Delphinium hybrids

'Blue Tit'   Raised by Blackmore and Langdon in 1960. Height to 1.4m; flowers 7cm across.

'Crown Jewel'   Raised by Blackmore and Langdon in 1979. Height to 2.8m; flowers 2.8cm across.

'Fanfare'   Raised by Blackmore and Langdon in 1960. Height to 1.8m; flowers 7.5cm across.

'Guy Langdon'   Raised by Blackmore & Langdon in 1955. Height to 2.0m; flowers 8.75cm.

'Leonora'   Raised by Latty in 1969. Height to 1.5m; flowers 7.5cm across.

'Lilian Bassett'   Raised by Bassett in 1984. Height to 1.5m; flowers 7.1cm across.

'Macaz'   Raised by McIntosh. A. M. 1984.

'Purple Triumph'   Raised by Blackmore and Langdon in 1960. Spike to 72cm long; flowers 7.5cm across.

'Sandpiper'   Raised by Latty in 1977. Height to 1.2m; flowers 8cm across.

'Shasta'   Raised by Bott. A. M. 1983.

'Spindrift'   Raised by Cowan in 1971. Height to 2m; flowers 8cm across.

'Strawberry Fair'   Raised by Blackmore and Langdon in 1967. Height to 2m; flowers 7cm across.

Delphinium 'Sandpiper'

Delphinium 'Purple Triumph'

Delphinium 'Crown Jewel'

Delphinium 'Honey Bee'

Delphinium 'Butterball'

Delphinium 'Can-Can'

Delphinium 'Blackmore's Blue'

Delphinium 'Turkish Delight'

Delphinium 'Loch Maree'

Delphinium 'Charles Gregory Broan'

Delphinium 'High Society'

The new red *Delphinium* seedlings behind bars in an experimental house at Wisley

New Delphinium hybrids at Wisley   Attempts to breed a hardy red border delphinium are still continuing. Ruys's breeding programme, begun in the 1920s, failed, but did produce the dainty 'Pink Sensation' (see p. 17). In 1953 Dr R. A. Legro began his breeding experiments at Wageningen in Holland, and this programme was moved to the Royal Horticultural Society's garden at Wisley in 1980. The original plants used were white cultivars of *D. elatum*, crossed with *D. nudicaule*, *D. cardinale* and *D. semibarbatum* (syn. *D. zalil*), to try to raise a yellow. The first stage in the programme was to produce tetraploid forms of the three wild species, but crosses between these and the already tetraploid *elatum* cultivars proved disappointing. Success was finally achieved by producing allotetraploid, and therefore fertile, seedlings of *nudicaule × cardinale* and *semibarbatum × cardinale*. When these were crossed with the *elatum* cultivar 'Black and White', a range of bluish seedlings was produced, but other colours appeared in the second generation, including an orange and a semi-double red, creams and yellows. The plants themselves were very beautiful, but short-lived, difficult to propagate and unreliable from seed as they produced a large proportion of inferior plants. To be valuable commercially, the new coloured plants have to be reliably perennial, hardy and able to be propagated in large quantities. This has finally been achieved, again with great difficulty, by tissue culture, and the first plants of the new hybrids should be ready for sale to the public by spring 1992, 39 years after the breeding programme was begun.

Delphinium cultivars

'Blackmore's Blue'   Raised by Blackmore and Langdon. Height to 1.65m; flowers 7.5cm across. A. M. 1947.

'Butterball'   Raised by Blackmore and Langdon before 1969. Height to 1.9m; flowers 7cm across.

'Can-Can'   Raised by McGlashan in 1986. Height to 2.0m; flowers 8.5cm across.

'Charles Gregory Broan'   Raised by Broan in 1967. Height to 1.2m; flowers 6.5cm across.

'High Society'   Raised by Pye before 1985. Height to 1.63m; flowers 9.2cm across.

'Loch Maree'   Raised by Cowan in 1968. Height to 2.4m; flowers 7.5cm across.

'Stalwart'   An old variety of great elegance, preserved at Kew. Height to 1.8m; flowers *c*.2cm across.

'Turkish Delight'   Raised by Blackmore and Langdon in 1967. Height to 1.7m; flowers 6.2cm across.

Blackmore and Langdon's hybrid   A seedling from Blackmore and Langdon, dating from the 1940s. This old one we have treasured in our own garden; it is reliably perennial, with rather small flowers of a good sky-blue, and stems to 2m.

An old, reliably perennial Blackmore and Langdon hybrid

Delphinium 'Stalwart' at Kew

Nymphaea alba near Maam Cross, Connemara

Nuphar lutea (L.) Sm. (*Nymphaeaceae*) **Yellow Water Lily** Native of Europe and N Asia, east to Japan, growing in lakes and rivers, often in moving water, flowering in June–August. Plant very invasive with creeping rhizomes. Leaves either submerged, floating or emergent; when floating ovate, thick or leathery, 12–40cm long. Flowers 4–6cm across, with 4–6 sepals, smelling of brandy and fruit decanter-shaped, hence the colloquial name 'Brandy-bottle'. For water up to 3m deep. Hardy to −20°C or less.

Nuphar polysepala Englem. Native of W North America, from California to Alaska, and east to Colorado and South Dakota, growing in ponds and slow rivers, flowering in April–September. Differs from the European *N. lutea* by having 7–9 sometimes reddish sepals, to 5cm long, and broadly oval leaves to 40cm long, either floating or emergent. A striking plant in shallow water, with its large emergent leaves. Hardy to −20°C.

Nymphaea alba L. (*Nymphaeaceae*) Native of Europe, from W Ireland and NW Africa eastwards to Turkey, Russia and Kashmir, growing in ponds, lakes and slow rivers, flowering in June–August. Plant with a stout rhizome, forming loose patches of floating leaves 10–30cm across. Flowers 5–20cm across, usually scented for the first day after opening, white. (The wild red form originated from Sweden, around Nerike.) Subsp. *occidentalis* Ostenf. is merely a small form, with flowers 5–12cm across and globose fruit, described from Connemara and Perthshire. Best in water 1–3m deep. Hardy to −20°C or less.

Nymphaea 'Froebeli' Raised by a Zurich nurseryman, Otto Froebel, in around 1898, by repeated selection of *N. alba* var. *rubra*. Leaves purplish. Flowers rather small but scented. Best in water 45–60cm deep.

Nymphaea 'Laydeckeri Fulgens' Raised by Marliac-Latour in 1895, and named after his foreman and son-in-law Maurice Laydecker. The 'Laydeckeri' hybrids are smaller than the 'Marliacea' hybrids, and are probably derived from *N. tetragona* Georgi, a dwarf species with flowers *c*.2.5cm across. In 'Laydeckeri Fulgens' the flowers are around 8cm across. For small pools and shallow water 30–60cm deep.

Nymphaea 'Marliacea Carnea' syn. 'Marliac Flesh' Raised by Marliac-Latour in 1887. Flowers large, *c*.20cm across, scented. Leaves large, purplish when young. Best in water 45–150cm deep.

Nymphaea 'Marliacea Chromatella' syn. 'Marliac Yellow' Raised by Marliac-Latour in 1887. Flowers yellow, 15cm across. Leaves speckled with maroon. Probably a hybrid with *N. mexicana* which has speckled leaves and yellow flowers. There are several 'Marliacea' hybrids, ranging in colour from deep-crimson 'Ignea' to white 'Albida'.

Nymphaea odorata Dryander **'William B. Shaw'** Raised by Dreer in *c*.1900. Flowers well scented, raised slightly above the water. *N. odorata* itself is native of North America from Newfoundland and Cape Cod to Kansas, Mexico and Cuba, growing in lakes, bog pools and slow rivers, flowering in June–September. Plant forming large clumps, with long, creeping rhizomes; leaves and flowers variable in size.

Nymphoides peltata

Nuphar lutea

Nymphaea 'Marliacea Carnea'

Nymphaea 'Marliacea Chromatella'

Nuphar polysepala

Nymphaea 'Froebeli'

Nymphaea odorata 'William B. Shaw'

'William B. Shaw' requires water 45–60cm deep. Others require variable depths, according to their size.

Nymphoides peltata (Gmel.) O. Kuntze (*Menyanthaceae*) Native of Europe, from N England and S Sweden eastwards to the Caucasus, N Asia and Japan, growing in lakes and slow rivers, flowering in June–August. Plant with a creeping rhizome, and floating leaves 3–10cm across. Flowers in 2–5-flowered groups, supported by a pair of leaves. Corolla *c.*3cm across, with wavy and ciliate lobes. Fruits flattened, with grey, flattened ciliate seeds. Related to Bogbean (vol. 1, p. 165), rather than waterlilies, but so similar in habit to a miniature waterlily that it is put on this page.

Nymphaea 'Laydeckeri Fulgens'

Nymphaea 'Gladstoniana' at Inverewe

'Madame Wilfron Gonnère'

'Gonnère'

Hardy Water Lily hybrids It is a measure of the indestructible nature of water-lilies, and the lack of modern interest in the hardy varieties, that of the 90 or so hybrids available in Europe at present, 66 were bred by M. Marliac-Latour, who had a nursery near Temple-sur-Lot, and raised hybrids between 1880 and 1920. More recent work has been done, mainly in America, and has concentrated on the spectacular subtropical species, whose tuberous roots require protection from frost in winter. Much of the early work was done by George Pring at the Missouri Botanical Garden from 1913 to 1930, and other hardy cultivars have been produced in North Carolina by Perry Slocum, whose first hybrid, 'Pearl of the Pool', was patented forty years ago, and who is still producing new hybrids.

'Amabilis' syn. 'Pink Marvel' Raised by Marliac-Latour in 1921. Flowers large, to 25cm across. Best in 45–60cm depth of water.

'Charles de Merville' Raised by Marliac-Latour in 1931. Flowers large. Best in 60–120cm of water.

'Escarboucle' syn. 'Aflame' Raised by Marliac-Latour in 1906. The best large red; flower large, up to 30cm across, scented. Best in deep water, 60–185cm deep.

'Gladstoniana' syn. 'Gladstone' Raised by Richardson in 1897. A hybrid of *N. tuberosa*. Flowers very large. Best in deep water, 60–250cm deep.

'Gonnère' syn. 'Crystal White' Raised by Marliac-Latour. Compact growing. Best in 45–75cm of water.

'James Brydon' syn. 'Brydonia Elegans' Raised by Dreer in 1902. Flowers large, scented. Leaves speckled. Best in water 45–90cm deep.

'Madame Wilfron Gonnère' Flowers large, with an extra-large number of petals. Best in 45–75cm of water.

'Masaniello' Raised by Marliac-Latour in 1908. Flowers scented, pink with crimson speckles. Best in 45–90cm of water.

'Mrs Richmond' Raised by Marliac-Latour in 1910. Flowers with a deep-red centre, pale on the edge. Best in 45–75cm depth of water.

'Norma Gedge' Raiser not recorded. Plant with a very long flowering season. Best in 30–45cm depth of water.

'Pink Opal' Raised by Fowler in 1915. Recognized by its spherical buds. Leaves brownish. Best in 45–75cm of water.

'Sioux' Raised by Marliac-Latour in 1908. Flowers open yellowish and become crimson as they age. Leaves with purple speckles. Best in 30–45cm depth of water.

'Mrs Richmond'

'Escarboucle'

Nymphaea 'James Brydon' in the water lily collection at Kew

'Charles de Merville'

'Pink Opal'

'Masaniello'

'Sioux'

'Amabilis'

'Norma Gedge'

Papaver orientale 'Goliath' at Sissinghurst

Papaver orientale 'Harvest Moon' from Blooms

Papaver orientale 'Ladybird'

Papaver orientale 'Picotee'

Papaver bracteatum Lindl.   Native of N Iran, the Caucasus and E Turkey, from Nigde north and eastwards, growing on rocky and grassy slopes at 2000–2500m, flowering in June–July (in late May in gardens in S England, usually earlier than the other species). Stems stiffer and taller than *P. orientale*, to 1.2m. Flowers with conspicuous bracts below the flower, and purplish-crimson petals with a black blotch, longer than broad. Stigma rays 14–20. There are two other species in this group: *Papaver lasiothrix* Fedde, which is the only species with spreading hairs on the peduncles, and has smallish, blood-red flowers with 6 petals, 4–5cm long; and *Papaver paucifoliatum* (Trautv.) Fedde, a more slender plant with leaves only at the base of the stem, and 4 brick-red, unspotted

petals 3–5cm long. It is found in the mountains at up to 2700m, in extreme NE Turkey and Transcaucasia. The double-flowered forms are nearest to this species.

Papaver orientale L. (*Papaveraceae*)   Native of the Caucasus, N Iran and NE Turkey south to Van, growing on rocky slopes and dry meadows at 1950–2800m, flowering in July. Roots fleshy, brittle and deep; stems few, 60–90cm, without bracts below the flowers, with appressed hairs. Flowers scarlet, with 4 petals 7–9cm long, each with a black spot, broader than long, at the base; stigma rays 10–16. Var. *parviflora* Busch has petals only 4.5–6cm long, without spots, and 7–13 stigmas. It is found in meadows and on grassy volcanic

slopes, from the Caucasus to NE Turkey, flowering in June–August.

***Papaver orientale* cultivars**

'Allegro Vivace'   Orange flowers with 4 petals; unspotted without bracts, fairly dwarf to 90cm.

'Goliath'   Very large, blood-red flowers with bracts and a dark spot. Close to *P. bracteatum*.

'Harvest Moon'   Flowers rather small, orange, unspotted. Stems *c.*1m.

'Ladybird'   Flowers very large with bracts and with a black blotch. 60cm. Early season.

Papaver 'May Queen'

Papaver orientale with cow parsley among long grass on a roadside in Scotland

Papaver 'Olympia'

Papaver 'Allegro Vivace'

Papaver 'Picotee'

Papaver 'Ladybird'

Papaver 'Picotee'

Papaver orientale specimens from Wisley, 1 June. ¼ life size

'May Queen'   Double, orange-red flowers with quilled petals and flexuous stems without bracts.

'Olympia'   Semi-double flowers with flat petals. Stems flexuous, without bracts.

'Picotee'   Petals frilled, with a white base and pinkish-orange tip; the proportion of orange and white is variable.

'Glowing Embers'

'Blue Moon'

'Pale Face'

'Cedric Morris'

'Sultana'

'Beauty of Livermere'

'Princess Victoria Louise'

Papaver orientale specimens from Wisley, 1 June. ⅓ life size

Papaver orientale 'Mrs Perry' at Crathes Castle, Aberdeenshire

Papaver 'Turkish Delight'

Papaver 'Cedric Morris'

Papaver 'Curlilocks'

Oriental Poppies Cultivated oriental poppies are now found in all shades of red, orange, pink, almost mauve and white. They were all bred from the four wild species from Turkey and the Caucasus, notably by Amos Perry at Enfield. In the 1930s even more colours and shapes were available than can be found today, including 'Waterloo', dark-crimson-suffused purple, with woolly leaves; 'Mahony' and 'Darkness', deep maroon; and 'Tulip', with long, tapering buds. All are easily grown in any good moist soil in full sun and are beautiful in a herbaceous border or in grass. They die back after flowering. They are best moved or planted in autumn, and are easily propogated by root cuttings. Even small pieces of broken root will make new plants. Hardy to −20°C or less.

'Beauty of Livermere' Flowers blood-red, with black blotch and large bracts to 120cm. Close to *P. bracteatum*, and probably the same as 'Goliath', p. 23.

'Black and White' Flowers white with black blotches. Stems *c*.80cm.

'Blue Moon' Flowers very large to 25cm across; bluish pink with basal blotches and large bracts. Stems to 100cm.

'Cedric Morris' Flowers very large, pale pink, with frilled petals and a large black centre; stems to 80cm, with bracts.

'Curlilocks' Flowers orange, somewhat nodding, with deeply serrated petals, with black blotches; stems *c*.70cm.

'Glowing Embers' Flowers orange-red with black blotches; stems to 110cm, with large bracts.

'Mrs Perry' Flowers medium, pale salmon pink with black blotches; stems *c*.90cm, with small bracts.

'Pale Face' Flowers very pale pink, with a white centre; stems *c*.90cm, without bracts.

'Princess Victoria Louise' Flowers very large, pale pink with dark blotches.

'Sultana' Flowers mid-pink with a faint darker base; stems *c*.60cm.

'Turkish Delight' syn. 'Turkenlouis' Flowers medium, pale salmon pink, unspotted; stems *c*.80cm, without bracts.

Papaver 'Black and White'

Meconopsis 'George Sherriff 600'

Meconopsis 'George Sherriff 600' at Inshriach, Aviemore

Meconopsis × beamishii at Branklyn, Perth

Meconopsis grandis

Meconopsis quintuplinervia

Meconopsis × beamishii Prain (*Papaveroceae*) A hybrid between *M. grandis* and *M. integrifolia*, and one of the few hybrids to have remained in cultivation for some time. It was first raised in Co. Cork in 1906, is often monocarpic and has large pale-yellow flowers in the axils of the upper leaves. *M. × sarsonii*, the cross between *M. betonicifolia* and *M. integrifolia*, is taller, with smaller flowers.

Meconopsis betonicifolia Franch. syn. *M. baileyi* Prain Native of SE Xizang, NW Yunnan and NE Burma, growing in woods and scrub, and along streams in alpine meadows at 3000–4000m, flowering in June–August. Stems to 1.5cm. Basal leaves oblong, truncate or slightly cordate at the base, usually obtuse or rounded at the apex. Upper stem leaves usually auriculate or cordate at base, amplexicaul in a whorl at the top of the stem. Flowers 1–6 in the uppermost whorl of leaves; petals *c*.5cm across and long, often purplish, on pedicels *c*.10cm at first opening, elongating in fruit. This species differs from *M. grandis* most clearly in its basal leaves, which are truncate or cordate at the base, not tapering into the narrow stalk. Easily raised from seed, and prefers a sandy, peaty soil, moist in summer. Sometimes this species is monocarpic, and it is said that preventing it flowering in its second year encourages the production of side shoots at the base. Hardy to −20°C.

Meconopsis grandis Prain Native of Bhutan and Sikkim, extending to W Nepal and S Xizang, growing on rocky hillsides and in scrub

at 3650–4800m, flowering in June–August. Reputed to be cultivated around shepherds' huts in Sikkim where the seeds are used for oil. Plant forming large clumps of stems to 120cm. Basal leaves elliptic, 15–25cm long, acute, cuneate or attenuate at base. Stem leaves become sessile and whorled at the top of the stem, sometimes cordate. Flowers 1–4 per stem, on pedicels 10–15cm; petals 4–7cm, often purplish. G. Sherriff 600 is a clone of this species, collected SW of Sakden in E Bhutan, and very close to *M. × sheldonii*. There is much discussion as to which of the cultivated forms are 'pure' *M. grandis*, and which are hybrids with *M. betonicifolia* (see *M. × sheldonii*). Generally *M. × sheldonii* has leafier stems, with the stem leaves cordate at the base, and more than 4 flowers per stem. *M. grandis* usually has longer pedicels, and narrower basal leaves which taper gradually with the stalk. For sandy, peaty soil, cool and moist in summer. Hardy to −20°C.

Meconopsis punicea Maxim. Native of NE Xizang, S Gansu and NW Sichuan, growing in damp hay meadows with willows or *Rhododendron*, and on grassy slopes, at 2800–4500m, flowering in June–August, usually in the shade. Plant forming small clumps, with leaves all basal, to 30cm long, but usually *c*.15cm. Flower stems to 6 for each rosette, up to 75cm, but usually *c*.30cm at flowering, elongating in fruit. Petals to 10cm long. This species was found by Rock & Wilson, but had died out in gardens until recently reintroduced into cultivation by Roy Lancaster under the

Meconopsis × *sheldonii* at Kildrummy Castle Garden, Aberdeenshire

Meconopsis 'Branklyn' at Branklyn

Meconopsis 'Crewdson Hybrids'

Meconopsis 'Slieve Donard'

Meconopsis betonicifolia

number 1630. Requires a very cool position and moist shade: it is likely to grow best in Scotland or in cool gardens in the mountains elsewhere. Hardy to −20°C.

Meconopsis quintuplinervia Regel   Native of NE Xizang, S Gansu, NW Sichuan to C Shensi, growing in alpine meadows on limestone, often among dwarf *Rhododendron* scrub, at 2200–4300m, flowering in ?June–August. Plant forming extensive clumps, with leaves up to 25cm long. Flower stems to 90cm, usually *c.*30cm. Flowers 1 per rosette, with petals 3.75cm long, pinkish to azure-blue. This dainty alpine species is happiest in places such as the peat beds in the Royal Botanic Garden, Edinburgh, growing in the open but shaded from the south, among dwarf shrubs. Hardy to −20°C.

Meconopsis × **sheldonii** G. Taylor   Many of the finest blue poppies in cultivation at present probably belong to this cross between *M.*

grandis and *M. betonicifolia*. It was first raised at Oxted in Surrey in 1937 and is a strong-growing perennial, with stems to 1.5m. Easy to grow, but liable to die if it becomes too hot and dry in summer. In warmer climates, such as E North America and SE England, a cool, shaded and sheltered position is required if it is to survive. Several named clones or forms are grown in gardens:

'Branklyn'   A robust plant to 1.8m, often with a hint of mauve in the very large flowers, and with leafy stems. Originally 'Branklyn' was a selection of 'G. Sherriff 600', a form of *M. grandis*, itself very close to *M.* × *sheldonii*; the plant shown here growing at Branklyn is possibly not the original.

'Crewdson Hybrids'   A good form with a neat habit derived from *M. betonicifolia*, and dark-blue flowers.

'Slieve Donard'   One of the earliest crosses, increased and sold by the Slieve Donard nursery in Northern Ireland. An elegant form with longer, more pointed petals than most.

Meconopsis punicea at Inshriach

Eschscholzia californica

Eomecon chionanthum at Edington, Wiltshire

Meconopsis villosa at Inverewe

Meconopsis cambrica in Derbyshire

Meconopsis cambrica 'Flore Pleno'

Meconopsis chelidonifolia at Sellindge, Kent

Glaucium flavum

Eomecon chionanthum Hance
(*Papaveraceae*)   Native of E China, in Guangxi (Kwangsi) growing on the banks of the Bamboo River, presumably under trees, flowering in April–July. Plant forming wide mats by far-creeping rhizomes. Leaves fleshy, with yellow juice, on petioles to 30cm, with blade 10cm across. Flower stems with few branches to 40cm; flowers 3.5–4cm across. Easily grown in moist, leafy soil, and can become a pest if it grows too well, but dislikes drought and cold, heavy soil. Hardy to −20°C or so.

Eschscholzia californica Cham.
(*Papaveraceae*)   Native of California, west of the Sierras and the west part of the Mojave desert, and of Washington and Oregon from the Columbia River southwards, growing on dunes, rocky hills and roadside banks at up to 2000m; commonly naturalized in S & W Europe and the Canaries; flowering in February–September. Usually perennial, although flowering in the first year from seed. Stems usually prostrate, 20–60cm high. Leaves glaucous. Petals deep orange to yellow, 2–6cm long. Capsule 3–8cm long. Variable and common in many habitats; the flowers often large and orange in spring, paler and smaller in late summer, and in shades of pink in cultivated annual strains. Easily grown as an annual, and perennial in mild winters and with well-drained soil. Hardy to −10°C.

Glaucium flavum Crantz (*Papaveraceae*)
Native of the coasts of most of Europe except the far north, in Ireland and in Britain from Arran southwards; naturalized inland in Switzerland, ?Hungary, Austria, Czechoslovakia, and Poland. Native also in the E Mediterranean, NW Africa and the Black Sea, growing on sandy shores and shingle banks, flowering from May–August. Perennial or sometimes biennial. Stems to 90cm, sparsely bristly-pubescent. Leaves greyish green. Flowers 6–9cm across. Seed pods linear, 15–30cm long. This species usually has yellow flowers. Red or orange flowers are found in the annual *G. corniculatum* (L.) Rud. which is common in S Europe, and in the perennial *G. grandiflorum* Boiss. & Huet, from Greece, east to Iran, a plant of semi-deserts, with flowers 8–12cm across, and red, black-spotted petals. All species require very well-drained, poor soil to survive the winter as perennials. Hardy to −10°C.

Meconopsis cambrica (L.) Vig.
(*Papaveraceae*)   Native of Britain, chiefly in Wales and also on Exmoor; and in Ireland, mainly in the Wicklow Mountains, in Co. Sligo, and on the Antrim coast; of W France and N Spain, and naturalized in Germany, Switzerland and Holland, growing in woods by rocky streams, on old walls and mountain rocks at up to 600m, flowering in June–August. A long-lived perennial with branching taproots. Stems 30–60cm. Flowers 4–8cm across.
'Aurantiaca'   Flowers orange. Common in cultivation, coming true from seed, in various shades of orange.
'Flore Pleno'   Flowers orange or yellow, double, coming true from seed.
'Francis Perry'   Flowers reddish-orange.
All three are easily grown in cool gardens, especially in north-facing shade.

Meconopsis chelidonifolia Bur. & Franch.
Native of W China, in W Sichuan, at 1800–

2750m, especially from Mount Omei to around Kangding (Tatsienlu), growing in scrub, flowering in July–August. A long-lived perennial, with stems to 1m, with leafy bulbils in leaf axils. Petals *c.*2.5cm long and wide. Capsule ellipsoid, splitting by 5–6 valves, not often produced in cultivation. *M. oliverana* Franch. & Prain   from E Sichuan and W Hubei has a capsule rather like that of *M. villosa* (q.v.), but is otherwise very similar to *M. chelidonifolia*. An elegant and attractive plant, requiring a moist position, sheltered from drying winds in summer, which shrivel and blacken the leaves. The stem bulbils form a convenient means of propagation. Hardy to −15°C, perhaps less.

Meconopsis villosa (Hook. fil.) G. Taylor syn. *Cathcartia villosa* Hook.   Native of E Nepal, Sikkim and Bhutan, often forming large clumps on shady rocks and by streams in *Tsuga* and *Abies* forest, and in forest clearings, at 2700–4000m, flowering in May–July. Stems 60–150cm. Basal leaves palmately 3–5-lobed, the lobes toothed. Flowers 1–5 per stem. Petals 2.5–3cm long and wide. Capsule cylindric, 40–80mm × 5–7mm, 4–7 valved, the valves splitting almost to the base. It is because of its distinct capsule that this species is sometimes placed in the genus *Cathcartia*. Easily grown in a moist, shaded and sheltered position, but not often seen in cultivation. It is liable to damage from warm, wet weather in winter.

Papaver lateritium Koch (*Papaveraceae*)
Native of NE Turkey, in the Çoruh valley at 1200–3000m, on hillsides, meadows and screes, flowering in July–August. Stems 30–60cm, usually *c.*40cm in cultivation. Leaves narrowly lanceolate, deeply double-toothed. Flowers orange, *c.*5cm across. Similar to *P. monanthum* Trautv. and *P. oreophilum* Rupr. from the Caucasus. 'Fireball' syns. 'Nana Plena' or 'Nana Flore Pleno' is possibly a double form or hybrid of this species, not of *P. orientale*. Both are long-lived perennials forming spreading clumps. For any well-drained soil. Hardy to −15°C.

Papaver spicatum Boiss. & Bal. syn. *P. heldreichii* Boiss.   Native of W & S Turkey, from Manisa to Anamur, on limestone screes and rocky mountains at 600–1400m, flowering in June. Stems 60–75cm. Leaves greyish white with appressed hairs, serrate-crenate. Flowers sessile or short-stalked towards the base, the terminal opening first; petals orange, unspotted; capsules glabrous. Easily grown in well-drained soil in full sun.

Papaver lateritium at Inshriach, Inverness-shire

Papaver spicatum at Windsor

Papaver lateritium 'Fireball'

Argemone munita

Argemone munita above Death Valley, California

Capparis spinosa near Tarsus, S Turkey

Argemone munita Dur. & Hilg. (*Papaveraceae*)
Prickly Poppy   Native of California in the
Coast Ranges from San Luis Obispo Co.
southwards to Baja California, and on the dry
eastern side of the Sierra Nevada north to Shasta
Co. and eastwards to Arizona, Nevada and
Utah, growing in scrub, chaparral, open pinyon
pine woodland and roadside desert margins at
up to 2500m, flowering in March–September.
Plant usually perennial with prickly, upright or
spreading stems to 150cm. Leaves prickly,
usually greyish. Flowers 5–13cm across. The
subspecies, four of which are covered in *A
California Flora*, differ primarily in the size and
distribution of their prickles. For very dry soil
in full sun. Hardy to −15°C, possibly less. *A.
mexicana* is a commonly cultivated annual, with
yellow flowers, now found throughout the
tropics.

Capparis spinosa L. (*Capparidaceae*) **Caper**
Native of the E Mediterranean and now found
throughout the Mediterranean region east to
Kashmir, growing in old walls, cliffs and rocky
roadsides, flowering in July–August. Plant with
annual usually spiny, trailing stems from a
shrubby base. Leaves rounded up to 4cm long.
Flowers *c*.7cm across. Much cultivated for its
aromatic buds which are eaten in sauces. For a
dry position in full sun. Hardy to −10°C
perhaps. *C. ovata* Desf., which has flowers with
much longer lower petals than upper, and
elliptic leaves, is possibly hardier.

Eucnide urens (Gray) Parry (*Loasaceae*) **Rock
Nettle**   Native of SE California, around Death
Valley, eastwards to Utah, Arizona and Baja
California, growing in dry rocky places and

open scrub at up to 1500m, flowering in April–
June. Plant with a woody base and stems to
60cm, forming a rounded bush. Stems and
leaves with long, barbed, stinging hairs.
Flowers with 5 petals, each 2.5–4cm long. For a
very dry position in sandy, rocky soil and full
sun. Hardy to −10°C or lower if dry. Most of
the family *Loasaceae* have stinging hairs, but
very beautiful flowers. 'Blazing Star', *Mentzelia*,
is the commonest genus in California, with 19
species, including *M. lindleyi* (syn. *Bartonia
aurea*), a commonly grown annual.

Hypericum cerastoides (Spach) Robson syn.
H. rhodoppeum Friv. (*Guttiferae*)   Native of S.
Bulgaria, Greece and NW Turkey, growing in
stony places and woods at up to 1500m,
flowering in April–July. Plant forming
spreading mats or with ascending stems to
30cm. Leaves 8–30mm, oblong to ovate, finely
pubescent. Flowers 2–4cm across, deep yellow.
Easily grown in well-drained, sandy soil,
preferably slightly acid. Hardy to −15°C or less.

Hypericum olympicum L. f. **minus** Hausskn.
'**Sulphureum**' syn. *H. polyphyllum* 'Citrinum'
hort.   Native of S Greece, in parts of Thessaly,
Euboea, Attica and the Peloponnese, growing
on rocky slopes and in dry scrub, flowering in
May–July. Plant with erect or sprawling stems
to 35cm from a woody base. Leaves glabrous,
narrowly elliptic, acute to rounded, greyish.
Flowers *c*.6cm across, deep yellow or pale in
'Sulphureum'. For well-drained soil in full sun.
Hardy to −15°C perhaps. Forma *uniflorum* D.
Jord. & Kuz. has rounder leaves and fewer
flowers (1–3) per stem. It also has a pale-yellow
form, 'Citrinum'.

Macleaya cordata (Willd.) R. Br. syn.
Bocconia cordata Willd. (*Papaveraceae*)   Native
of Japan, from Honshu southwards, of E China
and Taiwan, growing in grassy places, open
meadows and on the grassy floors of *Cryptomeria*
plantations, flowering in June–August. Plant
with spreading underground rhizomes and
upright stems to 2m or more. Leaves rounded,
deeply lobed, usually white beneath, to 25cm
long. Flowers whitish, with 2 sepals *c*.10mm
long, and 25–30 stamens. Capsules 2cm long.
M. microcarpa (Maxim.) Fedde has smaller
pinkish-brown or pinkish flowers, red in
'Kelways' Coral Plume', with 8–12 stamens,
and a more invasive root. Both are easily grown
in sun or partial shade. Hardy to −15°C or less.

Romneya coulteri Harvey (*Papaveraceae*)
Matilija Poppy   Native of S California from
Ventura Co. and the Santa Ana mountains south
to Baja California, growing in canyons and dry
riverbeds below 1200m, flowering in May–July
and later if watered. Plant with creeping
underground rhizomes and upright or leaning
stems to 2.5m; flowers to 20cm across. Two
varieties are recognized in California: var.
coulteri, which is not found along the coast, has
glabrous sepals, rather bare peduncles, and
lobes of leaves less than 12mm wide; var.
trichocalyx (Eastw.) Jepson has more slender
stems, narrower leaves, with lobes 3–10mm
wide, peduncles leafy to the top and bristly
buds. Most of the plants in cultivation are
probably hybrids between the two varieties. For
well-drained soil in a warm position in full sun.
Hardy to −15°C, or less if the rootstock is
covered.

Eucnide urens

Eucnide urens above Death Valley, California

Hypericum cerastoides

Hypericum olympicum 'Sulphureum'

Macleaya cordata

Romneya coulteri in a garden near Cambridge

Megacarpaea orbiculata at Amankutan, near Samarkand

Megacarpaea polyandra at Keillour Castle

Megacarpaea orbiculata (fruit)

Erysimum scoparium on Mount Teide, Tenerife

Crambe cordifolia in the University Botanic Garden, Oxford

Crambe cordifolia Stev. (*Cruciferae*)   Native of the N Caucasus, growing in steppes and open stony places, flowering in May–July. Plant with a very thick, woody rootstock, from which come a few much-branched stems making a huge frothy mass to 1.8m in diameter, with small, white flowers. Basal leaves thin, heart-shaped, bristly, shallowly lobed, *c.*35cm long. Flowers 12–14mm across, scented. Fruit firm, 4.5–5mm across. A fine plant for a huge border, in well-drained but good soil in full sun. Hardy to −20°C or less.

Crambe kotschyana Boiss.   Native of C Asia, in the Tien Shan, the Pamir-Alai, the Dzungarian Ala-tau, and in NW China (Sinjiang); also in SW Asia in the Badgis, in NE Iran and perhaps Afghanistan, growing on rocky slopes, grassy foothills and screes at 1400–4000m, flowering in March–May. Plant with several much-branched stems from a deep, woody rootstock. Basal leaves thick, less deeply lobed than *C. cordifolia*. Inflorescence to 2.5m tall and as much across. Fruit spongy, *c.*6mm across. *C. orientalis* L., which is widespread in Turkey and Iran, is similar but it forms a mound to 120cm in diameter, with small flowers 8–12mm across. For deep, well-drained, rather dry soil in full sun. Hardy to −20°C.

Crambe maritima L. **Seakale**   Native of Europe, including the British Isles, on the shores of the Baltic, the Black Sea and the Atlantic, but not the Mediterranean, on shingle beaches near the high-tide line, flowering in May–June. Stems and leaves form a mound to 50cm across from a hard, woody rootstock. Flower shoots to 60cm. Leaves very fleshy, fluted and wavy edged, with a glaucous bloom. Flowers 10–16mm across, scented. Fruiting stems breaking off and blowing like a tumbleweed. Fruits spongy, 12–14mm across, able to float in seawater without damage to the seed. Often grown as a vegetable but is also an attractive border plant, recommended by Gertrude Jekyll, growing best in sandy, very well-drained soil. Easily propagated by root cuttings. Hardy to −20°C.

Erysimum scoparium (Willd.) Wettst. (*Cruciferae*)   Native of the Canary Islands, especially Tenerife, growing on rocky volcanic slopes at *c.*3000m, flowering most of the year. Shrubby at the base to 30cm; stems to 50cm. Leaves thick and fleshy to 12.5cm long, 1cm wide, not toothed or with distinct fine teeth. 'Bowles' Mauve' (vol. 1 p. 47) is very similar to this species but has shorter, broader leaves and larger flowers. For very dry, poor soil in full sun. It will grow easily in richer, damper soil, but then is liable to rot in winter. Hardy to −15°C or lower when dry.

Megacarpaea orbiculata B. Fed. (*Cruciferae*) Native of C Asia, in the Tien Shan and the Pamir Alai, growing on rocky limestone hills at *c.*1800m, flowering in March–April. Rootstock thick and deep. Stems 50–100cm, widely branched. Young leaves fan-shaped, glaucous, plant probably monocarpic, growing for several years before flowering. Fruits almost circular, 2.5–3cm across. For well-drained but deep, rich soil and full sun, dry in summer. Hardy to −15°C.

Megacarpaea polyandra Benth.   Native of Kashmir to C Nepal, growing in alpine meadows and open forests, at 3000–4300m, flowering in June–July. Stems 1–2m. Flowers 1cm across; fruit 3.5–5cm across, of 2-headed lobes. Plant taking many years to flower from

Crambe kotschyana near Ferghana, C Asia

Crambe maritima at Dungeness, Kent

seed, perhaps monocarpic. Leaves pinnate, lobes 10–20cm long. Hardy to −20°C. Most of the eight or so *Megacarpaea* species are from C Asia.

Stanleya pinnata (Pursh) Britton (*Cruciferae*) Native of California, especially on the east side of the Sierra Nevada and in the south, east to North Dakota, Kansas, Arizona and Texas, growing in dry, stony places and desert slopes at up to 1800m, flowering in April–September. Plant subshrubby at the base, with many tall, upright stems to 1.5m. Lower stem leaves pinnatifid. Inflorescence remarkably *Eremurus*-like. Petals with the inner surface hairy, 12–16mm long. Seed pods 5–8cm long, curling or recurved. For dry, poor soil in full sun. Hardy to −20°C or less. This plant grows well in a warm, dry border at Kew.

Stanleya pinnata in Arizona

Sphaeralcea fendleri var. *venusta* at Kew

Alcea excubita Iljin (*Malvaceae*) Native of N Iran and E Turkey westwards to Malatya, growing on rocky hillsides at 600–2000m, flowering in June–July and later in gardens. Stems to 1.5m, few to several from a woody rootstock. Leaves and stems with dense stellate hairs. Upper leaves deeply 5–7-lobed. Petals white or pale yellow, to 5.5cm long. For a dry, sunny, well-drained position in full sun. Hardy to −20°C or less.

Alcea rugosa Alef. Native of S Russia and the Caucasus, south to Georgia and Armenia, east to N Iran and the Kopet Dağ, growing on dry hills and steppes, and in open woods, flowering in June–August. Stems to 2.5m from a stout, woody rootstock, purple spotted, bristly-hairy with stellate hairs. Upper leaves shallowly 3–5-lobed, the middle lobe longest. Flowers to 12cm across, pale yellow. For dry, well-drained soil in a full sun. Hardy to −20°C or less.

Sidalcea candida A. Gray (*Malvaceae*) Native of Nevada to Wyoming, south to S New Mexico, growing along streams and in moist mountain meadows, flowering in June–September. Stems upright or leaning to 90cm. Basal leaves rounded with 7 shallow lobes, upper deeply 7-palmate. Flowers *c.*2.5cm across, in an often dense spike. For any good soil in sun or partial shade. Hardy to −20°C or less.

Sidalcea malviflora (DC.) A. Gray ex Benth. Native of the coast of California, from Los Angeles north to Mendocino Co., growing on open grassy slopes and mesas (moist grassy hollows), flowering in May–July. Other subspecies (there are at least 10) grow at higher elevations northwards to Oregon. Stems several from a tough rootstock, to 60cm. Leaves 7–9-lobed. Petals to 2.5cm long, usually with pale veins. About 24 cultivars are grown now, including: 'Elsie Heugh', petals attractively fringed; 'Rose Queen', large, pink flowers and stems to 1.2m; 'Sussex Beauty', flowers very pale pink; 'William Smith', flowers deep pink. For any good soil in sun or partial shade. Hardy to −20°C perhaps.

Sidalcea oregana (Nutt.) Gray subsp. **spicata** (Repel) C. L. Hitchc. Native of W North America from Oregon south to N California (Modoc to Siskiyou Cos.), growing in coniferous forests in damp grassy places, flowering in June–August. Stems several, 80cm to 1m in cultivation, from a stout tap-root. Inflorescence many-flowered, spike like. Petals 10–20mm long. For moist soil in sun or partial shade. Hardy to −15°C or less.

Sphaeralcea emoryi Torr. (*Malvaceae*) Native of W North America, from N Baja California east to S Nevada and S Arizona, growing by fields and roadsides at below 1000m, flowering in March–May. Stems several, upright to 120cm, sometimes greyish. Leaves 3-lobed, usually twice as long as wide. Petals 10–20mm long, usually reddish, sometimes pinkish. *S. ambigua* Gray is similar, but has a more open inflorescence and leaves as long as wide. For well-drained, dry soil in full sun. Hardy to −10°C perhaps.

Sphaeralcea fendleri Gray var. **venusta** Kearney Native of N Mexico to Arizona (with other varieties in S Colorado and W Texas) growing in pine forest and evergreen oak scrub, usually along streams, at up to 2599m, flowering in June–October. Stems several from a stout rootstock to 1.5m. Leaves silky-silvery, with few but long-rayed stellate hairs. Petals 15–20mm, pinkish, rarely reddish. For well-drained, dry soil in a sunny, sheltered position. Hardy to −15°C, perhaps lower when dry.

Sphaeralcea laxa Woot. & Standl. Native of W Texas and Arizona, growing in scrub and on open hillsides on limestone at 600–1800m, flowering in March–November. Stems several, sprawling, from a stout rootstock. Leaves usually silvery, tomentose, often deeply dissected. Flowers in an open, long-branched panicle, to 5cm across. For well-drained, dry soil in full sun. Hardy to −15°C, perhaps less in dry climates.

Alcea rugosa at Leeds Castle, Kent

Sphaeralcea emoryi in Arizona

Alcea excubita near Lake Van, Turkey

Alcea rugosa

Sidalcea candida with *Melianthus major*

Sidalcea oregana subsp. *spicata*

Sidalcea malviflora 'William Smith'

Sphaeralcea laxa

Sidalcea malviflora 'Rose Queen'

Malva moschata

Althaea officinalis L. (*Malvaceae*) **Marsh Mallow**   Native of Europe, from S Ireland eastwards to C Asia and Afghanistan and south to Israel, growing in grassy places by the sea, and by ditches and salt marshes inland, flowering in June–September. Plant with lax stems to 2m from a stout rootstock. Leaves softly whitish, hairy. Flowers in groups in the leaf axils, 1.2–3cm across. For good, moist soil. Hardy to −25°C.

Kitabela vitifolia Willd. (*Malvaceae*)   Native of Yugoslavia and recorded also in the Kopet Dağ (Göktepe), growing in scrub, grassy places and in vineyards, flowering in June–August. Plant with a great clump of tall stems to 3m from a huge rootstock. Leaves up to 18cm across with 5–7 toothed, pointed lobes. Flowers *c*.4cm across, pinkish. For any soil in sun or partial shade. Hardy to −20°C perhaps.

Lavatera cachemeriana Cambess. (*Malvaceae*)   Native of the W Himalayas, from Pakistan to N India, growing in meadows and open places in forest at up to 3600m, flowering in July–September. Stems much branched, to 2m from a stout rootstock. Leaves 3–5 lobed. Flowers 5–8cm across, in the commonly cultivated variety with narrow, widely separate, petals with a pale centre. For any good soil in sun or partial shade. Hardy to −20°C perhaps. Now often considered a minor variant of *L. thuringiaca*.

Lavatera olbia L.   Native of SW Europe, from Italy and Sicily westwards to Spain, Portugal and North Africa, growing in hedges, by rivers and in damp places, flowering in May–September. Plant shrubby at the base, with stems to 2m or more in gardens. Lower leaves 3–5-lobed, upper leaves 3-lobed, with the lower lobes much reduced. Flowers pink, 3.5–7cm across, on very short stalks 2–7mm long. For well-drained soil in sun. Hardy to −15°C perhaps.

Lavatera thuringiaca L.   Native of Europe, from C Italy and Germany, eastwards to Russia and NW China and south to Turkey and NW Iran, growing in scrub by roadsides and by streams at up to 2800m in Turkey, flowering in July–October. Plant with annual stems to 1m.

Lavatera 'Barnsley' with *Phlox* and *Nicotiana* at Cockermouth Castle, Cumbria

Lavatera 'Barnsley'

Malva sylvestris 'Primley Blue'

Lavatera triloba in S Spain

Kitabela vitifolia at Axeltree Nursery, Kent

Lower leaves 3–5-lobed, upper leaves weakly 3-lobed. Flowers 4.5–10cm across on stalks 10–22mm long. For any good garden soil. Hardy to −20°C, perhaps less. The following are considered by Alan Leslie to be hybrids with *L. olbia*:
'Barnsley' A semi-albino form found by Rosemary Verey in a garden in Gloucestershire in *c.*1985. It is one of the best plant introductions of recent years. It will revert to pink if the top growth is killed.
'Kew Rose' A deep-pink flowered form, with purplish stems. A pure white is also known. The old variety 'Rosea' syn. *L. olbia* 'Rosea' differs from 'Kew Rose' in its paler flowers, hairier stems and paler leaves.

Lavatera triloba L. Native of C, S & E Spain, S Portugal and Sardinia, with subsp. *agrigentina* (Tineo) R. Fernandes in S Italy and Sicily, growing on rocky hillsides, often in damp, heavy or saline soils, flowering in April–June. Plant musk-scented, glandular, woody below, with upright stems to 1.5m with broad stiples. Leaves slightly 3-lobed, woolly or bristly-hairy. Flowers in clusters of 3–7, purplish pink or yellow, 4–7cm across. For rich soil in full sun. Hardy to −15°C perhaps.

Malva moschata L. (*Malvaceae*) **Musk Mallow** Native of Europe, from England and Poland south to Spain, NW Africa and Turkey (where it is rare), growing in grassy places, especially on road verges, flowering in June–September. Plant with several decumbent stems from a branching taproot. Leaves very deeply divided. Flowers pink or white in *f. alba*, 4–7cm across. Easily grown in any good soil in full sun. Hardy to −25°C or less.

Malva sylvestris L. Native of most of Europe, North Africa and Asia eastwards to NW China, growing in grassy places, on roadsides, flowering in May–October. Plant perennial or biennial, with upright or trailing stems to 150cm. Leaves with 3–7 rounded lobes. Flowers to 6cm across, usually pinkish purple, but bluish in 'Primley Blue' (shown here), a recent introduction. A large, upright form with fine, deep-purple flowers has been called *M. mauritiana* L. but is now generally considered part of the variable *M. sylvestris*. For any soil in full sun. Hardy to −20°C or less.

Lavatera olbia

Lavatera cachemeriana

Lavatera 'Kew Rose'

Althaea officinalis on Romney Marsh

Euphorbia schillingii

Euphorbia longifolia

Euphorbia schillingii at Washfield Nurseries, Hawkhurst, Kent

Euphorbia kotschyana Fenzl (*Euphorbiaceae*)
Native of W & S Turkey, W Iran, W Syria and Lebanon, growing in fir and cedar forest, oak scrub and on mountain steppes, at up to 2500m, flowering in May–August. Plant with several stems to 80cm from a woody rootstock. Leaves glossy above, glaucous beneath, to 8cm long. Raylet leaf cups 1–4cm across. Fruits pubescent or glabrous. Differs from *E. macrostegia* Boiss. mainly in its taller stems and narrower glossier leaves. For well-drained soil in sun or partial shade. Hardy to −15°C perhaps. J. & J. Archibald 47900.

Euphorbia longifolia D. Don   Native of the Himalayas, from W Nepal to Bhutan, growing

in mountain meadows and clearings in forest at 1680–3600m, flowering in May–June, according to altitude. Plant with creeping rhizomes and stems to 1m, forming spreading clumps. Stem leaves linear-lanceolate, 6–11cm long, 1–1.8cm across. Bracts yellow, ovate. Fruits warty. Styles deeply bifid. Close to *E. griffithii* (see vol. 1, p. 51), but without the red leaves and bracts. For moist soil in sun or partial shade. Hardy to −15°C, perhaps less. Schilling 2069.

Euphorbia palustris L.   Native of Europe, from Sweden and Spain, east to Siberia, the Caucasus and Turkey, growing by rivers and lakes, and in marshes, flowering in March (in the south) to August. Plant forming large clumps of stems to 1.5m, from a stout, woody rootstock. Rays and raylet leaves bright yellowish when young, with willowy side branches developing after flowering. Fruit tuberculate. For moist or wet soil in sun or partial shade. Hardy to −20°C or less.

Euphorbia schillingii A. Radcliffe-Smith   Native of E Nepal, in the Dudh Kosi valley south of Everest, growing on rocky slopes at 2500–3000m, flowering in July–September. Plant clump forming, with many branching stems to 1.0m tall, 30cm across. Leaves to 12cm long, c.2cm across. For moist but well-drained soil in sun or partial shade. Hardy to −20°C, perhaps less.

Euphorbia seguieriana Necker subsp. **niciciana** (Borbás) Rech. fil. syn. *E. niciciana* Borbás   Native of Yugoslavia, Greece and

Turkey, east to Pakistan, growing in dry scrub, by roadsides and on rocky hills, flowering in March–October. Plant with several upright stems to 60cm from a woody rootstock. Leaves rather leathery, linear or oblong-linear, acute, 1–4cm long, spreading. Rays up to 30. Differs from the rather similar *E. nicaeensis* (see vol. 1, p. 49) in its narrower leaves, more upright stems and more numerous rays. For any dry position in full sun. Hardy to −15°C, possibly less.

Euphorbia sikkimensis Boiss.   Native of the Himalayas in Sikkim and possibly Bhutan, growing in scrub and clearings in forest, at 2700–3300m, flowering in July. Plant with far-creeping rhizomes and glabrous stems to 1.2m. Young shoots beautifully marked, reddish. Stem leaves lanceolate, 10–12cm long, 2cm wide. Bracts rounded at apex, yellow. Close to *E. griffithii* but taller, with yellow, not red, rounded bracts and later flowering. For moist soil. Hardy to −20°C perhaps.

Humulus lupulus L. 'Aureus' (*Cannabidaceae*) Golden Hop   Found wild throughout Europe, W & C Asia (but native distribution uncertain), growing in scrub or hedges, flowering in June–August. Plant with a stout rootstock and annual climbing stems to 6m or more. Male and female flowers on separate plants, the male with conspicuous stamens, the female only forming hops. The golden-leaved form shown here has been known since 1889. It is male. For any soil, preferably in a warm, sheltered position. Hardy to −20°C or less.

Euphorbia sikkimensis

Euphorbia sikkimensis (young shoots)

Euphorbia seguieriana subsp. *niciciana*

Humulus lupulus 'Aureus' with *Lysimachia ciliata* at Cobblers, Sussex

Euphorbia palustris

Euphorbia kotschyana at Coldham, Kent

Polygonum bistorta 'Superbum' with *Allium giganteum* at the Culpepper Gardens, Leeds Castle, Kent

Polygonum macrophyllum

Polygonum bistorta subsp. *carneum* above Kasbegi, C Caucasus

Polygonum tenuicaule

Eriogonum compositum Douglas ex Benth. (*Polygonaceae*)   Native of W North America, from Idaho to Washington and south to California, growing on dry, rocky slopes at 1900–3500m, flowering in May–July. Plant branched and rather woody at the base, with flowering stems 10–50cm. Leaves with blades 2–10cm long, whitish beneath, cuneate to cordate. Primary umbel with lanceolate bracts; secondary umbels many-flowered. For dry, well-drained soil, in full sun. Hardy to −15°C, or less if dry. There are at least 150 species of *Eriogonum*, mostly in W North America, ranging from low shrubs to herbaceous perennials, annuals and cushion-like alpines. Flowers are commonly yellow, but may be red, or white to pink.

Polygonum affine D. Don syn. *Bistorta affinis* (D. Don) Greene (*Polygonaceae*)   Native of Afghanistan, east to Nepal and Sikkim, growing on rocky slopes and screes at 3000–4800m, flowering from June–September. Plant forming leafy mats, often up to 1m across. Stems 15–30cm. Leaves lanceolate, elliptic, the blade 4–8cm long. Flower-head 5–7.5cm long, with pink or red flowers. Best in rather shallow, peaty, but well-drained soil. Hardy to −20°C. 'Donald Lowndes' is a deep-pink form. 'Superbum' is said by Graham Thomas to be an even better clone.

Polygonum amphibium L. syn. *Persicaria amphibia* (L.) S. F. Gray   Native of Europe and Asia, from Ireland eastwards to Japan, south to the Mediterranean, and in North America from Quebec and Alaska south to Kentucky and California, growing in lakes, ponds, rivers and canals, flowering in July–September. Either an aquatic plant with floating ovate-oblong leaf blades and an emerging flower stalk, or a leggy marsh plant with oblong-lanceolate leaves. Flower-head 2–4cm, with pink or red flowers. An attractive aquatic for water from 1–3m deep. The leaves are often attacked by the black and yellow larvae of the water-lily beetle. Hardy to −25°C and less.

Polygonum bistorta L. syn. *Bistorta vulgaris* Hill   Native of Europe, from Ireland eastwards to Japan, southwards in the mountains to Turkey, growing in subalpine meadows, by rivers and on grassy roadsides, flowering from June–August. Plant forming extensive colonies, with a very thick rhizome. Stem 25–50cm. Leaves 5–15cm, broadly ovate, obtuse, truncate or subcordate at base. Flowers pink or white, on a spike 3–6cm long. Hardy to −25°C or less. An attractive clump-forming perennial for a moist border. 'Superbum' is a garden selection.

Polygonum bistorta L. subsp. **carneum** (Koch) Coode & Cullen syn. *P. carneum* Koch   Native of Caucasus and NE & E Turkey, growing in mountain meadows and open woods, at 1800–3600m in Turkey, flowering in June–August. Similar to *P. bistorta*, but generally smaller, with deep-pink, stalked flowers, in a more rounded, oblong-globose head. For moist soil in a cool position. Hardy to −20°C or less.

Polygonum macrophyllum D. Don syns. *Persicaria macrophylla* (D. Don) Trehane, *P. sphaerostachyum* auct. non Meissn.   Native of the Himalayas, from N India and Nepal to SW China, growing in damp alpine meadows at 1700–4870m, flowering in May–September. Plant forming spreading clumps. Stems 5–30cm; leaf blades ovate-lanceolate, 4–12cm × 2–3cm, or sometimes narrower, rounded or cordate at base. Flower spikes 2–7cm, erect; flowers 2–5mm, pink, pendent on the spike. For moist, peaty soil in sun or partial shade. Flowering in gardens in mid-summer. Hardy to −20°C. Dwarf forms, with narrower leaves and short flower spikes, are found at high altitudes.

Polygonum milletii Léveillé syn. *Persicaria milletii* (Léveillé) Trehane   Native of the Himalayas, from W Nepal to SW China, growing in scrub and on cliff ledges at 300–4700m, flowering in June–November. Plant tufted with many stems 20–60cm tall. Leaves lanceolate, 8–15cm × 0.7–4.5cm, acuminate, decurrent at base into the stalk. Flowers 5–6mm, crimson, on spikes 2.5–6cm long. Differs from *P. macrophyllum* in its larger crimson flowers, and longer leaf sheaths up to 10cm. For moist, well-drained soil in sun or partial shade. Hardy to −20°C.

Polygonum tenuicaule Biss. & Moore syn. *Persicaria tenuicaulis* (Biss. & Moore) Trehane Native of Japan, in Honshu, Shikoku and Kyushu, growing in woods and on shady banks, flowering in April–June. Plant mat-forming, with short, thick rhizomes. Leaves 3–8cm × 2–3cm, oblong-ovate. Stems 7–15cm. Flower spikes 2–3.5cm long. For a moist, shaded position; an attractive small ground-covering plant. Hardy to −15°C perhaps.

Polygonum affine   *Polygonum amphibium*

Eriogonum compositum in N California

Polygonum milletii

Gypsophila 'Rosy Veil' in the ruins at Cockermouth Castle, Cumbria

Gypsophila paniculata 'Flamingo'

Gypsophila acutifolia

Gypsophila paniculata 'Bristol Fairy'

Gypsophila acutifolia Stev. ex Spreng.
(*Caryophyllaceae*)   Native of the N Caucasus
and southern Russia northwards to Romania
(introduced) and the Ukraine (possibly
introduced), growing in dry, sandy places and
on stony slopes, flowering in July–September.
Plant with a stout, deep rootstock, and
branching stems to 170cm long. Leaves linear-
lanceolate to lanceolate, acuminate.
Inflorescence glandular, the pedicels 1–4mm
long. *G. perfoliata* L. has similar flowers, but
longer pedicels which are glabrous and ovate,
amplexicaul leaves. For well-drained soil in full
sun. Hardy to −20°C or less.

Gypsophila bicolor Freyn & Sint. syn. *G.
paniculata* L. subsp. *bicolor* Freyn & Sint.
Native of E Turkey, the S Caucasus, Iran and C
Asia, growing in steppes, in open woods and
cornfields, flowering in May–July. Differs from
G. paniculata in its green, not glaucous leaves,
denser inflorescence and calyx teeth orbicular-
cordate, finely toothed. For dry, well-drained
soil in full sun. Hardy to −20°C or less.

Gypsophila paniculata L.   Native of E
Europe, from C Austria and Bulgaria eastwards
to the Caucasus, C Asia and NW China,
growing in grassy sandy steppes and stony
places, flowering in July–August. Stems few to
several from a deep, stout rhizome, forming a
mound of stiff, thin stems 1.5m high. Leaves
usually glaucous and glabrous. Pedicels 3–6mm
long. Flowers white or pink, double in
'Flamingo' (pink) and 'Bristol Fairy' (white),
the petals linear-spathulate, 3–4mm long. For
well-drained soil in a dry and sunny position.
Hardy to −20°C or less, but intolerant of winter
damp.

Gypsophila 'Rosy Veil' correctly
'Rosenschleier'   A hybrid between *G.
paniculata* and *G. repens* 'Rosea' raised by K.

Saponaria ocymoides in S France

Gypsophila bicolor in a cornfield near Lake Van, SE Turkey

Foerster in 1933. It forms a mound of trailing
stems to 100cm across, with double flowers
opening white, becoming very pale pink,
produced in July–August. For very well-
drained soil in full sun. Hardy to −20°C or less.

Saponaria × lempergii hort. **'Max Frei'**
(*Caryophyllaceae*)   A hybrid between *S. cypria*
and *S. haussknechtii*, with numerous softly
glandular-hairy stems to 30cm and masses of
flowers *c*.1.5cm across. For well-drained soil in
a dry position in full sun. Hardy to −15°C
perhaps.

Saponaria ocymoides L.   Native of Europe,
from N Spain and S France to Italy, S Germany
and Yugoslavia, growing on sunny slopes and
rocks, usually limestone, in the foothills up to
c.2300m in the Alps, flowering in July. Stems
creeping to 50cm or more. Flowers purplish-
pink or rarely white, 7–12mm across. For a
well-drained, sunny, dry position on a wall or
edge of border creeping over a path. Hardy to
−15°C, perhaps less.

Saponaria officinalis L. **Soapwort**   Native of
most of Europe, though often an escape from
cultivation, eastwards to Turkey and the
Caucasus, growing most commonly on grassy
roadsides but also by streams and in damp
woods, flowering in June–August. Naturalized
in North America. Plant with upright stems to
70cm from creeping underground rhizomes,
forming spreading patches. 'Rosea Plena' is the
commonest with double, pale-pink flowers.
'Rubra Plena' has dark-pinkish-red flowers.
There is also a double white. Flowers scented,
to 20mm across. Easily grown but invasive,
though intolerant of shade in cultivation. Hardy
to −20°C. Used in the past as soap and still
valuable for treating especially delicate, ancient
fabric.

Saponaria × lempergii 'Max Frei' at Kew

Saponaria officinalis 'Rubra Plena'

Saponaria officinalis

Saponaria officinalis 'Rosea Plena'

A form of *Dianthus deltoides* at Coldham, Kent

Dianthus deltoides in Finland

Dianthus superbus

Dianthus superbus on grassy dunes near Shari, Hokkaido

Dianthus 'White Loveliness'

Dianthus gratianopolitanus at Cheddar

Dianthus knappii at the Royal Botanic Garden, Edinburgh

Dianthus 'Glory Lyonnaise'

Dianthus 'Green Eye'

Dianthus 'Ursula Le Grove'

Dianthus deltoides L. (*Caryophyllaceae*)
Maiden Pink   Native of most of Europe from
Scotland eastwards to Finland and N Russia,
but absent from the Mediterranean region,
growing in dry, grassy places, flowering in
June–September. Plant with very many
sprawling stems to 45cm, from a slender,
creeping rootstock. Leaves usually green; on
sterile shoots oblanceolate 10–15mm long, on
flowering shoots longer and more acute.
Flowers usually solitary, *c*.1.8cm across,
unscented. For light soil in full sun. Hardy to
−20°C or less. Several named cultivars are
grown, including a pure white, and a fine red,
'Steriker', introduced by Valerie Finnis.

Dianthus ferrugineus Mill.   Native of the
Mediterrranean region, from S France to
Yugoslavia and Albania, growing on stony hills
and scrub, flowering in June–July. Plant with
several lax stems to 50cm from a woody
rootstock. Leaves very narrow. Flowers in
dense heads, *c*.3cm across. Epicalyx scales with
a long point. There are numerous very similar
species with tall stems and heads of reddish-
magenta flowers; *D. carthusianorum* L. is the
commonest, and differs from *D. ferrugineus* in
its broader, short, pointed epicalyx scales. For
any well-drained soil in full sun. Hardy to
−15°C perhaps.

Dianthus gratianopolitanus Vill. **Cheddar
Pink**   Native of Europe from England, only
found in Cheddar Gorge, east to Poland and the
W Ukraine, growing on limestone rocks and
cliffs, flowering in June–July. Plant tufted with
sterile rosettes and flowering stems to 20cm.
Leaves glaucous. Flowers to 3.5cm across,

clove-scented. For well-drained soil in a sunny
position. Hardy to −20°C.

Dianthus knappii (Pant.) Aschs. & Karnitz ex
Borbás   Native of W Yugoslavia, growing in
grassy places and scrub, flowering in June–
August. Plant with few rather lax stems to
40cm. Inflorescence with usually 2 heads, each
crowded with several flowers, *c*.2cm across.
This untidy plant, interesting as the only
yellow-flowered *Dianthus*, was used in breeding
the yellow-flowered pinks. For well-drained soil
in sun or partial shade. Hardy to −15°C.

Old *Dianthus* cultivars
'Glory Lyonnaise'   An old cultivar of
unknown origin. Stems to 30cm.
'Green Eye'   Origin unknown. Stems to 20cm.
'Ursula Le Grove'   Raised by the Revd. C.
Oscar Moreton and named after his daughter.
Stems to 30cm.
'White Loveliness'   Stems *c*.25cm; well
scented. Probably a hybrid of *D. superbus*,
raised by Allwoods in 1928.

Dianthus superbus L.   Native of Europe,
from France and Holland eastwards to Russia
and E Siberia, south to Japan and Taiwan,
growing in damp, grassy places, on dunes, in
open woods and in mountain meadows,
flowering in June–October. Plant with usually
green leaves, decumbent sterile shoots and
flowering stems to 90cm. Flowers 3.5–6.5cm
across; largest in subsp. *speciosus* (Rchb.) Pawl,
the montane subspecies; the petals always
deeply laciniate. For any well-drained, peaty
soil in sun or partial shade, and a cool position.
Hardy to −20°C and below.

Dianthus ferrugineus

DIANTHUS

'Pheasant's Eye'   'Eileen'   'Lady Glanville'

'Painted Beauty'   'Queen of Sheba'   'Kesteven Chambery'

'Hollycroft Fragrance'   'Farnham Rose'   'Gravetye Gem'

'Dewdrop'   'Glory Lyonnaise'   'Musgrave's Pink'

'Brympton Red'   'Inchmery'   'Arthur'

Specimens from Ramparts Nursery, 4 June. ⅔ life size

Dianthus **cultivars** (pinks) These have been bred for many centuries from *D. caryophyllus* and *D. plumarius*.

Double-flowered pinks

'Alice' Raised by Allwoods in 1930. Stems *c*.32cm. Well scented.
'Bat's Double Red' Raised by T. Bat in the 18th century. Stems *c*.17cm.
'Bridal Veil' Known since the 17th century. Stems *c*.35cm. Well scented.
'Heidi' C. Frickart 1959. Stems *c*.20cm.
'Hope' Raised by Allwoods in 1946. Stems *c*.25cm. Well scented.
'Laced Joy' Raised by Allwoods in 1947. Stems *c*.30cm.
'Laced Romeo' Raised by Allwoods in 1963. Stems *c*.30cm. Well scented.
'London Delight' Raised by F. R. McQuown before 1946. Stems *c*.25cm. Well scented.
'London Poppet' Raised by F. R. McQuown in 1946. Stems *c*.25cm. Variable.
'Mrs Sinkins' Raised by J. Sinkins in 1868. Stems *c*.20–25cm. Flowers untidy but wonderfully scented.
'Old Crimson Clove' Known since the 16th century. Stems *c*.25cm. Well scented.
'Old Pink Clove' An old cultivar of unknown origin. Stems weak, to 40cm. Well scented.
'Paisley Gem' Raised by J. Macree around 1798. Stems *c*.30cm. Well scented.
'Prudence' Raised by Allwoods before 1953. Stems *c*.30cm.
'Rose de Mai' *C*.1820. Stems *c*.25cm.
'Sam Barlow' An old variety, known since the early 19th century, resembling Mrs Sinkins in form. Compact.
'Sops-in-Wine' An old cultivar of unknown origin. Stems *c*.17cm.
'Sweetheart Abbey' An old cultivar from Sweetheart Abbey in SW Scotland; *c*.25cm.
'White Ladies' An old cultivar of unknown origin. Stems *c*.25cm. Well scented.

Single and semi-double pinks

'Arthur' Raised by Allwoods in 1920. Stems *c*.28cm. Well scented.
'Brympton Red' Raiser not recorded, pre-1960. Stems *c*.25cm. Well scented.
'Constance Finnis' Raised by C. S. Finnis pre-1969 and named by her daughter, Valerie. Well scented. White, with clear crimson markings.
'Dewdrop' Raised by Allwoods before 1932. Stems *c*.15cm. Well scented.
'Eileen' Raised by Allwoods before 1927. Stems *c*.25cm. Well scented.
'Farnham Rose' Soft maroon, with flecks and blotches. Well scented.
'Glory Lyonnaise' An old cultivar of unknown origin. Stems *c*.30cm.
'Gravetye Gem' Raised by W. E. Th. Ingwersen before 1940. Well scented.
'Hollycroft Fragrance' Raised by Hollycroft Nurseries before 1979. Stems *c*.15cm. Well scented.
'Inchmery' Raised in the 18th century. Stems *c*.28cm. Well scented.
'Kesteven Chambery' Raised by A. E. Robinson *c*.1970. Stems *c*.15cm.
'Lady Glanville' Raised in *c*.1840. Stems *c*.25cm. Well scented.
'Musgrave's Pink' syn. 'Charles Musgrave' Raised *c*.1730. Stems *c*.20cm. Well scented.
'Painted Beauty' An old cultivar of unknown origin. Stems *c*.20cm.
'Pheasant's Eye' An old cultivar known since 1671. Stems *c*.30cm. Well scented.
'Queen of Sheba' Early 17th century. Stems *c*.25cm. Well scented.

'White Ladies'

'Sam Barlow'

Dianthus 'Constance Finnis' at Wisley

Dianthus 'Rose de Mai' at Bressingham Gardens

Dianthus 'Old Pink Clove'

Dianthus 'Bat's Double Red'

A collection of pinks with *Allium christophii* at Northbourne Court, Kent

'Prudence'

'London Delight'

'Paisley Gem'

'Alice'

'London Poppet'

'London Poppet'

'Laced Joy'

'Old Crimson Clove'

'Heidi'

'Hope'

'Laced Romeo'

'Sweetheart Abbey'

'Sops-in-Wine'

'Bridal Veil'

'Mrs Sinkins'

Specimens from Ramparts Nursery, Essex, 4 June. ⅔ life size

DIANTHUS

Dianthus 'Doris', one of the most popular pinks

'Diane'   'Doris'   'Constance'

'Helen'   'Achievement'

'Iceberg'   'Brilliance'   'Haytor White'

'Widecombe Fair'   'Show Ideal'

'Freckles'   'Freckles'/'William of Essex'   'William of Essex'

Specimens from Ramparts Nursery, Essex, 4 June. ⅔ life size

Modern garden pinks

'Achievement'   Raised by Allwoods before 1959; stems 22cm, well scented.

'Annabelle'   Raised by Th. Charli. before 1957, stems 30cm.

'Anthony'   Raised by P. A. Fenn in 1967; stems 20cm.

'Brilliance'   Raised by P. A. Fenn in 1975; long flowering season, stems 20cm.

'Constance'   Raised by Allwoods before 1955; stems 30cm.

'Desmond'   Raised by Mrs D. Underwood in 1978, strong-growing, stems 25cm.

'Diane'   Raised by Allwoods in 1964; a sport of 'Doris', stems 26cm.

'Doris'   Raised by Allwoods before 1954; vigorous and well scented, stems 26cm.

'Freckles'   Raised by C. H. Fielder in 1948. Well scented, stems 20cm.

'Gaiety'   Raised by Lindabruce Nurseries in around 1955, stems 25cm.

'Golden Cross'   Raised by J. Galbally before 1972; stems 25cm.

'Gran's Favourite'   Raised by Mrs D. Underwood; well scented, stems 25cm.

'Haytor White'   Raised by C. Wyatt in 1971; well scented, robust, stems 33cm.

'Helen'   Raised by Allwoods before 1948; well-scented, stems 30cm.

'Houndspool Cheryl' syn. 'Cheryl'   Raised by J. Whetman in 1980; stems 27cm.

'Houndspool Ruby' syn 'Ruby Doris'   Raised by J. Whetman in 1977; stems 27cm.

'Iceberg'   Raised by C. H. Fielder in 1950; well scented, with a second crop of flowers; stems 33cm.

'Kesteven Kirkstead'   Raised by A. E. Robinson; stems 15cm.

'Pink Bouquet'   Raised by Mrs D. Underwood in 1958; well scented, with a second crop of flowers; stems 22cm.

'Pink Mrs Sinkins'   Raised by C. Turner before 1908; well scented, stems 30cm.

'Polly Piggott'   A modern variety of unrecorded origin; stems 25cm.

'Portrait'   A modern variety of unrecorded origin; good on light soil, stems 25cm.

'Ruth'   Allwoods before 1933; stems 27cm.

'Show Ideal'   Raised by Allwoods in 1945; strong-growing, stems 30cm.

'Thomas'   Raised by C. Wyatt in 1977; stems 25cm.

'Valda Wyatt'   Raised by C. Wyatt in 1977; stems 25cm.

'Widecombe Fair'   Raised by C. Wyatt in 1974. Well scented and an unusual apricot colour; stems 30cm.

'William of Essex'   Raised by Ramparts Nursery in 1982, a sport of 'Freckles' (q.v.); well scented, stems 10cm.

'Winsome'   Raised by C. H. Fielder in 1947; strong-growing, stems 25cm.

Dianthus 'Golden Cross' at Wisley

Dianthus 'Thomas'

Dianthus 'Haytor White'

Dianthus 'Pink Mrs Sinkins'

'Gaiety'   'Houndspool Ruby'   'Annabelle'

'Pink Bouquet'   'Winsome'

'Portrait'   'Anthony'   'Houndspool Cheryl'

'Polly Piggott'   'Gran's Favourite'

'Desmond'   'Valda Wyatt'   'Ruth'

Specimens from Ramparts Nursery, Essex, 4 June. ⅔ life size

Dianthus 'Kesteven Kirkstead' at Wisley

Sedum spectabile 'Carmen' with Small Tortoiseshell butterflies

Sedum telephium subsp. telephium in NW England

Sedum 'Sunset Cloud' at Wisley

Sedum maximum 'Atropurpureum'

Sedum alboroseum 'Medio-variegatum'

Sedum 'Ruby Glow'

Cotyledon orbiculata L. var. *oblonga* (Haw.)
DC. (*Crassulaceae*)   Native of S Africa, from
the N Transvaal to Lesotho and SE Cape
Province, growing in rocky places on cliffs and in
dry scrub at up to 3000m, flowering throughout
the year. Plant forming rosettes of obovate,
fleshy, white leaves to 20cm long; flowering
stems to 1m, with pendent flowers *c*.3cm long.
For well-drained soil in full sun. Hardy to
−10°C, or probably less, with the protection of a
pane of glass.

Sedum aizoon L. **'Aurantiacum'**
(*Crassulaceae*)   Native of N Japan in Hokkaido
and Honshu, in E Siberia, Mongolia and in N
and NW China (N Sinjiang), growing on dry
grassy slopes, in scrub and by rocky streams,
flowering in July–September. Stems to 50cm
from a stout, branching rhizome forming
spreading clumps. Leaves usually alternate.
Flowers 10–13mm across in heads about 6cm
across, yellow, or reddish in bud and fruit in
'Aurantiacum'. For good soil in sun or partial
shade, moist in summer. Hardy to −25°C.

Sedum alboroseum Baker **'Medio-variegatum'**
syn. *S. erythrostictum* Miq.   Native of E Siberia,
N China and ? Japan, flowering in July–October.
Similar to *S. spectabile* (q.v.), but differing in its
greenish flowers, alternate or opposite leaves and
inflorescence with longer lowest branches. The
variegated form is the one usually seen.

Sedum **'Ruby Glow'** syn. *S. cauticola*
'Robustum'   A hybrid between *S. cauticola*
Praeger and *S. telephium* L.; it forms sprawling
clumps of stems to 25cm, very grey leaves, with
deep purplish flowers in July–August. Hardy to
−15°C.

Sedum spectabile Boreau   Native of Korea and
NE China (Heilonjiang), flowering in July–
September. Stems to 70cm from a stout,
branched rootstock, forming dense clumps.
Leaves fleshy, glaucous, opposite or whorled.
Flowers in a head *c*.12cm across, with flowers
each 10mm across, with stamens longer than the
petals; much visited by butterflies. 'Carmen' is
one of several cultivars in various shades of
mauve-pink. 'Iceberg' has white flowers. All do
best in rich, sandy soil, with ample water in
summer. Hardy to −20°C.

Sedum **'Sunset Cloud'**   A hybrid between
'Ruby Glow' (q.v.) and *S. telephium* subsp.
maximum 'Atropurpureum' (q.v.) raised by Jim
Archibald of 'The Plantsmen' in around 1970.
Leaves purplish grey; stems to 30cm, sprawling.
'Vera Jameson' is similar.

Sedum telephium L. subsp. *maximum* (L.)
Krosker   Native of Europe, from France
eastwards to N Turkey and the Caucasus,
growing in dry, rocky places and open pine forest
at up to 2300m, flowering in July–September.
Stems few, erect to 45cm, from a stout rootstock.
Leaves broadly ovate, amplexicaul, to 4cm wide.
Inflorescence very dense; flowers 6–10mm
across, usually greenish white, rarely pink. In
'Atropurpureum' the leaves are deep purple.
Hardy to −15°C.

Sedum telephium L. subsp. *telephium*   Native
of Europe, from Ireland and Spain eastwards to
China, Siberia and Japan, growing in open grassy
places in woods and scrub, flowering in August–
September. Stems few, to 50cm tall, usually
erect, from a stout rootstock. Leaves oblong,
toothed, truncate at its base. Flowers purplish
pink, rarely white. For good, well-drained soil
not too dry. Hardy to −20°C.

Cotyledon orbiculata var. *oblonga* at 3000m on Carlyle's Hoek, NE Cape Province

Sedum aizoon 'Aurantiacum'

Sedum telephium subsp. *maximum*

Lathyrus grandiflorus Sibth. & Sm. (*Leguminosae*) Native of S Italy, Sicily, Greece and the S Balkan peninsula, and NW Africa, growing in scrub in the mountains, flowering in May–July. Stems from a suckering and invasive rootstock, pubescent, ridged but not winged, to 1.5m. Leaves with 1 pair of ovate leaflets and a simple or 3-branched tendril. Flowers 1–4 on a stalk 2.5–3cm across. Pods with 15–20 seeds, but rarely formed in gardens. A pretty but invasive plant, difficult to remove once it is established. It is best in a narrow bed at the base of a hedge, or where it can hang down over a wall, and not be in danger of swamping other plants.

Lathyrus japonicus Willd. subsp. **maritimus** (L.) P. W. Ball **Sea Pea** Native of the colder coasts of the N Hemisphere, south to the Scilly Isles, to New Jersey and to Del Norte Co., California, and by the Great Lakes, growing on shingle and on sand dunes (var. *acutiformis* (Bab.) Pedersen) flowering in June–August. Stems to 90cm, creeping, from a deep rootstock. Stipules broadly hastate. Leaves rather fleshy and leathery when growing by the sea, but losing this character when growing in gardens, glaucous, with 3–4 pairs of obovate leaflets, usually with small tendrils. Flowers up to 15cm on a stalk, around 1.8cm across, purplish or bluish. For deep, moist and well-drained soil in a cool position.

Lathyrus latifolius L. **Everlasting Pea** Native of Europe, except the north, from France to Spain and Portugal, east to Poland, S Russia and the Caucasus (commonly naturalized in England, Belgium and Germany, in E North America, and in N California) growing in scrub, grassy roadsides and waste places, flowering in May–July. Stems scrambling or climbing to 3m, from a stout and sometimes suckering rootstock, glabrous or pubescent, winged. Leaves with 1 pair of linear to ovate leaflets, to 15 × 5cm, and branched tendrils. Flowers 5–15 on a stalk, 2–3.5cm across, usually purplish pink, but also white, white with pink veins or pale pink with darker veins. Pale-coloured forms have been given various names such as 'White Pearl' ('Weisse Perle'), 'Pink Pearl' ('Rosa Perle'), 'Blushing Bride', etc., and can be grown with difficulty from cuttings, but similar plants can be raised from seed. Easily grown in any soil in warm position. A beautiful plant with a very long flowering season.

Lathyrus laxiflorus (Desf.) Kuntz. Native of Europe from S Italy to Greece, SW Russia, the Caucasus, Turkey, Syria and N Iran, growing in woods, scrub and shady roadsides, flowering in June–July. Plant forming clumps from a tuberous rootstock. Stems scrambling to 50cm, with leaf-like stipules. Leaves with 1 pair of broadly elliptic or lanceolate leaflets 1–4cm long without a tendril. Flowers 1.5–2cm long, usually bicoloured. For well-drained soil in sun or partial shade. Hardy to –15°C.

Lathyrus mulkak Lipsky Native of C Asia, in the Pamir-Alai, in the districts of Saravshan, Hissar, Darvas, etc., growing in scrub at around 3000m, flowering in June–August. Plant with climbing stems to 2m, from a deep, branched rhizome. Flowers 25–30mm across. This beautiful species is not easy to grow, and requires a very well-drained but deep, rich, sandy soil in full sun. Hardy to −15°C or less.

Lathyrus grandiflorus, a rampant weed in a border

Lathyrus japonicus subsp. *maritimus* growing on shingle at Dungeness, Kent

Lathyrus sylvestris at Dungeness, Kent

Lathyrus latifolius with Santolina at Cockermouth

Lathyrus rotundifolius

Lathyrus laxiflorus

Lathyrus latifolius 'White Pearl'

Lathyrus mulkak

Lathyrus rotundifolius Willd.   Native of the Crimea, growing in pine forests, flowering in June–July. Subsp. *miniatus* (Bieb. ex Stev.) Davis, from the Caucasus, N Iran and N & E Turkey, grows in scrub, wet meadows and corn fields, flowering in June–July. Stems glabrous to 2m, from a perennial stock. Leaves with 1 pair of rounded obovate, elliptic or suborbicular leaflets, and branched tendrils. Flowers up to 10 on a stalk, deep pinkish purple or reddish, 1.5–2.5cm across. Subsp. *miniatus* is said to have longer leaflets, stouter, more broadly winged stems and a larger calyx with longer teeth. It is not clear to which subspecies the cultivated plants shown here belong, but the bright-reddish-flowered plant is probably subsp. *miniatus*. For any soil in sun or partial shade.

Lathyrus sylvestris L. **Narrow-leaved Everlasting Pea**   Native of most of Europe, including England, NW Africa, N Turkey and the Caucasus, growing in woods, scrub, shady woodside banks and on shingle by the sea, flowering in June–August. Stems winged, climbing, from a stout rootstock, to 2cm or more; stipules narrowly lanceolate. Leaves with one pair of linear or narrowly lanceolate leaflets to 15cm long, 2cm wide, with branched tendrils. Flowers usually flesh-pink, 1.3–2cm across, up to 12 on a stalk. As rampant as the commoner *L. latifolius*, but with smaller flowers.

Lathyrus tuberosus L. **Fyfield Pea**   Native of most of Europe, from France and Spain eastwards to Russia and Siberia and southwards to Turkey and W Iran, growing in grassy places, water meadows, hedges or corn fields, flowering in June–August. Plant spreading by thin underground rhizomes which have small edible tubers. Stems not winged, to 100cm. Leaflets 1 pair, elliptic to broadly oblanceolate, c.30cm long, with one tendril. Stipules lanceolate, semi-sagittate. Stems with 3–9 flowers, 12–20mm across. For any soil in full sun; slightly invasive but with a long flowering period; suitable for meadow gardens or for a rough bank.

Lathyrus latifolius, a veined seedling at Dungeness, Kent

Lathyrus tuberosus

Lathyrus latifolius

Galega officinalis 'His Majesty'

Galega orientalis

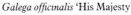

Hedysarum coronarium with a lead tank at Edington, Wiltshire

Hedysarum hedysaroides above St Luc, the Valais

Galega officinalis L. syns. *G. bicolor* Hausskn., *G. coronilloides* Freyn & Sint. (*Leguminosae*) **Goat's Rue** Native of C & S Europe, the Caucasus, Turkey and Lebanon, east to C Asia and W Pakistan, growing in scrub, woods, marshy fields and roadsides, flowering in June–September. Often naturalized on roadside banks in England. Plant with rather lax stems to 1.5m. Leaflets in 4–10 pairs. Inflorescence with 30–50 flowers, 10–15mm across, variable in colour from white, to purple or bicoloured. 'His Majesty' is one of the selected clones of *G.* × *hartlandii*, a hybrid between *G. bicolor* and *G. officinalis*. *G. bicolor* Hausskn. is now considered merely a colour form of *G. officinalis*, so the name *G.* × *hartlandii* is unnecessary. Other colour selections are 'Alba', 'Candida' and 'Lady Wilson'. Easily grown in sun or partial shade.

Galega orientalis Lam. Native of the Caucasus, growing in subalpine meadows, on riverbanks, in scrub and open forest, flowering in May–June. Plant with upright stems to 1.5m, and spreading by creeping underground rhizomes. Leaflets 30–60cm long, acuminate. Flowers bluish, usually larger than *G. officinalis*. Pods deflexed. A beautiful, if rather invasive, plant for the large herbaceous border or meadow, flowering in late May or June, and growing well in E Scotland. Hardy to −20°C.

Hedysarum coronarium L. (*Leguminosae*) Native of the W Mediterranean east to Sicily, and naturalized elsewhere, growing in grassy places, moist in spring, flowering in March–May. Plant with erect or leaning stems to 1m. Leaflets 15–35mm long, in 3–5 pairs. Flowers 12–15mm long, reddish purple or carmine. Pod splitting into rounded, prickly segments. For well-drained soil in a sunny position. Sometimes grown as a fodder crop in S Europe. Hardy to −15°C perhaps. Photographed in the Old Vicarage Garden, Edington, Wiltshire.

Hedysarum hedysaroides (L.) Schinz & Thell. syn. *H. obscurum* L. (*Leguminosae*) Native of the Alps and Carpathians, east to Romania, Siberia and Japan (Rebun Island), growing in subalpine meadows, stony mountainsides or cliffs at 1200–2500m in the Alps, flowering in July–August. Plant forming spreading clumps, with single stems up to 20cm tall. Leaflets in 4–6 pairs. Flowers 15–25mm long. For well-drained soil, moist in summer. Hardy to −20°C.

Ononis spinosa L. **Spiny Restharrow** (*Leguminosae*) Native of England and most of Europe except the far north and north-east, south to Turkey, Syria and east to Iran and Pakistan, growing in chalk and limestone grassland, stony hillsides and open pine forests, flowering in May–August. Plant with few stems to 80cm, woody and spiny towards the base, often sticky with glands. Leaflets *c*.1.5cm long. Flowers 10–20mm long. Shown here is subsp. *spinosa*, found mainly in N & W Europe. Easily grown in well-drained soil, or in a sunny meadow. Other species of Restharrow are shrubby with yellow or pink flowers, annuals or creeping perennials (*O. repens* L.).

Trifolium rubens L. (*Leguminosae*) Native of C Europe, from N Spain to C Russia, Romania,

Trifolium rubens, one of the largest clovers

and Albania, growing in dry, open woods and scrub, flowering in June. Plant with numerous upright stems from rhizomes, to 60cm tall. Leaflets up to 7cm long. Flower-heads to 8cm long, cylindrical, with purple or white flowers. One of the showiest clovers, easily grown in a sunny rather dry position. Hardy to −20°C or lower. Other native species are good for meadow gardens. *T. pratense* L., the common red clover, is easily grown and very common as a fodder crop. *T. medium* L., the Zigzag Clover, forms spreading clumps by underground stems. It is tolerant of more shade and usually found on rather heavy soil.

Vicia canescens Lab. subsp. **variegata** (Willd.) Davis syn. *V. variegata* Willd. (*Leguminosae*) Native of E & NE Turkey, Soviet Armenia and NW & N Iran, growing in grassy places, abandoned fields, and on banks at 1600–2800m, flowering in June–July. Plant forming patches of erect stems to 80cm. Leaves greyish hairy, though even more silvery in other subspecies. Flowers lilac or bluish, 17–25mm long, 3–18 in a long-stalked, dense raceme. Seed pods usually hairy. For well-drained soil in a sunny position; shown here growing on a ledge on the rock garden at Kew. Hardy to −20°C. Related to *V. cracca*, the tufted vetch, a beautiful and common climbing plant of hedges throughout Europe.

Vicia sylvatica L. **Wood Vetch**   Native of Europe, from Ireland and Scotland east to Siberia, and south in the mountains to France, Albania and S Russia, growing on wood edges, scrub and on coastal cliffs and shingle, in June–August. Plant climbing with stems to 2m. Leaflets 5–12 pairs, usually 6–9, oblong-elliptic. Tendrils branched. Flowers up to 18 on the raceme, 15–20mm long, white with bluish veins. For well-drained moist soil and a cool position. Hardy to −20°C and below.

Vicia unijuga A. Br. (*Leguminosae*)   Native of E Siberia, N China, Korea, Sakhalin and throughout Japan, growing in scrub and grassy places, flowering in June–October. Plant with many stems, 60–100cm tall, without tendrils. Leaflets 2, 4–7cm long. Flowers 12–15mm long, bluish purple. For a sunny or partly shaded position, moist in summer. Hardy to −20°C.

Vicia sylvatica in Finland

Vicia unijuga at Kew

Vicia canescens subsp. *variegata* on the rock garden at Kew

Ononis spinosa on chalk downs in Wiltshire

Aruncus dioicus by the Japanese Bridge at Wisley

Cardiandra alternifolia near Kyoto, Japan

Filipendula ulmaria 'Aurea'

Aruncus dioicus (Walter) Fernald syns. *A. silvester* Kostel, *A. vulgaris* Raf. (*Rosaceae*) Native of E North America, from Pennsylvania to Iowa, south to Georgia and Missouri, and in Europe from Belgium and the Pyrenees eastwards to the Caucasus and Siberia, N China and Japan (where it is particularly variable), growing in damp woods, in shady places and by streams usually in mountain areas, flowering in June–August. Plant forming very large clumps of stems to 2m. Leaves to 1m long, 2-pinnate, with ovate leaflets. Flowers 5mm across, usually unisexual. For any moist soil in partial shade. Hardy to −20°C or less. A handsome plant, like a giant *Astilbe*.

Cardiandra alternifolia Sieb. & Zucc. (*Hydrangeaceae*)   Native of S Honshu, Shikoku and Kyushu, growing in moist woods in the mountains, flowering in July–September. Plant with erect stems to 70cm, like an herbaceous hydrangea, with alternate, narrowly ovate, acuminate leaves. Calyx lobes 2–3, petal-like, on sterile flowers around the margin of the inflorescence. Fertile flowers *c*.6mm across. For moist, peaty soil in partial shade. Hardy to −15°C perhaps.

Deinanthe caerulea Stapf (*Hydrangeaceae*) Native of Hubei, growing in wet places on shady cliffs, flowering in July–August. Stems few to 45cm, from a tufted rootstock. Leaves *c*.15cm long. Flowers 2cm across white, pale blue or purple. For a cool, sheltered, moist position in shade, protected from drying wind. Hardy to −20°C perhaps.

Filipendula kamtschatica (Pall.) Maxim. (*Rosaceae*)   Native of Japan in Hokkaido and N Honshu and of E Siberia, growing along streams in the mountains, often in large quantity, flowering in June–September. Plant forming large clumps of stems to 2m. Leaves with a large, round terminal leaflet, 15–25cm across, palmately 5–lobed, deeply double-toothed. Lateral leaflets very small or absent. Flowers 6–8mm across, white or pale pink. For moist soil in sun or partial shade. Hardy to −25°C.

Filipendula ulmaria (L.) Maxim **'Aurea' Golden-leaved Meadow Sweet**   Native of Europe, from Iceland south to Portugal and east to SE Turkey (Hakkari), the Caucasus, Siberia and NW China, growing in grassy bogs, wet ditches and by streams often in willow scrub, flowering in May–September. Plant forming clumps, and often covering large areas. Stems to 2m. Leaves aromatic, emerging golden in 'Aurea', with 3–5 pairs of leaflets. Flowers to 10mm across, creamy-white. For moist soil; the golden-leaved form needs shade if the leaves are not to scorch. All need ample moisture. Hardy to −20°C or less.

Filipendula rubra (Hill) Robinson **'Venusta'** syn. **'Magnifica' Queen-of-the-Prairie**   Native of E North America, from Pennsylvania to Michigan and Illinois, south to Georgia and Kentucky and Iowa, and naturalized in New England, growing in meadows and prairies, flowering in June–August. Plant with several stems to 2.5m. Leaves irregularly pinnate, with the terminal leaflet large, 7–9 lobed, incised and toothed. Lateral leaflets also incised into 3–5

Kirengeshoma koreana

Francoa ramosa

Francoa sonchifolia

Kirengeshoma palmata

Deinanthe caerulea in Sussex

lobes. Flowers bright pink. For good, moist soil in full sun. Hardy to −20°C or less.

Francoa ramosa D. Don (*Saxifragaceae*)
Native of Chile, in the region of Valparaiso, flowering in December–January. Plant forming small clumps of softly-hairy evergreen leaves, sometimes producing a leafy stem to 20cm. Flowering stems to 90cm, branched below, with loosely arranged white flowers; petals often spotted. For a warm sheltered position. Hardy to −5°C perhaps. It is likely that this species, *F. sonchifolia* and *F. appendiculata* Cav. are merely forms of one very variable species.

Francoa sonchifolia Cav.   Native of Chile, growing in rather dry areas, in rock crevices on the sides of gorges overhanging water, flowering in December–January. Plant forming mats of softly hairy evergreen leaves from creeping rhizomes. Flowering stems to 60cm unbranched, with a rather compact inflorescence of pink flowers. For a warm sheltered position in sun or partial shade. Hardy to −10°C perhaps. The hardiest species.

Kirengeshoma palmata Yatabe
(*Hydrangeaceae*)   Native of Japan in Shikoku and Kyushu, growing in woods in the mountains, flowering in August. Plant with several stems to 120cm from a stout rhizome. Leaves 10–20cm long and as wide, with shallow, long-pointed lobes. Flowers with fleshy petals *c*.3cm long. *Kirengeshoma koreana* Nakai from Korea is little different, often more erect to 2m or more, with more open flowers. Both require moist leafy soil in partial shade, with ample water in later summer. Hardy to −20°C.

Filipendula kamtschatica

Filipendula rubra 'Venusta'

63

'Bressingham Beauty'

'Weisse Gloria'

'Cattleya'

'Betsy Cuperus'

'Federsee'

Astilbe rivularis

Specimens from the Savill Gardens, Windsor, 20 July. ¼ life size

Astilbe rivularis var. myriantha

Astilbe 'Deutschland'

Astilbe 'Fanal'

Astilbe 'Jo Ophurst'

Astilbe   All Astilbes require wet or moist peaty soil in partial shade, and make valuable late-flowering plants for the bog garden, with delicate leaves to contrast with bold foliage plants such as *Hosta*, the closely related *Rodgersia* and *Ligularia*. All are hardy to −20°C and less.

Astilbe × arendsii Arends (*Saxifragaceae*)   A group of hybrids between *A. davidii*, *A. astilboides*, *A. japonica* and *A. thunbergii*, raised by Georg Arends at Ronsdorf, Germany, from 1909 until 1955. Cultivars include:
'Cattleya'   Raised by G. Arends in 1953. Height *c*.90cm.
'Fanal'   Raised by G. Arends in 1933. Height *c*.60cm. Early-flowering.
'Granat'   Raised by G. Arends in 1920.
'Weisse Gloria' syn. 'White Gloria'   Raised by G. Arends in 1924. Height *c*.60cm. Early-flowering.

Astilbe × hybrida hort. ex Iev. & Lus.   A group of hybrids between *A. chinensis* and other species, sometimes included under *G. × arendsii*. Cultivars include:
'Betsy Cuperus'   Very graceful, spreading habit, to 1.2m high. Raised by B. Ruys in 1917.
'Bressingham Beauty'   Rich pink with horizontal or slightly drooping side branches; stems to 1m. Raised by Alan Bloom.
'Jo Ophurst'   Upright side branches give this a

Astrilbes at Longstock Park Gardens, Hampshire

stiff effect; stems to 90cm. Close to *A. chinensis* var. *davidii*, and late-flowering. Raised by B. Ruys in 1916.

Astilbe japonica (Morr. & Decne.) A. Gray
Native of Japan, in S Honshu, Shikoku and Kyushu, growing on moist rocks in ravines in the mountains, flowering in May–June. Stems to 80cm; flowering panicles 10–20cm long, dense; flowers white. Cultivars include:
'Deutschland'   Stems around 50cm; flowers pure white. Raised by G. Arends in 1920.
'Federsee'   Stems around 60cm. Raised by P. Theobolt in 1939.

Astilbe rivularis Buch.-Ham. ex D. Don
Native of the Himalayas, from Pakistan to SW China, in Yunnan, growing in scrub by streams at 1800–3300m, flowering in July–September. Plant with few stems 1–2m tall, from a stout rootstock. Leaves 2–3-pinnate, with ovate, pointed leaflets 2.5–10cm long. Inflorescence pyramidal, 30–60cm, with unbranched, upward-pointing side branches. Sepals and stamens 5, petals absent, carpels 2. In habit like *Aruncus dioicus*, but that is dioiceous, has 5 petals, numerous stamens in the male flowers, and 3 carpels in the female. *Astilbe rivularis* var. *myriantha*, from SW China, differs in the more branched and drooping side shoots of the inflorescence. It makes a very large and graceful late-flowering specimen.

Astilbe 'Granat' on the rock garden at Kew

Astilbe chinensis 'Purpurlanze'

Astilbe simplicifolia 'Bronze Elegans'

Astilbe chinensis 'Pumila'

Rodgersia pinnata 'Superba'

Astilbe chinensis (Maxim.) Franch. & Sav. var. *taquetii* (Léveillé) Vil. **'Purpurlanze'** (*Saxifragaceae*)   Native of E China, growing in damp woods and along shady streams, flowering in August, the last of the *Astilbes* to flower. Plant with upright stems to 1.2m. Leaflets broadly lanceolate with brownish stalks. Inflorescence with erect side branches; flowers magenta-purple. 'Pumila', sometimes considered a hybrid, has paler-pink flowers and stems to 45cm, and is close to the wild type of *A. chinensis*. For moist soil in sun or partial shade. Hardy to −20°C.

Astilbe simplicifolia Mak.   Native of Honshu, found only in Sunya and Sagama prefectures, where it is rare. A dwarf plant with simple basal leaves to 8cm long, with 3 or 5 lobes, deeply double-toothed. Inflorescence loose to 30cm, with spreading branches and white flowers. Numerous crosses have been made using this species, e.g. 'Bronze Elegans', which has pink flowers but retains the loose inflorescence and lobed, sharply toothed leaflets. For a moist, sheltered position, in partial shade. Hardy to −15°C perhaps.

Peltiphyllum peltatum (Torr.) Engl. syn. *Darmera peltata* (Torr.) Voss (*Saxifragaceae*) Native of California, from Tulare Co. northwards to S Oregon, growing by the banks of mountain streams below 1800m, in yellow pine and mixed evergreen forest, flowering in April–July before the leaves emerge. Stems 30–100cm, from a stout, creeping rhizome. Leaves 30–60cm across, peltate. Petals 5–7mm long. There is a dwarf form, 'Nanum', with leaves only 30cm high, 25cm across. *Astilboides tabularis* (Hemsl.) Engl. (syn. *Rodgersia tabularis*) (not shown), from NE China and North Korea, has rather similar peltate leaves, paler, of a smoother texture, up to 90cm across. The flowers are *Astilbe*-like, in a plume to 1.5m tall, produced in June–July.

Rodgersia aesculifolia Batalin (*Saxifragaceae*) Native of W China, in Gansu, Hupei and Sichuan, growing in damp woods and along streams in scrub at 1500–3200m, flowering in June–July. Plant with a creeping rootstock and basal leaves to 45cm across. Leaflets 7, to 25cm long, coarsely toothed. Inflorescence to 1.8m,

with white flowers. For moist, peaty soil in sun or partial shade. Hardy to −20°C. Leaves like *R. pinnata*, but always palmate; sepals accrescent after anthesis; leaf with idumentum along the veins and on the teeth beneath. Sepals not accrescent after anthesis and leaves with indumentum on the veins only are the distinguishing characters of *R. henrici*.

Rodgersia pinnata Franch. **'Superba'** syn. *Astilbe pinnata* (Franch.) Franch.   Native of W China, in Yunnan and S Sichuan, growing in moist, grassy places in scrub, open forest and by streams at 2100–3650m, flowering in June–July. Plant with a stout, shortly creeping rhizome. Leaves to 1m, usually partially pinnate, with 5–9 rugose leaflets, to 20cm long, glabrous above. Inflorescence 60–120cm; flowers white, pink, yellowish or reddish. For peaty soil in sun or partial shade. Hardy to −20°C. 'Superba' is a good form, with bright-pink flowers and leaves purplish when young. It often has palmate leaves, and may be a hybrid with *R. aesculifolia*.

Rodgersia podophylla A. Gray syn. *Astilbe podophylla* (A. Gray) Franch.   Native of Japan, in Hokkaido and Honshu, and of Korea, growing in moist woods in the mountains at 700–2000m, flowering in June–August. Plant with a stout, creeping rhizome, in time forming large clumps. Leaves palmate with 5 rather thin leaflets, the longest to 35cm long, with 3–5 shallow lobes towards the apex. Flowering stems to 1.3m; flowers white, with long acuminate sepals. For most soil in shade or a cool, sunny place by water, away from hot, drying wind. Hardy to −20°C or less.

Rodgersia sambucifolia Hemsl.   Native of W China, in Yunnan and S Sichuan, growing on mossy rocks often of limestone, in pine forest at 2700–3350m, flowering in June–July. Plant with shortly creeping rhizomes. Leaves pinnate or rarely irregularly pinnate, with 8–11 leaflets, with glandular hairs on the surface. Flowers white or pink; stamens and styles equal to or shorter than the sepals at anthesis. For moist, rich soil in sun or partial shade. Hardy to −20°C perhaps. The leaves of this really do look like *Sambucus*, with 6 pairs of sharply toothed leaflets and a sessile terminal one.

Rodgersia podophylla by a stream in Kent

Rodgersia sambucifolia

Peltiphyllum peltatum (leaves)

Peltiphyllum peltatum (flowers only)

Rodgersia podophylla in autumn colour at Kildrummy Castle

Rodgersia aesculifolia by a stream near Baoxing, Sichuan

Lythrum salicaria in a wet meadow in Connemara

Epilobium angustifolium f. *albiflorum* at Bracken Hill, Kent

Lythrum salicaria 'Firecandle'

Lythrum virgatum at the Royal Botanic Garden, Edinburgh

Epilobium dodoneaei

Cuphea cyanea Mocino & Sesse (*Lythraceae*) Native of Mexico in the Sierra Madre Oriental, flowering in July–September. Stems to 45cm from a woody rootstock. Leaves evergreen in mild climates. Flowers *c*.20mm long. For a warm, sheltered position in full sun. Hardy to −10°C, especially in very well-drained soil. Most *Cuphea* species are more tender and require protection from frost, but may be used for summer bedding.

Epilobium angustifolium L. syn. *Chamaenerion angustifolium* (L.) Scop. (*Onagraceae*) **Rosebay Willowherb** Native of most of Europe, N Asia and North America, south to Carolina and Arizona in the mountains, growing in woods and on grassy roadsides, especially in areas recently cleared of trees or burned, flowering in June–September. Plant with stems to 2m or more from strongly creeping underground rhizomes, forming large patches. Leaves to 20cm long, narrowly lanceolate, up to 5.5cm broad in var. *macrophyllum* (Hausskn.) Fern. Flowers with petals 21–22cm long, normally magenta, more rarely in shades of pink, and occasionally white in f. *albiflorum* (Dumort.) Hausskn. (shown here) with whitish sepals; flowers also white, but with red sepals in f. *spectabile* (Simmons) Fern. Rosebay Willowherb appears to be more variable in North America than in Europe, though pink- and white-flowered forms are recorded in both continents. The white form is an attractive plant for a wild garden or a position where its invasive rhizomes will not become a nuisance. Hardy to −20°C or less.

Epilobium dodoneaei Vill. syn. *E. rosmarinifolium* Haenke.   Native of Europe, from Germany and S France to W Russia and Greece, growing on river gravel and in moist screes, at up to 1500m in Turkey, flowering in August–September. Stems 30–85cm from a creeping rootstock, forming spreading patches. Leaves 2–2.5cm long, to 3.5mm wide, linear, sparsely pubescent with spreading hairs. Flowers 3.0–3.5cm across. The closely related *E. stevenii* Boiss., from the S Caucasus, N Iran and Turkey, has wider, 4–8mm,. silky-hairy leaves. For any good, well-drained soil in full sun. Hardy to −20°C.

Epilobium glabellum Forster fil.   Native of New Zealand, from the East Cape southwards, growing in riverbeds, grassland, and mountain sides at up to 1800m, flowering in December–February, or June–August in the northern hemisphere. Stems to 30cm, creeping or upright from a slender rootstock. Leaves ovate, finely toothed, opposite or alternate. Flowers 6–25mm across, white or yellowish in 'Sulphureum'. For moist soil in a cool position in sun or partial shade. Hardy to −15°C perhaps.

Limonium chrysocephalum (Regel) Lincz (*Plumbaginaceae*)   Native of C Asia in NW China (Sinjiang), growing in dry, stony steppe and desert, flowering in May. Plant with many upright stems to 30cm from a tough, woody rootstock. Leaves linear. Flowers *c.*10mm long. For well-drained, dry soil in full sun. Hardy to −25°C or less, and tolerant of summer heat and drought.

Limonium latifolium (Sm.) Kuntz.   Native of SE Europe from Bulgaria and Romania to S Russia, growing in steppe and dry grassland, flowering in July–September. Plant with rosettes of spathulate to elliptical leathery, evergreen leaves, to 60cm long and 15cm wide, from a tough, deep rootstock. Flowering stems to 80cm, much branched, with whitish hyaline bracts and a small purple corolla *c.*6mm long. For sandy, well-drained soil in full sun. Hardy to −15°C, possibly less in a dry climate.

Lythrum salicaria L. (*Lythraceae*) **Purple Loosestrife**   Native of Europe, from Ireland south to North Africa and eastwards to India, China and Japan, growing in wet meadows, shallow water and reed swamps, flowering in July–September. Stems several from a stout rootstock, to 180cm tall. Leaves ovate to narrowly lanceolate, opposite or in whorls of 3, truncate or semi-amplexicaul at the base. Flowers with 12 stamens, and petals 10mm long. 'Feuerkerze' syn. 'Firecandle' has more pinkish-red, less magenta flowers than the usual wild form. For wet soil in sun or partial shade. Hardy to −25°C or less.

Lythrum virgatum L.   Native of C Europe, from NW Italy and E Russia, southwards to Greece, Turkey, the Caucasus and east to C Asia and NW China, growing in marshes and shallow water, flowering in June–August. Stems several from a stout rootstock to 200cm, branched above. Leaves linear-lanceolate, tapered towards the base. Petals 6–9mm long. A much more graceful plant than the commoner *L. salicaria*. For wet soil in sun or partial shade. Hardy to −20°C or less. Less purple- and more pinkish-flowered named clones are cultivated, such as 'Rose Queen'.

Limonium chrysocephalum in a cold desert near Sairam Nor, Sinjiang

Epilobium glabellum   *Cuphea cyanea* at Sissinghurst Castle

Limonium latifolium with *Artemisia* 'Powys Castle' at Wisley

Oenothera tetragona 'Clarence Elliott' at Edington, Wiltshire

Oenothera missouriensis

Oenothera fruticosa

Oenothera tetragona

Oenothera acaulis Cav. syn. *O. taraxifolia* hort. (*Onagraceae*)   Native of C Chile, from Coquimbo to Concepción, where it is common, growing in gravelly places and disturbed ground, flowering in November–March, or May–September in the north. Plant with short, branching stems to 15cm high, forming a twiggy mass or sometimes stemless, and deeply cut, dandelion-like leaves. Flowers opening in the late evening, *c*.9p.m., fading to pinkish by daybreak, to 7.5cm across, on a tube 5–12.5cm long. For poor soil, well-drained, in full sun. Hardy to −10°C perhaps.

Oenothera caespitosa Nutt.   Native of N Mexico and from California northwards on the east of the Sierras to Utah and E Washington, growing on dry stony slopes, in open scrub and pinyon pine woods in very dry areas, at 1000–3000m, flowering in April–August. Plant tufted with a thick rootstock and stemless or with short stems to 20cm. Leaves usually hairy, linear-lanceolate, toothed and wavy edged, tapering into a winged stalk. Flowers opening at night, white, fading pink, with a tube up to 10cm long and petals to 4cm long, pollinated by hawkmoths. A very beautiful plant for a sheltered and dry, sunny position. Hardy to −15°C or less, but intolerant of winter damp and often short-lived. Shown here is subsp. *caespitosa*, which includes var. *eximea*.

Oenothera 'Clarence Elliott'   A distinct form of *O. tetragona* (see below) with purplish foliage and red buds; flowers yellow, *c*.6cm across. 'Fyrverkeri' ('Fireworks') and 'Glaber' are similar but less purple. Stems *c*.50cm. For good soil in full sun. Hardy to −20°C or less.

Oenothera fruticosa L.   Native from Florida to Oklahoma north to New England, New York, Tennessee and Missouri, growing in marshes, meadows and wood margins, in sandy places and even in coastal salt marshes, flowering in May–August. Plant with erect or ascending stems to 100cm from a compact rootstock. Leaves lanceolate, oblong or linear. Flowers with calyx pubescent but not glandular. Flowers 3–5cm across. Capsule clavate, tapering to a slender stalk. For any good soil in sun or partial shade. Hardy to −20°C or less.

Oenothera acaulis

Oenothera speciosa at Edington, Wiltshire

Oenothera missouriensis Sims   Native of Missouri and Kansas, south to Texas, growing in rocky or sandy places, flowering in May–September. Plant with a deep root and short, decumbent leafy stems to 30cm. Flowers 6–12cm across; fruit ellipsoid to suborbicular, 5–8cm long, with broad wings. Seeds in one row, crested. A fine dwarf species with large flowers for well-drained soil in full sun. Hardy to –15°C.

Oenothera rosea Ait.   Native of S Arizona and Texas, south through Mexico to Bolivia and naturalized elsewhere, e.g. South Africa, growing in canyons and river valleys, flowering in April–August. Stems to 60cm, upright or sprawling, flowering the first year. Leaves shallow-toothed to pinnatifid. Flowers pink, open in the daytime, small, up to 2cm across. For a hot, sunny position. Hardy to – 10°C perhaps, but easily raised from seed.

Oenothera speciosa Nutt.   Native of Missouri and Kansas, south to Texas and Mexico, and naturalized in other parts of SE United States, from Virginia to Florida, growing in dry fields and prairies, flowering in May–July. Plant with creeping underground rhizomes and stems to *c*.30cm. Leaves oblong-lanceolate to linear, with large triangular teeth or almost pinnatifid; flowers nodding in bud, opening in the evening, 4–8cm across, white or pale pink. Capsule obovoid, 9-ribbed; seeds in more than 2 rows. For well-drained soil in full sun. Hardy to – 15°C or less, but intolerant of winter damp, especially in rich soil.

Oenothera tetragona Roth   Native of New York to Illinois, south to Georgia and Tennessee, growing in marshes, meadows and damp scrub, flowering in May–August. Stems to 1m, usually *c*.45cm from a compact rootstock. Leaves lanceolate or linear to ovate in var. *fraseri* (Pursh) Munz. Flowers with glandular hairs on the calyx and ovary, to 6cm across. Capsule ellipsoid or oblong with a short stalk, 4-angled. For any good soil in full sun. Hardy to – 20°C or less.

Oenothera caespitosa subsp. *caespitosa* at Edington, Wiltshire

Oenothera rosea

Aciphylla aurea

Aciphylla squarrosa (inflorescence)

Heracleum mantegazzianum

Aciphylla squarrosa

Levisticum officinale

China (Heilonjiang), growing in grassy places and open woods in the mountains, flowering in August–September. Stems few from a thick rootstock, 1–2m tall. Leaves with inflated purplish sheaths. Flowers deep purple, in umbels to 12cm across. Fruits 8 × 5mm. For good, leafy soil, moist in summer, flowering in 2 years from seed. The specimen shown here was grown in the very dry summer of 1989, so is rather small. Hardy to −20°C or below.

Gunnera magellanica Lam. (*Gunneraceae*) Native of the Falkland Islands, SW Argentina, S Chile to 35°30′S and along the Andes to 1°N, growing in damp grassy places, flowering in October–February. Plant creeping to form extensive patches. Leaf stalks 1.5–20cm; leaves up to 5.5cm × 9cm, toothed. Male flowers (shown here) on slender stalks to 12cm, the female stouter, finally with scarlet fleshy fruits. Hardy to −10°C or lower.

Gunnera manicata Lindl. ex Andre   Native of S Brazil, in the Serro do Mar, growing by streams in grassland and on wet rocks in the mountains at 700–1200m, flowering in May–June in gardens in the north, December in the wild. Plant huge, with a large creeping rhizome and leaves 1.5–5m across, on prickly petioles to 2.5m tall. Differs from *G. tinctoria* in its larger size and slender, flexuious inflorescence branches, over 15cm long. For rich, wet soil. Hardy to −10°C, with protection.

Gunnera tinctoria (Molina) Mirbel syn. *G. chilensis* Lam.   Native of Chile, from Valparaiso southwards, reported also from Ecuador and Columbia, and naturalized in W Ireland, W France and the Azores, growing in damp places and by streams and lakes, flowering in June–August. Plant slowly spreading, forming dense clumps. Leaf stalks to 1.5m, with stiff spines. Leaf blades, to 1.5m across, cordate, deeply lobed and toothed. Flowers minute, on *c*. 12 cm long branches on a compound inflorescence to 1m. The rootstock is rather tender, surviving *c*. −10°C, and so requires protection in autumn by piling the dying leaves over the growing points.

Heracleum mantegazzianum Somm. & Lev. (*Umbelliferae*) **Giant Hogweed**   Native of the Caucasus, growing in damp places by streams, flowering in June–August and often naturalized by rivers in the rest of Europe. Often perennial, but sometimes biennial or monocarpic. Stems to 5m, up to 10cm in diameter, red-spotted. Leaves to 3m long, pinnate, coarsely toothed. Umbels to 1.5m across. A statuesque plant for the wild garden, indeed one of the largest of all hardy perennials. The plant contains a poison which can cause the skin to burn when exposed to sunlight. The witch hunts directed at this plant, as a 'triffid', are quite unjustified. It is less dangerous than wild hemlock or the common rue.

Hydrocotyle verticillata Thunb. (*Umbelliferae*)   Native of North America, from California to Texas and from Massachusetts to Florida, mainly in the south and along the coast; and widespread in C & S America, growing in marshy places, and in shallow water, flowering in April–September. Plant creeping to form large patches. Leaves to 5cm across.

Levisticum officinale Koch **Lovage** (*Umbelliferae*)   Native of SE Iran and Afghanistan, growing by streams and in wet places at 2500–3400m, but widely naturalized in Europe, especially in the mountains. Plant forming clumps of stems to 2.5m. Leaves strongly aromatic, rather curry-like, lobes long-cuneate at the base, toothed and lobed at the apex.

Aciphylla aurea W. R. B. Oliver (*Umbelliferae*)   Native of New Zealand, in South Island, growing on the east of the mountains in subalpine and mountain grassland, flowering in November–February. Plant forming rosettes of leaves with flat segments *c*.7mm across, usually golden-green, finely toothed. Inflorescence *c*.80cm. For well-drained, peaty soil in sun. Hardy to −15°C.

Aciphylla squarrosa Forster & Forster **Common Spaniard**   Native of New Zealand, in North and South Islands, from East Cape to N Canterbury, growing in subalpine tussock grassland, by roadsides and on abandoned meadows, flowering in November–January, or June–July in the northern hemisphere. Plant forming large spiny tussocks of several rosettes, up to 1m tall; flower stalk 60–200cm; male and female flowers on separate inflorescences, sweetly scented. Easily grown in moist but well-drained soil in full sun. Hardy to −15°C or less.

Angelica gigas Nakai (*Umbelliferae*)   Native to Japan (Shikoku and Kyushu), Korea and N

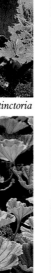

Gunnera tinctoria

Gunnera magellanica

Gunnera manicata at Wisley

Gunnera tinctoria naturalized in Connemara

Hydrocotyle verticillata

Gunnera by the lake at Stancome Park, Gloucestershire

Pimpinella major 'Rosea' at Old Rectory Cottage, Berkshire

Myrrhis odorata by the River Don, Aberdeenshire

Chaerophyllum hirsutum 'Roseum'

Selinum tenuifolium

Chaerophyllum hirsutum L. **'Roseum'** (*Umbelliferae*)   Native of S Europe, from France and Spain to Poland, SW Russia and Greece, growing in grassy places and scrub in the mountains, flowering in June–July. Plant with several stems from a deep branching rootstock up to 120cm. Leaves softly hairy, with overlapping segments. Umbels *c*.6cm across; flowers white or pink in 'Roseum', with ciliate petals. *C. roseum* M. Bieb., from the Caucasus, Soviet Armenia and Georgia, regularly has pink flowers: it is almost glabrous, with stems to 70cm. Both are easily grown in rich, moist soil in sun or partial shade. Hardy to −20°C or less.

Ferula communis L. syn. *F. chiliantha* Rech. fil. (*Umbelliferae*)   Native of the Mediterranean region from Spain, North Africa and the Canary Islands east to the Lebanon, growing in rough ground, in rocky places, and by roadsides, often in soil which is damp in spring, flowering in April–June. Stems usually solitary from a stout root, up to 2.5m. Leaves with linear lobes up to 5cm long, all green and up to 0.8mm wide in subsp. *communis*; glaucous beneath and 1–3mm wide in subsp. *glauca* (L.) Rouy & Camus; leaf sheaths of uppermost leaves very large, inflated and leathery. Umbels without bracts (the related genus *Ferulago* has well-developed bracts and bracteoles), *c*.8cm across. Fruit elliptic to suborbicular, flattened. Easily grown in a well-drained border, but sometimes dying after flowering. Hardy to −10°C, possibly lower with protection for the top of the rootstock.

Ferula kuhistanica Korov. syn. *F. jaeschkeana* auct. non Vatke   Native of C Asia in the Tien Shan, and Pamir Alai, in both of which it is widespread, growing in grassy places among limestone rocks, in soil moist in spring, dry in summer, at 1200–3500m, flowering in May–June. Plant with robust stems to 2m or more from a stout tuberous root. Leaf segments flat, rather thin in texture, *c*.5cm wide. Umbels to 20cm across. A fine plant for a sunny position, dry in summer, when it becomes quite dormant. Hardy to −20°C or less. *F. jaeschkeana* Vatke, from the W Himalayas at 2400–3600m, is very

similar, but taller and more slender, with narrower leaf segments 1–2cm wide. I have had a plant increasing in size for several years without flowering and hope that when it finally flowers it will not prove to be monocarpic.

Myrrhis odorata (L.) Scop. (*Umbelliferae*) **Sweet Cicely**   Native of the Alps, Pyrenees, Apennines and W Greece, Albania and W Yugoslavia, commonly naturalized elsewhere in N Europe, growing in damp woods and hedges, by streams and rivers and on damp, grassy roadsides, flowering in May–July. Plant with several stems from a deep-branching rootstock, up to 120cm tall and wide. Leaves softly hairy, smelling sweetly of aniseed. Umbels *c*.5cm across. Hardy to −20°C or below. A beautiful plant for a cool position, more reliably perennial, with longer-lasting, fresh, green leaves, and at the same time less invasive than the common Cow's Parsley or Queen Anne's Lace. *Anthriscus sylvestris* (L.) Hoffm, a black-leaved form of *A. sylvestris*, called 'Raven's Wing', has appeared recently.

Pimpinella major (L.) Huds **'Rosea'** (*Umbelliferae*)   Native of most of England, SW Ireland and S Scotland, south to Portugal and east to the Caucasus, growing on grassy roadsides, in hedges and scrub, flowering in June–July. Stems several, 50–120cm, from a stout rootstock. Basal leaves simply pinnate, the segments toothed, subcordate. Upper leaves small, with sheath-like petioles. Flower umbels 6cm across. Easily grown in any good soil, preferring rather moist conditions. Hardy to −20°C.

Selinum tenuifolium Wall. ex C. B. Clarke (*Umbelliferae*)   Native of the Himalayas, from Kashmir east to Bhutan, growing in scrub and mountain meadows, at 2700–4000m, flowering in July–September. Plant with many stems to 150cm, forming handsome clumps. Leaves very finely divided into elliptical segments. Umbels 5–8cm across, with white-edged, toothed bracteoles as long as the flowers. A fine plant for the border or for growing in damp grass. Hardy to −20°C.

Ferula kuhistanica in the Amankutan hills near Samarkand, overlooking the Oxus valley

Ferula communis near Ronda, S Spain

Ferula kuhistanica (young inflorescence)

'Rosea'

'Rubra'

'Rosensymphonie'

Astrantia major

'Sunningdale Variegated'

'Shaggy'

Astrantia major
subsp. *carinthiaca*

Astrantia maxima

Specimens from Beth Chatto and Wisley, 20 June. ½ life size

Astrantia major 'Rosea'

Astrantia major at Cedar Tree Cottage, Sussex

Alepidea natalensis in the Drakensberg

Astrantia major 'Rubra'

Sanicula caerulescens near Ya-an, Sichuan

Alepidea natalensis Wood & Evans (*Umbelliferae*)   Native of South Africa in the Drakensberg mountains in Natal, growing in damp, rocky grassland, on bare rock and peat and in shallow streams at up to 2400m, flowering in January–February. Plant with few stems of 45cm rising from a rosette of ovate leaves. Flower-heads *c.*1cm across. With its tight head of small flowers and petal-like bracts this genus of *c.*25 species, mainly in South Africa, resembles the northern hemisphere *Astrantia*. For moist, peaty soil in full sun.

Astrantia major L. subsp. **carinthiaca** Arcangeli syn. *A. major* subsp. *involucrata* Koch (*Umbelliferae*)   Native of the Alps, Pyrenees and NW Spain, growing in alpine meadows, flowering in July–September, or June in gardens. Subspecies *carinthiaca* differs from subsp. *major* in its longer bracteoles, around twice as long as the umbel. The commonest cultivar is called 'Shaggy' syn. 'Margery Fish', with its whitish bracteoles, sharply toothed, to 3.5cm with green edges. Another form, shown here, with paler flowers and only the tips of the bracteoles green, is sometimes wrongly labelled 'Carniolica'. *A. carniolica* Jacq., from the SE Alps in Austria, Italy and Yugoslavia, has bracteoles shorter than the umbel, and central leaf lobes not divided to the base. Easily grown

in good soil in sun or partial shade. Hardy to −20°C.

Astrantia major L. subsp. **major** **Masterwort**   Native of much of Europe from NW Spain, the Pyrenees and Alps and from the Black Forest south to Bulgaria and east to W Russia, and sometimes naturalized in Britain, growing in damp meadows and open woods, flowering in June–September. Plant forming large clumps of upright stems to 1m, branched near the top. Basal leaves 3- to 5-lobed, the lobes themselves lobed and coarsely toothed. Bracteoles petal-like, white, greenish or pinkish, surrounding and more or less equalling the dense umbel of small greenish flowers. Easily grown in good soil, moist in summer, in sun or partial shade. Hardy to −20°C. There are several selected varieties of this subspecies in cultivation; shown here are:
'Alba'   With white, green tipped bracteoles.
'Rosea'   Deeper pink.
'Rosensymphonie'   A good rose pink.
'Rubra'   The darkest, purplish-red.
'Sunningdale Variegated'   An excellent foliage plant with a neat mound of leaves with a good white edge and patches of pale green. Fresh new leaves are produced throughout the summer.

Astrantia maxima Pallas   Native of the Caucasus, south to NW Iran and NE Turkey,

west to Ordu, growing in woods and damp meadows at 1300–2400m in Turkey, flowering in July–August. Plant forming widely spread mats of leaves 3-lobed to the base; lobes toothed, 3–10cm long. Bracteoles 9–12, elliptic to ovate, pinkish, 1–3cm long, 3–12mm wide, longer than the umbel. Usually a rather small plant with 3-lobed leaves and a short, often unbranched flowering stem. Subsp. *haradjianii* (Grintz) Rech. fil. from C Turkey from Ladik and Ulu Dağ south to Adana and Isparta has 3- or 5-lobed basal leaves, shorter, narrower bracteoles which are green and white, and more branched stems. It grows in drier places, in conifer forest and scrub, flowering in June–July. Both are easily grown in sun or partial shade, subsp. *maxima* preferring a cool position. Hardy to −20°C.

Sanicula caerulescens Franch. (*Umbelliferae*) Native of China, in W Sichuan and Yunnan, growing in damp scrub and woodland, flowering in May. Plant with a compact rootstock. Leaves deeply 3–5 lobed, with the lobes toothed, 5–8cm across. Flowers very small, sky-blue. Hardy to −15°C perhaps. For a moist and sheltered woodland position in shade. *S. europaea* L., a native of Europe, is found in woods and shady banks, especially on chalk and limestone soils. It has attractive dark-green leaves and white flowers.

Eryngium variifolium

Eryngium billardieri near Erzurum, E Turkey, October

Eryngium billardieri B. Delaroche syn. *E. orientale* Stapf & Wettst. (*Umbelliferae*) Native of E Turkey, Lebanon and Soviet Armenia east to Kashmir, growing on mountain steppes and rocky slopes at 1400–3810m in Turkey, flowering in July–October. Basal leaves bluish green, leathery, in a rosette, the blades deeply divided with broad linear segments, to 15cm long. Stems several, 40–75cm, stiff, with tripartite leaves. Bracts 5–7, 2.5–5cm long, linear-lanceolate, with a spiny tip. For dry, well-drained soil in full sun. Hardy to −25°C.

Eryngium bourgatii Gouan Native of the Pyrenees, to Spain and NW Africa, with subsp. *heldreichii* (Boiss.) Davis in S Turkey and Lebanon, growing in dry rocky places, usually on limestone, at up to 2400m in Turkey,

flowering in July–August. Basal leaf blades much divided and spiny, 3–7cm across. Stem leaves similar. Stems 15–45cm. Bracts 7–15, linear-lanceolate, spiny, 3–5-veined, 2–5cm long in subsp. *bourgatii*, 7-veined and to 6cm long in subsp. *heldreichii*. Heads 1.5–2.5cm across, ovoid-globose, or depressed-globose (1.2–1.5cm across in subsp. *heldreichii*). For well-drained soil in full sun. Hardy to −15°C, perhaps less. 'Oxford Blue' has especially good colour.

Eryngium decaisneanum Urban syn. *E. pandanifolium* Cham. & Schlecht. Native of South America, in S Brazil, Argentina, Uruguay and Paraguay, growing in marshes and wet fields, flowering in gardens in late summer. Stems 1.5–4m. Basal leaves sword-shaped,

1.5–2.5m long, 2.5cm wide, undivided, with slender spines along the edge. Flower-heads 6–10mm long, 4–8mm across, often purplish. Bracts *c*.2cm. For any good, rich soil in full sun. Hardy to −10°C.

Eryngium horridum Malme. Native of Brazil and Argentina, in wet or dry grassland, and on the Pampas, flowering in November–January, in summer in the north. Plant to 3m; basal leaves to 1m long, 3cm wide. Heads nearly globose, 9–12mm across. For any good soil in full sun. Hardy to −10°C perhaps.

Eryngium maritimum L. Native of the coasts of W Europe, the Mediterranean and the Black Sea, growing on sand dunes, flowering in June–September. Leaves leathery, glaucous, with large, triangular, spiny teeth. Stems widely branched, to 35cm. Bracts 5, ovate, with broad teeth tipped with spines. Flower-heads 1.5–3cm across. A familiar seaside plant, but good in the garden too, needing deep, well-drained, sandy soil in a hot, dry position. Hardy to −15°C, perhaps less.

Eryngium paniculatum Cav. & Domb. Native of S. Chile and Argentina in Patagonia, growing in grassy places, flowering in summer. Stems to 1.5m. Basal leaves spiny on the edge, to 35cm long, 1.5cm wide. Flower heads 8–15mm across. For any good soil in full sun. Hardy to −10°C perhaps.

Eryngium variifolium Coss. Native of North Africa, in Morocco, growing in the mountains, flowering in June–August. Plant with a clump of rosettes of fleshy leaves, green through the winter. Leaf blades ovate, cordate, crenate, *c*.5cm long, with pale veins. Stems *c*.45cm, stiff, upright. Bracts 6–7, *c*.4cm long, unequal, linear, white, with a stiff terminal spine and 1–2 lateral spines. Flower-heads rounded, *c*.1.5cm wide. For any good, moist soil in full sun. Will grow in short grass. Hardy to −15°C, perhaps less, but then not evergreen.

Eryngium decaisneanum at the Chelsea Physic Garden

Eryngium paniculatum at the Chelsea Physic Garden

Eryngium maritimum

Eryngium bourgatii

Eryngium horridum

Eryngium
× *tripartitium*

Eryngium amethystinum

Eryngium
agavifolium

Eryngium × *zabelii*

Eryngium eburneum

Specimens from Beth Chatto, Unusual Plants, 7 August. ¼ life size

Eryngium agavifolium at Wakehurst Place, Sussex

Eryngium eburneum with white Agapanthus

Eryngium agavifolium Griseb. (*Umbelliferae*)
Native of Argentina, in the province of
Cordoba, growing on stony hills and river
banks, flowering in January–March, and in
summer in the north. Stems *c*.2m. Leaves 75–
50cm long, spiny-toothed. Bracts small.
Flower-heads 5cm long, 2.5cm across. For well-
drained but not dry soil in full sun. Hardy to
−10°C perhaps.

Eryngium alpinum L.   Native of the Jura and
the Alps, from France to C Yugoslavia, growing
in subalpine meadows usually on limestone at
1500–1800m, flowering in July–August. Plant
with a rosette of stalked basal leaves with the
blade 8–15cm × 5–13cm, ovate-cordate,
toothed. Stems 30–70cm, with deeply cut
leaves. Bracts 3–6cm, more than 25, very finely
divided, 2–4cm long. For well-drained, stony
soil in full sun, but not too dry. Hardy to −20°C
or less.

Eryngium amethystinum L.   Native of SE
Europe, from Italy to Greece and Crete,
growing in dry, stony places, flowering in July–
August. Plant with tough, leathery basal leaves
with lamina 10–15cm long, below, palmate-
lobed above, pinnate below with a broadly
winged stalk. Bracts 5–9, 2–5cm long, linear-
lanceolate, with 1–4 pairs of spines. For dry,
well-drained soil in full sun. Hardy to −15°C
perhaps. The best forms are a very good blue.

Eryngium eburneum Decne.   Native of S
Brazil, Argentina, Paraguay and Uruguay,
growing in marshes and wet, grassy places,
flowering in October–May, but in late summer
in the north. Stems to 1.5m. Leaves to 1m long,

3–5cm wide, with thin spines, evergreen.
Flower-heads 15–20mm long. For good, moist
soil in full sun. Hardy to −15°C perhaps.

Eryngium planum L.   Native of Europe, from
Germany and Austria eastwards to Russia, the
Caucasus and C Asia, growing in dry places,
roadsides and rocky slopes, flowering in July–
September. Plant forming large clumps of stems
to 1m or more in gardens. Basal leaves with
blade 5–10cm × 3–6cm, oblong to ovate-
oblong, cordate, toothed. Middle leaves
undivided; upper leaves only deeply lobed.
Bracts 6–8, 1.5–2.5cm long. Flower head ovoid-
globose, 1–2cm long. For well-drained soil in a
sunny position. If grown in too rich soil, the
plant needs staking before the stems have
flopped. Hardy to –25°C or less.

Eryngium × tripartitum hort. non L.
Probably a hybrid between *E. planum* and a
species with divided basal leaves such as *E.
amethystinum*. The basal leaves are more
coarsely toothed than those of *E. planum*; the
stem leaves are deeply 3–5-lobed. The small
heads are a good blue. For sunny, dry soil.
Hardy to −20°C perhaps.

Eryngium × zabelii hort. ex Hegi   A group of
hybrids between *E. alpinum* and *E. bourgatii*,
named in 1926. They differ from *E. alpinum* in
having variably lobed basal leaves and more
rounded flower-heads, produced in July–
August. The old selections, 'Jewel' and
'Violette', both raised in 1913, are still
occasionally available; both have large, blue
flower-heads.

Eryngium alpinum with variegated mint

Eryngium planum

Galax urceolata in the Valley Gardens, Windsor Great Park

Lysimachia ephemerum at Edington, Wiltshire

Lysimachia clethroides

Lysimachia nummularia 'Aurea'

Lysimachia thyrsiflora in Finland

Galax urceolata syn. *G. aphylla* (*Diapensaceae*) **Beetleweed** Native of E North America, from Virginia and West Virginia, south to Georgia and Alabama, growing in dry, open woods, mainly in the mountains, flowering in late May–July. Plant forming mats of creeping rhizomes, with red roots and leathery evergreen leaves 3–16cm wide, on slender petioles. Flowering stems to 80cm; flowers 3–4mm across. For leafy soil in shade or partial shade, and acid soil. Hardy to −20°C.

Lysimachia ciliata L. syn. *Steironema ciliata* (L.) Raf. (*Primulaceae*) Native of North America, from Quebec to British Columbia, south to Florida, Texas and Colorado, growing in damp woods and by lakes and rivers, flowering in June–August. Plant spreading by underground rhizomes with stems to 1.2m. Leaves ciliate on the petioles. Flowers 1.5–2.8cm across, on thin axillary shoots. For any moist soil in sun or shade. Hardy to −25°C or less. There are five other species in this group in North America, mostly with narrower leaves, and seldom seen in gardens.

Lysimachia clethroides Duby Native of Japan, in all the islands, of Korea, N & E China and Indochina, and naturalized in Holland, growing on sunny, grassy hills at low altitudes, flowering in June–July. Plant with upright flowering stems to 100cm, and creeping rhizomes, forming large clumps. Leaves alternate, acuminate often chlorotic when young. Flowers 8–12mm across. Distinct in the raceme which is nodding in bud, becoming erect as the flowers open. Hardy to −25°C or less. For any good soil. *L. barystachys* Bunge, also from E Asia, has obtuse or subacute, not acuminate leaves, but is otherwise very similar.

Lysimachia ephemerum L. Native of W Portugal, S, C & E Spain and SW France, in the Pyrenees and Corbières, growing in damp, grassy places, especially by springs, and by streams, flowering in June–July. Plant forming clumps of upright stems to 1m or more. Leaves glaucous in 4 rows. Flowers *c*.1cm across. For any good soil that is not too dry, in sun or partial shade. Hardy to −15°C or less. A very handsome plant for a moist border.

Lysimachia nummularia L. 'Aurea' **Creeping Jenny** Native of most of Europe, south to Spain and Turkey in Europe, and east to Russia and the Caucasus, growing in damp woods, in fens, and on the banks of streams and lake shores, flowering in April–September. Naturalized in North America. Stems creeping and rooting to 70cm long or more. Leaves 12–25mm long, bright yellowish green in 'Aurea' (shown here). Flowers yellow, on short stalks in the leaf axils, 9–12mm long, cup-shaped. Hardy to −25°C or less. A distinct leaf shape and colour to contrast with other shade-loving foliage plants.

Lysimachia punctata L. Native to SE & EC Europe, from W Austria and N Italy eastwards to W Turkey and widely naturalized elsewhere in Europe and in NE North America, growing in shallow water in ditches, marshes and on river banks, flowering in May–September. Plant with shortly creeping rhizomes and upright stems to 150cm, forming large patches. Leaves in whorls of 2–4. Flowers 20–24mm across, 2–7 in a whorl. For any good, moist soil in sun or partial shade. Hardy to −20°C or less. *L. verticillaris* Spreng., sometimes included in *L. punctata*, is found in N & E Turkey, the Caucasus, Crimea and N Iran. It differs in its longer petioles, broader leaves 27–45mm wide, and 4–14 flowers in each whorl.

Lysimachia thyrsiflora L. syn. *Naumbergia thyrsiflora* (L.) Reichb.   Native of Europe, from England eastwards across Siberia to Japan, and of North America, from Alaska to Quebec south to California, Colorado and West Virginia, growing in marshes, bogs and cold swamps, flowering in May–July. Stems to 80cm from creeping rhizomes. Leaves lanceolate to elliptic. Flowers 3–5mm long, crowded into dense spikes. For wet soil in sun or partial shade. Hardy to −25°C or less.

Lysimachia vulgaris L. **Yellow Loosestrife**
Native of most of Europe and NW Africa, east to Turkey, N Iraq, Siberia and China, to Japan (var. *dahurica* (Ledeb.) Kunth), and naturalized in North America, growing in marshes, streams and in shallow water in reedswamps, flowering in April–September. Stems to 120cm, from a creeping rootstock, spreading by stolons. Leaves opposite or in whorls of 3–4. Flowers 12–15mm across, cup-shaped. Easily grown in wet soil in sun or partial shade. Hardy to −25°C or less.

Pyrola asarifolia Michx. (*Pyrolaceae*)   Native of North America, from Newfoundland west to Yukon, south to Prince Edward Island and New England, and along the Rockies from Indiana to New Mexico, growing in woods and scrub, usually on limestone, flowering in June–August. Plant with creeping underground rhizomes and round leaves to 6.5cm across. Flowering stems to 35cm with up to 20 flowers. Flowers 8–16mm across, crimson to pale pink, with rather thin calyx and petals. Style curved. For moist, loose, leafy soil, not too acid, in shade or partial shade. Hardy to − 25°C or less.

Pyrola rotundifolia L.   Native of NE North America, from Greenland to Quebec and Nova Scotia, with var. *americana* (Sweet) Fern south to South Dakota and Georgia; and of Europe, from Iceland and Scotland, south to C Spain and east to the Altai and Siberia in the north, to Turkey and the Elburz Mountains in N Iran, growing in bogs, fens and woods, especially of beech, often on limestone, and in dune slacks (subsp. *maritima* (Kenyon) E. F. Warburg) in NW Europe, flowering in June–September. Plant with creeping underground rhizomes and rosettes of rounded leaves to 5cm across. Flowering stems to 40cm. Flowers white, scented, 12–18mm across with a thick calyx and stiff, leathery petals. Style curved, 7–8mm long (5–7mm in subsp. *maritima*). For peaty or leafy but not very acid soil, moist in summer. Hardy to −20°C or less.

Lysimachia vulgaris

Lysimachia ciliata

Lysimachia clethroides

Lysimachia punctata

Specimens from Sellindge, Kent, 20 August. ⅓ life size

Pyrola rotundifolia

Pyrola asarifolia in Arizona

Lysimachia vulgaris

Asclepias incarnata

Asclepias tuberosa

Asclepias cordifolia in N California

Asclepias syriaca at Logan Botanic Garden

Asclepias cordifolia (Benth.) Jeps.
(*Asclepiadaceae*)   Native of California in the
Coast Ranges and the Sierra Nevada, from Kern
Co. northwards to Oregon and in W Nevada,
growing in chaparral, scrub and pine forest, at
up to 1800m, flowering in May–July. Stems to
80cm, sprawling, from a stout, woody
rootstock. Leaves mostly opposite, cordate-
amplexicaul, ovate, acute. Flowers dark red-
purple, 16–18mm across. For dry, well-drained
soil in full sun and a warm position. Hardy to
−15°C perhaps.

Asclepias incarnata L. **Swamp Milkweed**
Native of North America, from Quebec west to
Manitoba and Wyoming, south to Long Island,
South Carolina, Texas and New Mexico,
growing in marshes, wet scrub and on lake
shores, flowering in July–September. Plant with
few or several upright stems to 1.5m. Leaves
oblong-lanceolate to ovate, with ascending, not
transverse, veins. Umbels usually several.
Flowers c.8mm across, pink, purplish or rarely
white. Hoods 2–3mm high. For any good soil in
full sun. Hardy to −25°C or less.

Asclepias syriaca L. **Common Milkweed**
Native of North America, from New Brunswick
west to Saskatchewan, south to North Carolina,

Kansas and Georgia, growing in scrub, by
roadsides and in waste places, flowering in
June–August. Stems softly pubescent, to 2m
from stout creeping rhizomes. Leaves
lanceolate-oblong to broadly oval, to 26cm long,
to 18cm across, greyish with fine hairs beneath.
Flowers scented, in rounded umbels, each
flower 12–18mm across, purplish or greenish,
with obtuse hoods, 3–4mm high. For any good
soil in full sun. Hardy to −25°C and less. The
young shoots and half-grown seed pods are
edible.

Asclepias tuberosa L. **Butterfly-Weed**
Native of North America, from S Ontario and
New York west to Minnesota, south to
Colorado, Arizona and N Mexico, and to
Florida in the east, growing in dry, grassy
places, flowering in June–September. A variable
species with stems upright, roughly hairy, to
90cm from a tuberous rootstock. Leaves from
linear to lanceolate or oblong-ovate, sessile or
with a short petiole. Flowers yellowish to
orange, or red, c.12mm across; hoods erect,
oblong. For dry soil in full sun. Hardy to
−20°C.

Calystegia pulchra Brummitt & Heywood
(*Convolvulaceae*)   Native habitat unknown but

probably from NE Asia or a garden hybrid; now
naturalized in Europe from Ireland and
Scotland, eastwards to Poland, Sweden and
Czechoslovakia, growing in hedges and scrub,
flowering in July–September. Plant with fleshy
underground rhizomes and climbing stems to
3m or more. Leaves sagittate, the sinus oblong
with more or less parallel sides. Bracteoles
overlapping, saccate at the base, obtuse to
emarginate at the apex. Flowers pink, 50–70mm
long. Very similar to *C. sepium* subsp. *americana*
(Sims) Brummitt, which is found in similar
habitats in W Europe; it also has pink flowers,
but only 40–55mm long. A double-flowered
form of the Chinese *C. pubescens* Lindl. is also
grown in gardens. All require careful siting in
the garden because of their rampant roots.
Hardy to −20°C, probably less.

Convolvulus althaeoides L. (*Convolvulaceae*)
Native of S Europe and around the
Mediterranean, but commoner in the west and
naturalized in S California, growing on
roadsides, and rocky slopes usually on
limestone, flowering in April–May and later in
gardens. Plant with creeping underground
rhizomes and trailing or climbing twining stems
to 1m or more. Lowest leaves produced in
winter, hastate; upper leaves, on the twining

Solanum xantii var. *montanum* above Bishop, California

Ipomopsis subnuda in Arizona

Calystegia pulchra in Ireland

Ipomopsis aggregata

Ipomopsis aggregata in California

Convolvulus althaeoides in S Spain

stems, deeply lobed, but lobes not reaching the midrib. Flowers 27–38mm long, rich pink; outer sepals 8–10mm. *C. elegantissimus* Mill. (syn. *C. tenuissimus* Sibth. & Sm.), from the E Mediterranean, has more silky-hairy leaves, divided to the midrib, shorter outer sepals (4–7mm long), and usually paler pink flowers. Both need very well-drained soil in full sun and will happily naturalize in old walls, though they are rather too rampant for a choice position. Hardy to −15°C perhaps.

Ipomopsis aggregata (Pursh) V. Grant syn. *Gilia aggregata* (Pursh) Spreng. (*Polemoniaceae*) **Skyrocket**   Native of W North America, from Oregon to S California, east to W Texas and N Mexico, and north to North Dakota, growing on dry, rocky slopes in sagebrush, scrub and clearings in pine forest at up to 3000m in California, flowering in June–September. A very variable plant, usually a short-lived perennial, sometimes biennial, with a rosette of deeply divided pinnate leaves with a musky scent and flowering stems to 80cm. Flowers 2–3.5cm long, varying in colour from magenta and crimson to red with yellow mottling or all yellow (pale pink or white in subsp. *attenuata* (Gray) V. & A. Grant). For well-drained, dry soil in sun or partial shade. Hardy to −15°C,

or less if dry in winter. Easily raised from seed.

Ipomopsis subnuda (Torr.) V. Grant syn. *Gilia subnuda* Torr.   Native of N Arizona, New Mexico, Utah and Nevada, growing on sandy or rocky hills at 1500–2500m, flowering in June–July. Plants often biennial with stems to 60cm. Leaves glandular-pubescent, entire to shallowly pinnatifid. Flowers in small groups, the corolla tubular, 12–20mm long. For dry, well-drained soil in full sun. Hardy to −15°C, or less if dry.

Solanum xantii Gray var. **montanum** Munz (*Solanaceae*)   Native of E California, from San Bernardino north to Nevada Co. on the east of the Sierra Nevada, growing on dry slopes in the conifer forest zone at 1500–2750m, flowering in May–September. Stems to 40cm, often prostrate from a woody rootstock. Leaves greyish, pubescent, ovate. Flowers 1.5–2.5cm across. Berries greenish, 9–10mm across. For well-drained, dry soil in full sun. Hardy to −15°C if dry. Other varieties of *S. xantii* found in S California, Arizona and Baja California are subshrubby, up to 90cm high and found in scrub and chaparral at lower altitudes.

'Mother of Pearl'

'Cherry Pink'

'Rijnstroom'

'Mary Fox'

'Dodo Hanbury-Forbes'

'Fujiama'

'Sandringham'

'Skylight'

Phlox specimens from the Savill Gardens, Windsor, 28 August. ½ life size

Phlox 'Fujiama'

Phlox 'Prospero' in the Culpepper Garden, Leeds Castle, Kent

Phlox paniculata often called *P. decussata*
Introduced to Europe from North America in
1730. Several cultivars were developed during
the 19th century, some possibly by hybridization
with *P. carolina*, but mainly by selection of
colour forms of the original species and
varieties. The greatest advances in the raising of
new cultivars were made by Capt. B. Symons-
Jeune in the 1950s. He aimed not only for large
flowers, but also for pure colours, scent and
disease resistance. All the large-flowered border
Phlox require full sun, rich soil and plenty of
water, with liquid feed at the root. Mildew,
which can be a problem, can best be avoided by
making sure that air circulation is good, and
that the roots do not suffer from drought. All
are hardy to at least −25°C, and flower in July–
September. (See also vol. 1, p. 67.)

'Alison Jane'   Raised by A. Goatcher & Son,
Sussex, before 1960. Stems to 70cm. Flowers
3.8cm across. Panicles 7.5–10cm long.
'Cherry Pink'   Raiser not recorded. Height up
to 90cm.
'Dodo Hanbury-Forbes' (syn. 'Dorothy
Hanbury-Forbes')   Raised by Capt. B.
Symons-Jeune and introduced by Bakers
Nurseries. Flower stems stout, *c*.90cm; panicles
c.15cm long and wide. Flowers 4–4.5cm across.
'Europa'   Raiser not recorded. Height to
75cm.
'Fujiama' (syn. 'Mount Fuji')   Raised in the
USA, this has sturdy stems up to 1m, with large
heads of pure-white flowers from mid-
September onwards.
'Le Mahdi'   A strong grower, and an old
variety, known since 1933. Flowers deep
purplish blue.
'Mary Fox'   Raised by Alan Bloom; stems to
80cm, healthy and robust.
'Mother of Pearl'   Raised by Alan Bloom.
Height to 120cm. Flowers 3.75cm across, freely
produced, in panicles to 20cm long and wide.
'Prospero'   Raised by K. Foerster in 1956.
Height to 90cm.
'Rijnstroom'   An old, and reliable, variety.
Height up to 80cm.
'Sandringham'   An old variety, raised by R.
M. Bath Ltd of Wisbech before 1953, with
stems up to 1m.
'Silver Salmon'   Raised in Germany before
1965. Height to 90cm.
'Skylight'   Raiser not recorded. Height to 90cm.

Phlox 'Le Mahdi'

Phlox 'Europa'

Phlox 'Alison Jane'

Phlox 'Silver Salmon'

Onosma tauricum at Edington, Wiltshire

Onosma frutescens in S Turkey

Solenanthus circinnatus near Frunze

Onosma albo-roseum at Edington, Wiltshire

Macromeria viridiflora in Arizona

Moltkia doerfleri

Arnebia densiflora on limestone hills near Malatya, C Turkey

Arnebia densiflora (Nordb.) Ledeb. syn.
Macrotonia cephalotes (DC.) Boiss.
(*Boraginaceae*) Native of Greece, in the
Peloponnese (Aroania Oros), and of Turkey,
from Bursa south to Adana and east to
Erzinçan, growing on limestone and igneous
rocks and cliffs, at 750–2600m, flowering in
May–August. Plant tufted with several dense
rosettes of narrowly lanceolate basal leaves, and
flowering stems to 40cm. Flowers 12–16mm
across, 35–45mm long. A beautiful plant, but
very difficult to grow; although I have collected
seed and raised seedlings on several occasions,
the plants have always rotted before flowering.
They will require well-drained soil in full sun,
kept, if possible, dry and cold in winter. Hardy
to −25°C, probably less.

Arnebia pulchra (Roem. & Schult.)
Edmondson syns. *A. echioides* (L.) Boiss.,
Echioides longiflora (K. Koch) I. M. Johnston
Native of the N Caucasus, N Iran and NE
Turkey, growing in rocky places and roadsides
at 1525–3000m in Turkey, flowering in June–
July. Plant with stout rootstock, and few
sprawling stems to 45cm. Leaves stiffly hairy.
Flowers 18–25mm across, 20–24mm long, with
blackish spots which fade as the flower ages. For
well-drained soil in full sun. Hardy to −20°C or
less.

Macromeria viridiflora DC. (*Boraginaceae*)
Native of New Mexico and E Arizona to N
Mexico, growing on rocky slopes and in valleys
in pine forest and in scrub, at 1000–2750m,
flowering in July–September. A bristly plant
with several stems to 90cm. Flowers to 4cm
long, with stamens shortly exserted. Leaves
5–12cm long, broadly lanceolate. For well-
drained soil in full sun. Hardy to −15°C. Used

by the Hopi Indians, dried and mixed with wild
tobacco, for rain-bringing ceremonies.

Moltkia doerfleri Wettst. (*Boraginaceae*)
Native of NE Albania, growing in rock crevices,
flowering in May–June. Plant with a horizontal
rhizome and several upright stems to 50cm.
Leaves lanceolate, acute. Flowers 19–25mm
long, deep purple, the anthers not exserted. For
well-drained soil in full sun. Hardy to −20°C or
so.

Onosma albo-roseum Fisch. & Mey.
(*Boraginaceae*) Native of Turkey, N Syria and
N Iraq, growing on rocky slopes and cliffs on
limestone, at up to 2550m, flowering in April–
July. Plant with erect or ascending stems from a
central rootstock. Leaves obovate to oblong,
whitish, with dense appressed bristly hairs.
Flowers 18–30mm long, broadly campanulate.
For well-drained soil in full sun, in a crevice,
wall, or in a scree garden. Hardy to −15°C.

Onosma frutescens Lam. Native of C & S
Greece, W & S Turkey, and W Syria, growing
on limestone slopes and rocks at up to 1600m,
flowering in March–June. Plant bristly, with
somewhat woody, spreading stems and oblong-
lanceolate leaves. Flowering stems several, more
or less upright. Flowers 18–20mm long. For
well-drained soil in full sun, in a crevice or
similar position. Hardy to −10°C perhaps.

Onosma tauricum Pallas ex Willd. Native of
Yugoslavia and Romania, south to Turkey and
Syria, and east to the Caucasus and the Crimea,
growing on rocks, old walls, stony slopes and
steppes, flowering in March–June. Plant with
bristly stems and leaves, and several spreading
flowering stems from a central rootstock. Stem

leaves linear-lanceolate or linear-oblong.
Flowers 22–25mm long, white, yellow or cream.
For well-drained soil in full sun, preferably in a
crevice in paving, in a wall or in a scree garden.
Hardy to −15°C.

Solenanthus circinnatus Ledeb.
(*Boraginaceae*) Native of E Turkey and N Iraq
eastwards to Afghanistan and Siberia in the
Tien Shan and the Altai, and in NW China,
growing in scrub and alpine meadows in rich
soil, at up to 2800m in Turkey, flowering in
May–June. Plant with several stems to 100cm,
from a stout rootstock. Basal leaves broadly
ovate, 10–30cm long, to 20cm wide. Flowers
purplish, 5–7mm long, with whitish, long-
exserted stamens and style. For well-drained,
rich soil, dryish in summer. Hardy to −20°C or
less.

Arnebia pulchra in the Caucasus

Verbena macdougallii in Arizona

Verbena bonariensis with *Crocosmia* 'Lucifer' at Bressingham Gardens, Norfolk

Verbena corymbosa at Axeltree Nursery, Rye, Kent

Chelone glabra in New York State

Chelone glabra L. (*Scrophulariaceae*) **Balmony**, **Turtle-head** Native of Newfoundland, west to Ontario and Minnesota, south to Georgia, Alabama and Missouri, growing in wet places, in woods, clearings and by streams, flowering in late July–October. Stems to 2m, from a stout rootstock, finally forming large patches. Leaves tapering or rounded at base, with almost no petiole. Sepals with scarious margins. Flowers usually white. For moist, rich soil in sun or partial shade. Hardy to −20°C or less.

Chelone obliqua L. Native of Tennessee south to Florida and Mississippi, growing in wet woods and cypress swamps, flowering in late August–October. Differs from *C. glabra* in its lanceolate, slender-stalked leaves, purplish flowers, and sepals with very faint scarious margins and rounded, not acuminate bracts. For moist, good soil in sun or partial shade. Hardy to −20°C perhaps. The very similar *C. lyonii* Pursh has broader leaves, rounded at the base, on longer stalks, and a more sharply ridged upper lip to the flower.

Verbena bonariensis L. (*Verbenaceae*) Native of South America, in S Brazil, Argentina, Uruguay and Paraguay, growing in wet fields and waste places, flowering in late summer. Stems few, upright, square in section to 100cm tall. Leaves few, sessile, clasping the stem. Inflorescence with long, leafless branches. Flowers purple *c*.1mm across, in flat-topped cymes. For any good soil in full sun. Hardy to −10°C, possibly less, and often appearing again the following spring after sowing itself, if killed in a cold winter.

Verbena corymbosa Ruiz & Pav. Native of S Chile and Argentina, flowering in June–August in the north. Plant with upright stems to 100cm with far-creeping underground rhizomes. Leaves oblong or ovate, to 6cm long, sometimes lobed near the base. Flowers pale bluish mauve. Best in moist soil in full sun.

Verbena hastata in New York State

Chelone obliqua in Harry Hay's garden, Surrey

Verbena hastata L. **Simpler's Joy**　Native of
North America, from Nova Scotia and New
Brunswick south to Florida, Texas and from
British Columbia to California, growing in
marshes, damp scrub and by lakes and rivers,
flowering in June–September. Stems erect from
a tufted rootstock, to 150cm. Lowest leaves
sometimes hastate, but often lanceolate to
narrowly ovate. Inflorescence of numerous
narrow spikes. Flowers violet blue, pink in f.
rosea, or white, 3–4.5mm across. For good,
moist soil in full sun. Hardy to −20°C or less.

Verbena macdougallii Heller　Native of
Arizona, New Mexico and W Texas to S
Wyoming, growing in grassy places in open pine
forest at around 2000m, flowering in June–
October. Plant with erect, stiffly hairy stems to
90cm. Leaves coarsely toothed to 10cm long.
Flowers 6mm across. For any rich soil in full
sun. Hardy to −20°C.

Verbena rigida Spreng. syn. *V. venosa* Gillies &
Hook.　Native of Argentina and S Brazil. Plant
with many upright stems to 60cm from tuberous
roots. Leaves oblong, sessile, amplexicaul,
rough, irregularly toothed. Flower spikes in
threes, congested, the lateral being long-
stalked. Flowers purple to magenta, about 8mm
across. For any good soil in full sun. Hardy to
−10°C, but the tubers should be protected from
freezing.

Verbena tenera Spreng. syn. *V.* 'Hektor'
Native of S America, in Brazil and Argentina,
and naturalized in S California, flowering in
April–October in the north. Stems slender,
trailing, rooting at the nodes. Leaves with three
main divisions, dissected into linear lobes.
Flowers in short heads, bluish purple, rarely
white, the open flowers over-topping the buds,
6–8mm across. 'Mahonettii' has deep-purple
flowers with a white stripe. For any good soil in
full sun, moist in summer. Hardy to −10°C.
Easily grown, but can suffer from aphids in a
dry spring.

Verbena tenera at Wisley

Verbena rigida at Hawstead, Suffolk

Eremostachys lehmanniana

Phlomis bracteosa, avoided by grazing ponies, in Kashmir

Eremostachys laciniata

Phlomis russelliana at the Chelsea Physic Garden

Eremostachys speciosa near Tashkent

Phlomis lychnitis in S France

Phlomis tuberosa on the steppes near Stavropol, growing with *Paeonia tenuissima* and *Plantago media*

Phlomis tuberosa (detail)

Eremostachys laciniata (L.) Bunge
(*Labiatae*)   Native of S & E Turkey, W Syria,
Transcaucasia and Iran east to C Asia, growing
on steppes, in oak scrub and dry meadows at up
to 2200m in Turkey, flowering in May–July.
Stems 1–2m from a tuberous rootstock. Leaves
deeply laciniate, hairy, 15–30cm long. Flowers
white, cream or pinkish, often speckled with
red on the lip, 3–4cm long. Calyx not enlarging
in fruit. (In *E. molucelloides* Bunge, from C
Turkey east to Mongolia, the calyx becomes
large and bell-shaped and acts as an aid for the
dispersal of the seeds by the wind.) For dry,
well-drained, but good soil in full sun, with
water in autumn and spring only. Hardy to
−25°C.

Eremostachys lehmanniana Bunge   Native of
Soviet C Asia, growing on dry, rocky hillsides,
flowering in May–June. Plant with a clump of
stems to 1m from a tuberous rootstock; leaves
c.15cm long, hairy, deeply lobed. Flowers deep
pink. For dry, well-drained soil in full sun.
Hardy to −25°C.

Eremostachys speciosa Rupr.   Native of C
Asia and the W Himalayas, growing on rich,
grassy slopes and steppes, flowering in May–
June. Stems few to 60cm, from a tuberous
rootstock. Leaves green, pinnatifid, serrate.
Flowers on stout spikes in condensed whorls.
Calyx very woolly; corolla hairy. For a well-
drained, sandy soil, rather dry in summer and
winter. Hardy to −25°C.

Phlomis bracteosa Royle ex Benth.
(*Labiatae*)   Native of the Himalayas, from
Afghanistan to SW China, growing in grassy
places among rocks at 1200–4000m, flowering in
July–August. Stems several, 20–80cm, from a
stout rootstock. Leaves 5–10cm long. Flowers
1.5–2cm long, with a short tube and a large,
elongate upper lip. For good, but well-drained
soil in full sun, with water in summer. Hardy to
−25°C.

Phlomis lychnitis L.   Native of S France, as
far north as the Ardêche, of Spain and Portugal,

growing in dry scrub, garrigue and on rocky
hills, flowering in May–July. Plant spreading by
underground suckers. Stems 30–50cm, from a
woody base. Leaves puberulent, with stellate
hairs, to 7.5cm long. Flowers in whorls of 4–10,
c.2.5cm long. For dry, well-drained soil. Hardy
to −10°C, perhaps less.

Phlomis russelliana (Sims) Benth. syn. *P.
viscosa* hort.   Native of Turkey, mainly in the
north, from Istanbul to Rize, growing in woods
and clearings, and in hazel scrub, at up to
1700m, flowering in May–September. Plant
with stems 30–90cm, spreading above and
below ground. Leaves ovate, cordate, crenate.
Whorls distant on the spike; calyx stellate
tomentose, with spreading teeth; corolla yellow,
30–35cm long. For any good soil in sun or
partial shade. Hardy to −20°C.

Phlomis samia L.   Native of Greece, S
Yugoslavia and SW & S Turkey, growing in
pine and cedar forest, usually on volcanic soil,
flowering in June–August. Plant forming large
clumps of spreading stems to 1m. Leaves
8–20cm long, lanceolate-ovate to broadly ovate,
crenate or serrate. Flowers 30–35mm long, with
upper lip helmet-shaped. A vigorous species for
fairly dry, partially shaded places as well as in
full sun. (see p. 96)

Phlomis bovei Noë subsp. **maroccana**   Maire
syn. *P. samia* L. subsp. *maroccana* Maire is a
similar-looking plant found in the mountains of
Morocco. Hardy to −15°C perhaps.

Phlomis tuberosa L.   Native of C & SE
Europe, N & E Turkey, N Iran and Siberia,
growing on steppes, dry meadows and stony
hills, flowering in June–July. Plant with
spherical tubers formed as nodules on the root
system, and stems to 120cm or more tall. Leaves
green, ovate, cordate, to 25cm long. Flowers
14–40 per whorl, with the corolla 15–20mm
long, the upper lip longer than the lower. Easily
grown and totally deciduous in winter. Hardy to
−25°C.

Phlomis samia

Nepeta grandiflora

Stachys officinalis 'Rosea' (p. 97)

Nepeta × faassenii

Nepeta govaniana

Nepeta 'Six Hills Giant'

Specimens from Wisley, 20 July. ⅓ life size

Melissa officinalis L. (*Labiatae*) **Lemon Balm** Native of S Europe and North Africa, east to the Caucasus and N Iran, but commonly naturalized in disturbed ground further north, growing in open woods, scrub and on rocky slopes by streams, flowering in June–September. Plant with upright stems to 1m, from a shortly creeping, woody rootstock. Leaves rough, usually lemon-scented. Flowers 9–14mm long. For any soil in sun or partial shade, and useful in dry difficult places, though it can seed so freely as to be a nuisance. 'Aurea' has golden-variegated leaves. Hardy to −15°C, perhaps less. For *Melittis* see p. 208–9.

Nepeta × faassenii Bergmans ex Stearn (*Labiatae*) A hybrid between the Caucasian *N. racemosa* Lam. syn. *N. mussinii* Spreng. ex Henckel and *N. nepetella* L., a species from Europe and North Africa. It is a useful edging plant for hot, dry borders on an alkaline soil, with silvery leaves, and stems around 30cm, flowering throughout the summer.
'Six Hills Giant' Taller and tougher, with stems to 1m, and deep-blue flowers.

Nepeta govaniana Benth. Native of the Himalayas, from Pakistan to N India (Uttar Pradesh), growing in moist places in open woodland, flowering in August–September. A sweetly aromatic plant of great beauty with branched stems to 1m, and flowers to 30mm, on long pedicels, often in pairs. For moist, mildly acid soil in a cool position. Hardy to −15°C.

Nepeta grandiflora M. Bieb. Native of the Caucasus, growing in grassy meadows and scrub, flowering in May–June. Plant with several stems to 1m; leaves 5cm long, cordate, crenulate. Flowers in an elongated spike, lavender-blue, 1.5cm long. For any good soil in full sun. Hardy to −20°C.

Nepeta persica Boiss. Native of Iran, growing on dry, rocky hills, flowering in June–August. Plant compact, to 10cm, with grey, hairy, ovate leaves to 1.5cm long. Flowers in tight whorls. For dry soil in full sun. Hardy to −10°C. (See also p. 208.)

Nepeta sibirica L. syn. *N. macrantha* Fisch. ex Benth. Native of Siberia, growing in grassland, flowering in June–July. Stems to 1m, with smooth lanceolate leaves, 8cm long. Inflorescence branched. Flowers c.4cm long, with a straight corolla tube. For good soil in full sun. Hardy to −25°C.
'Souvenir d'André Chaudron' syn. 'Blue Beauty' A short stocky form of *N. sibirica*, with a longer flowering season.

Scutellaria amoena C. H. Wright (*Labiatae*) Native of China, particularly in Yunnan around Kunming and Lijiang, growing in dry scrub on limestone at c.1500m, flowering in April–May. Stems upright, tufted, to 20cm, from a shortly creeping rootstock. Leaves oblong, obtuse. Flowers c.15mm long. For well-drained soil in sun or partial shade. Hardy to −15°C perhaps.

Scutellaria incana K. Spreng. syn. *S. canescens* Nutt. Native of E North America, from New Jersey south to North Carolina, west to Kansas and Alabama, growing in open woods, scrub and grassland, flowering in June–August. Stems to 120cm; leaves grey, ovate, 7.5–12cm long. Flowers 15–25mm long. For any soil in sun or light shade. Hardy to −25°C.

Nepeta 'Six Hills Giant' at Crathes Castle, Aberdeenshire

Nepeta persica

Nepeta sibirica

Nepeta 'Souvenir d'André Chaudron'

Melissa officinalis

Nepeta govaniana

Scutellaria incana at Wakehurst Place, Sussex

Scutellaria amoena near Lijiang, Yunnan

Stachys officinalis 'Rosea'

Specimens from the Chelsea Physic Garden, 11 July. ¼ life size

Stachys byzantina
'Primrose Heron'

Stachys byzantina
(two forms)

Phlomis samia (p. 93)

Stachys thirkei

Ballota pseudodictamnus

Nepeta cataria

Marrubium peregrinum

Ballota pseudodictamnus (L.) Benth. (*Labiatae*)   Native of Crete, Kithira and Cyrenaica, growing on rocks and rough ground, flowering in May–July. Plant very woolly, yellowish grey. Calyces conspicuous, 7–8mm across; corolla small, usually white, 14–15mm. Subsp. *lycia* Hub.-Mor., from SW Turkey, has the fruiting calyx 8–10mm across. *Ballota acetabulosa* (L.) Benth. from S Greece, the Aegean islands and SW Turkey, has flatter calyces to 20mm across and larger flowers 15–18mm, white with purple spots; the whole plant is greyer and larger. Both need well-drained position in full sun. Hardy to −10°C.

Hyssopus officinalis L. **'Rosea'** (*Labiatae*) **Hyssop**   Native of S Europe, east to the Caucasus and N Iran, growing on dry hills and on rock ledges, at up to 2200m in N Turkey, flowering in July–August. Plant very variable in hairiness, calyx and leaf shape. Stems numerous, to 60cm. Leaves linear, aromatic, to 5cm long. Flowers 7–13mm long, usually bluish, but also purplish, pink or white. The pink form, shown here, was grown by Philip Miller in the Chelsea Physic Garden in the 18th century. For a dry, sunny place. Hardy to −25°C.

Marrubium peregrinum L. (*Labiatae*)   Native of SE Europe, from Austria to Greece and Russia south to the N Caucasus and W Turkey, growing in dry, open places, flowering in June–August. Stems yellowish, to 60cm. Leaves whitish hairy, especially beneath. Flowers small, hairy outside. For a dry place in full sun. Hardy to −25°C.

Nepeta cataria L. (*Labiatae*) **Catnip** or **Catmint**   Native of Europe, from S England east to Siberia, the Himalayas, China and Korea, and naturalized in North America and Japan, growing in scrub, hedges and on dry, grassy banks, often on limestone, flowering in July–August. Plant much loved by cats, with upright stems to 1m. Leaves grey-pubescent, c.5cm long. Flowers white with bluish spots, 6–7mm long. 'Citriodora' has lemon-scented foliage. For well-drained soil in a warm position. Hardy to −25°C.

Stachys coccinea at Harry Hay's, Surrey

Hyssopus officinalis 'Rosea'

Stachys macrantha (bicoloured form)

Stachys byzantina at Crathes Castle, Aberdeenshire

Prunella grandiflora

Prunella grandiflora subsp. *pyrenaica*

Stachys macrantha

Prunella grandiflora (L.) Scholler (*Labiatae*)
Native of most of Europe, growing in grassland, usually on alkaline soils, flowering in June–September. Plant forming spreading mats with upright stems to 60cm, usually *c.*30cm. Flowers 25–30mm long, usually bluish, but also reddish, pink and white in garden forms. The inflorescence, without a pair of leaves at the base, distinguishes this species. Subsp. *pyreniaca* (Gren. & Godr.) A. & O. Bolos syn. *P. hastifolia* Brot., found on acid soils in SW France, Spain and Portugal, has larger flowers and hastate leaves; both need good, moist soil in full sun. Hardy to −25°C.

Stachys byzantina C. Koch syns. *S. lanata* Jacq., *S. olympica* Briq. (*Labiatae*) **Lambs' Ears** Native of N Turkey, the S Caucasus and N Iran, growing on rocky hills, in juniper scrub and waste places, flowering in June–September. Whole plant densely woolly, with rosettes of basal leaves to 10cm long, and ascending flowering stems to 1m. Flowers pink, 12–14mm long. Calyx teeth erect, sometimes slightly recurved. For a hot, dry, sunny position. Hardy

to −20°C. Several distinct forms are grown in gardens: 'Primrose Heron' has yellowish leaves under the wool; 'Cotton Boll' syn. 'Sheila Macqueen' has flowers proliferating to form woolly balls up the stem.

Stachys coccinea Jacq. Native of W Texas, New Mexico, S Arizona and Mexico, growing in canyons and by streams in rich soil at up to 2400m in Arizona, flowering in March–October. Plant usually forming spreading patches of stems to 30cm tall. Leaves triangular-ovate, sparingly hairy. Flowers 18–21mm long. For good, well-drained soil in full sun. Hardy to −10°C, perhaps less.

Stachys macrantha (C. Koch) Stearn syn. *S. grandiflora* Benth. non Host Native of the Caucasus, NE Turkey and NW Iran, growing in meadows, on rocky slopes and in scrub, at 1600–3000m, flowering in June–September. Plant spreading slowly to form dense clumps, with upright stems to 45cm. Flowers 30–35mm long, purplish pink, rarely pure, pale pink. For any good soil in sun or light shade. Hardy to

−20°C. There are pink 'Rosea', white 'Alba', and a bicoloured form in cultivation, and 'Robusta'.

Stachys officinalis (L.) Trevisan syn. *Betonica officinalis* L. **Wood Betony** Native of Europe, from Ireland and Scotland east to Siberia and south to Turkey and N Iran, growing on moist grassy banks, in meadows and in openings in forest, flowering in June–September. Plant with slender, erect stems to 45cm. Flowers in dense spikes, usually reddish purple, rarely pink. An attractive plant for the wild garden or meadow, and characteristic of heathy roadside banks on heavy soils. Hardy to −25°C or less.

Stachys thirkei C. Koch. Native of the Balkan peninsula and Italy to W Turkey, growing on bare hills and waste ground, flowering in May–September. Plant with mats of tight rosettes of grey-green or densely white-tomentose leaves, with a rugose upper surface. Calyx teeth longer than those of *S. byzantina*, spreading. Flowers magenta. For a dry position in full sun, and dislikes winter wet. Hardy to −15°C.

Salvia nemorosa 'Superba'

Salvia buchananii

Salvia buchananii Hedge (*Labiatae*)   Found in the 1950s in a garden of an English family in Mexico City. Provenance unknown, but probably S Mexico or C America. Stems to 60cm. One of the most beautiful half-hardy species, with distinct dark-green, ovate, leathery leaves and flowers to 5cm long, velvety-hairy above. Flowers from July onwards, and best in rich, moist soil. Hardy to −10°C.

Salvia chamaedryoides Cav.   Native of the mountains of Mexico. A low creeping plant, with stems herbaceous below ground, becoming hard and woody above; stems *c*.30cm, spreading 60cm or more. Leaves elliptic, with fine hairs *c*.1cm long. Flowers with a short tube and bottom lip widely open. For hot, dry rocky places, flowering in late summer. Hardy to −10°C.

Salvia farinacea Benth. **Mealy Cup Sage**
Native of Texas and New Mexico, growing on dry hillsides, flowering in summer. Stems to 45cm; leaves ovate-lanceolate, 2.5–7.5cm long. Flowers in tight whorls, 1.2cm long, hairy. 'Alba' has green bracts and white, hairy flowers. For dry soil in full sun. Hardy to −15°C.

Salvia miltiorrhiza Bunge   Native of NE China, and common near Beijing, growing in light woodland and clearings, flowering in May. Plant to 1m, with a large, orange-red tuber below ground and recognized by its leaves, which are pinnate with 5 leaflets. It is praised for its alleged medicinal qualities, which include a remedy for cancer.

Salvia nemorosa L. **'Superba'**   The clone 'Superba' was selected at the turn of the century from the species which is native of C & E Europe and SW Asia, from E Turkey and Iran to the Caucasus and Afghanistan, growing on rocky slopes, in dry meadows and rough ground, flowering in June–September. Stems forming clumps to 1m or more tall, with a stiff, upright habit; flower spikes to 15cm long, with dark-blue flowers and reddish-purple bracts. Flowering in gardens is from midsummer onwards and the effect is prolonged by the persistence of the bracts. Hardy to −20°C.

Salvia pratensis L. **Meadow Sage** or **Common Clary**   Native of most of Europe, including Britain, where it is not as common as it used to be, south to Morocco, and east to Russia, growing in meadows, flowering in June–July and spasmodically later. Stems to 90cm, usually less; leaves wrinkled 7.5–15cm long. Flowers with calyx often tinted dark blue, and with

Salvia × sylvestris 'Mainacht'

Salvia pratensis in a subalpine meadow in Switzerland

Salvia chamaedryoides

Salvia farinacea 'Victoria'

corolla rich blue, pink or white, the upper lip prominently curved, to 2.5cm long. For well-drained but good soil. Hardy to −25°C.

Salvia sclarea L. **Clary Sage**   Native of SE Europe and SW Asia, growing in dry rocky places, flowering in July–August. A short-lived perennial or biennial; in its first year from seed it produces a rosette of pubescent leaves which are broadly ovate, wrinkled and up to 22cm long. Flowering stem to 1m, very large and much branched, produced the following year. Bracts very prominent, pinkish, lilac or white, sometimes with a greenish tinge. Flowers to 2.5cm long, with the upper lip strongly curved downwards. *S. sclarea* is known as Clary Sage on account of its alleged value as an aid to clear sight. Var. *turkestanica* Moltet is a form with exceedingly large bracts, probably not in cultivation. The whole plant is strongly aromatic. For dry, well-drained soil in full sun. Hardy to −20°C.

Salvia spathacea Greene **Pitcher Sage**   Native of California, from Solano Co. near San Francisco along the Coast Ranges south to Orange Co., growing in scrub, chaparral and open woods, flowering in March–May. Plant viscid, forming low, ground-covering mounds by means of creeping underground rhizomes. Leaves hastate, 10–15cm long, rugose above and hairy beneath. Flower-spikes 60–90cm high; corolla 4cm long, deep reddish-purple. Sometimes called 'Hummingbird Sage' in reference to its pollinator. For any soil in sun or partial shade. Hardy to −10°C perhaps.

Salvia × sylvestris L. **'Mainacht'** syn. 'May Night'   Sometimes found under the name *S. nemorosa*, this German hybrid between *S. pratensis* and *S. nemorosa* has given some excellent clones; 'Mainacht' has larger flowers than *S. nemorosa*, of rich indigo-violet, enclosed in reddish-purple bracts, in mid- to late summer. Hardy to −20°C.

Salvia uliginosa Benth.   Native of Brazil, Uruguay and Argentina, growing in damp grassland, flowering in August–October in the north. Stems to 2m high, forming large clumps a metre or more thick by means of fleshy underground stolons. Leaves lanceolate, to 7cm long, both stems and leaves slightly viscid. Flowers on small spikes at the top of each branch; corolla mid-blue 2cm long, the lower lip having a white patch. For any good sandy soil that is not dry in summer. Hardy to −10°C, possibly less, but in danger from slugs in winter, which eat the fleshy rhizomes.

Salvia spathacea in Santa Barbara Botanic Garden

Salvia miltiorrhiza near Beijing

Salvia uliginosa

Salvia sclarea

Salvia forskahlei

Salvia campanulata on the plain at Lijiang, early May

Salvia bulleyana Diels (*Labiatae*)   Native of W
China, especially in Yunnan, in the Dali and
Lijiang mountains, growing on rocky meadows,
flowering in June–July. Plant forming clumps of
bold leaves 60–90cm across, the blades cordate
or hastate, *c.*10cm long. Flowering stems to 1m,
with flowers in pairs up the spike, with the
corolla yellow, 2.5cm long, while the lower lip
has a distinctive brown or purplish blotch,
mimicking a bumble bee as an aid to
fertilization. For well-drained soil in full sun.
Hardy to −15°C or less?

Salvia campanulata Wall.   Native of the
Himalayas, from N India to SW China, growing
on rocky hillsides or grassy meadows at 2500–
4000m, flowering in May–July. Plant with a
tuberous rootstock. Leaves ovate, to 12cm long.
Flower spike to more than 30cm. Flowers in
pairs with large calyces. Flower colour very
variable, ranging from cream to yellow, pink or
blue. For well-drained soil in full sun, moist in
summer. Hardy to −15°C or less?

Salvia castanea Diels   Native of the
Himalayas in W China, described from Lijiang,
growing in open turf on limestone, flowering in
July–August. Plant forming clumps 90cm tall,
60cm across. Leaves ovate, glutinous, softly
hairy, to 15cm long. Flowers dark brownish-
maroon, 2.5cm long, with an expanded corolla
tube. For well-drained soil, with plenty of
moisture in the growing season, but may suffer
from too much moisture when dormant in
winter. Hardy to −20°C.

Salvia forskahlei L.   Native of Bulgaria and N
Turkey along the Black Sea, growing on dry
hillsides, bare meadows and in deciduous
woodland, at up to 1900m, flowering in June–
September. Plant forming large, almost woody,
ground-covering clumps, with ovate or cordate
rather rough leaves. Flowers in spikes to 100cm
high. Corolla violet-blue with white streaks on
the lower lip, which is strongly deflexed. For
rich soil in sun or partial shade. Hardy to
−15°C.

Salvia glutinosa L. **Jupiter's Distaff**   Native
of Europe, from the Alps east to the Caucasus,
Turkey and N Iran, growing in scrub and in
moist places in deciduous forest, flowering in
July–October. The closely related *S. nubicola*
Sweet, from C Asia, can scarcely be regarded as
a separate species, as it differs only in the more
reflexed lower lip. This plant is very sticky all

Salvia bulleyana

Salvia glutinosa

Salvia hians

Salvia hians in Kashmir, July

over, in common with many herbaceous species from Asia. Plant making a handsome clump to 1m high and wide. Leaves heart-shaped, large, to 20cm long. For full sun or partial shade in any good soil. Hardy to −20°C or less?

Salvia hians Royle   Native of the Himalayas, from Pakistan to Bhutan, and common in Kashmir, growing on rocky open slopes at 2000–3000m in single clumps, flowering in June–September. Plant covered in sticky glands, producing an aromatic oil which is very pleasantly scented. Leaves ovate, cordate, 8–13cm long; flower spikes normally 60cm high. Flowers to 3cm long, with an inflated tube and spreading lips. For good, rich soil in full sun. Hardy to −20°C.

Salvia hydrangea DC.   Native of NE Turkey, Soviet Armenia and Iran, growing on dry, rocky slopes, pastures and roadsides, at up to 2000m, flowering in June–August. Plant spreading by stems running below the ground, and layering itself from horizontal branches above ground, creating a mat to 60cm across, from which many flowering branches emerge to 50cm tall. Leaves pinnatisect, with 2–3 pairs of small lobes and a large lanceolate or linear terminal lobe to 4cm long. Flowers c.22mm long, pink to magenta. For dry, well-drained soil in full sun. Although cold-tolerant, this species often dies in damp temperate winters. Hardy to −25°C if dry.

Salvia multicaulis Vahl   Native of SW Asia, from Iran and Turkey to Syria and Sinai, growing in dry scrub, on steppes and rocky limestone slopes, at up to 2600m, flowering in April–July. Plant shrubby, nearly deciduous in winter. Stems to 15cm high; leaves oblong to suborbicular, c.4cm long, wrinkled and a good substitute for garden sage for cooking. Flowers pink or violet, enclosed in large reddish calyces which expand when the seeds develop. For well-drained, dry soil in full sun. Hardy to −25°C or less?

Salvia przewalskii Max.   Native of China, especially in W & NW Sichuan, growing on rocky slopes and seasonal stream beds, in rather dry valleys, flowering in August–September. Plant with several hairy stems to 1.2m. Leaves ovate, cordate, to 15cm long, hairy on both surfaces. Calyx glandular, viscid; corolla tube swollen to 2.5cm long, pale pink to rose-purple coloured. For well-drained soil in full sun. Hardy to −20°C or less?

Salvia multicaulis

Salvia castanea

Salvia hydrangea

Salvia przewalskii

Monarda didyma
'Prärienacht'

'Beauty of Cobham'

'Croftway Pink'

Physostegia virginiana
'Summer Spire'

Physostegia virginiana
'Summer Snow'

Monarda didyma
'Cambridge Scarlet'

Monarda didyma
'Schneewittchen'

Specimens from Beth Chatto, Unusual Plants, 17 August. ⅓ life size

Monarda didyma L. (*Labiatae*) **Bergamot, Oswego Tea**   Native of E North America, from New York to Michigan, and in the mountains south to Georgia and Tennessee, growing in moist woods and scrub, flowering in late June–August. Plant pleasantly aromatic, forming clumps of upright stems to 1.5m. Leaves softly hairy or smooth, toothed, to 14cm long, with a short stalk. Flowers in a terminal head, with red-tinged bracts. Corolla 3–4.5cm long, vermilion to scarlet, glabrous or nearly so. For a border or partial shade in a wild garden, in good, rich soil. Hardy to −25°C, or less. The cultivars, most of which are probably of hybrid origin, include the following. They are more tolerant of dry conditions than the wild species, but are still likely to suffer from mildew when too dry at the root.

'Beauty of Cobham'   Pink flowers and purplish foliage.

'Cambridge Scarlet'   Raised by Prichard before 1913. Stems 90cm.

'Croftway Pink'   Stems around 90cm.

'Prärienacht' syn. 'Prairie Night'   Raised by Kayser & Siebert in 1955. 'Blaustrumpf' syn. 'Blue Stocking' is another purple.

'Schneewittchen' syn. 'Snow Maiden'   Raised by K. Foerster in 1956. Stems *c*.60cm.

Monarda fistulosa L. **Wild Bergamot**   Native of NE North America from Quebec to Minnesota, south to Georgia, Alabama, Louisiana and E Texas, growing in dry scrub and wood edges, flowering in July–August. Var. *menthaefolia* (Graham) Fern. is found further west to British Columbia and along the Rockies to N Mexico. Plant forming clumps of stems 50–150cm tall. Leaves greyish, triangular-ovate to lanceolate, sessile. Bracts often pink-tinged. Flowers lilac, pink or whitish, pubescent, with the tip of the upper lip bearded. For any good soil in sun or part shade. Hardy to −25°C or less.

Monardella purpurea Howell (*Labiatae*)   Native of California in Del Norte Co., north to SW Oregon, growing on dry, stony slopes at 300–1200m, flowering in July–September. Plant small, glabrous, with stems to 15cm from a woody base. Leaves 1.5–3cm long. Flower-heads 1.5–2cm across. Bracts purplish; flowers *c*.2cm long. For a dry, warm position in full sun. Hardy to −10°C perhaps.

Physostegia virginiana L. (*Labiatae*) **False Dragonhead**   Native of E North America, from Quebec to Minnesota, south to North Carolina, Tennessee and Missouri, growing on river banks, in damp scrub and wet meadows, flowering in June–September. A rampant plant, spreading by white, fleshy stolons to form clumps several metres across when happy. Stems upright to 1m. Leaves to 12.5cm lanceolate, sharply toothed. Flowers 2–3cm long, inflated at the mouth. The pedicels are malleable, remaining fixed when moved, hence the name 'Obedient Plant'. There are several named clones:

'Summer Snow'   Shorter than most, 45–60cm.

'Summer Spire'   Stems to 1m; 'Vivid' (not shown) has stiffer stems, *c*.50cm, and deep-pink flowers. 'Bouquet Rose' has paler flowers. For good, moist soil in full sun. Hardy to −25°C.

Monarda didyma (pink form) in North America

Monarda 'Cambridge Scarlet'

Monarda fistulosa at Harry Hay's, Surrey

Monardella purpurea from Del Norte Co. at Harry Hay's, Surrey

Penstemon jamesii

Penstemon baccharifolius

Penstemon isophyllus (p. 107)

Penstemon clutei

Penstemon superbus

Penstemon glaber

Penstemon strictus

Specimens from Green Farm Plants, 4 August. ⅕ life size

Penstemon barbatus

Penstemon barbatus 'Coccineus'

Penstemon alluviorum Pennell
(*Scrophulariaceae*)   Native of S Indiana and S
Illinois to Missouri and south to Mississippi and
Arkansas, growing in marshes, river valleys and
damp hillsides, flowering in May–June. Stems
to 1.5m. Leaves pubescent, the lowest
acuminate, serrate. Inflorescence sparsely
glandular. Flowers 1.7–2.3cm long, upper lobes
curved upwards. *P. digitalis* Nutt. is similar but
has a very glandular inflorescence and flowers to
3cm long. For moist, rich soil in full sun. Hardy
to −15°C or less.

Penstemon baccharifolius Hook.   Native of
Texas, in the Trans-Pecos area, and in Mexico
to San Luis Potosi, growing in crevices of
limestone rocks, flowering in June–July? Plant
subshrubby at the base, with flowering stems to
c.60cm. Leaves 2.5–5cm long, thick and
leathery. Inflorescence glandular. Flowers 2.5–
3.2cm long, the staminode glabrous. For well-
drained, dry soil in full sun. Hardy to −10°C or
lower if dry.

Penstemon barbatus (Cav.) Roth.   Native of
Colorado to Nevada and south to Mexico, at up
to 3000m, growing on low hills and dry
canyons, in pinyon pine, oak or aspen forest,
flowering in June–October. Plant with several
stiff, upright stems to 90cm. Leaves often
glaucous, sometimes hairy. Flowers bright red,
rarely pink. Corolla strongly 2–lipped, the lower
lip reflexed usually hairy; upper lip projecting.
Anthers hairy or glabrous. For well-drained soil
in warm position in full sun. Hardy to −20°C if
dry. 'Coccineus' is the clone commonly grown.
It has fewer glaucous leaves and more branching
stems than the type.

Penstemon centranthifolius Benth. **Scarlet
Bugler**   Native of California, in the Coast
Ranges from Lake Co. southwards, and in
Lower California, growing in dry places in
chaparral, often with *Romneya*, below 2000m,
flowering in April–July. Stems woody to 120cm
tall. Leaves entire, glaucous, lanceolate, the
upper amplexicaul. Flowers 25–35mm, to 6mm
wide, the lobes scarcely spreading. Staminode
glabrous. For dry soil in full sun. Hardy to
−10°C.

Penstemon clutei A. Nelson   Native of
Arizona, around Sunset Crater, growing in
volcanic ash at c.1900m, flowering in June–July.
Stems to 1.8m. Leaves finely toothed, perfoliate
above, glaucous. Flowers inflated from a narrow
base, 9–12mm wide. Staminode not exserted.
For dry, well-drained soil in full sun. Hardy to
−15°C perhaps, if dry.

Penstemon glaber Pursh   Native of South
Dakota, to Nebraska, Wyoming and ?Arizona,
growing in dry, open places, grasslands, and
prairies in stiff, stony soil and on limestone,
often with *Artemisia*, flowering in June–July.
Plant forming small clumps of several stems
30–60cm tall. Leaves oblong to lanceolate,
5–10cm long. Flowers c.3cm long, deep blue.
Staminode glabrous or spreading, finely hairy.
For any good, well-drained soil in full sun.
Hardy to −20°C, or less if dry.

Penstemon jamesii Benth.   Native of SW
Colorado, S Utah, W New Mexico and N
Arizona, growing in sandy places, in pinyon
pine Juniper and *Pondorosa* pine forests at
1300–2000m, flowering in May–June. Stems to
60cm. Leaves scattered, linear, sometimes with
few teeth. Corolla to 22mm long, swollen at the
throat, and hairy inside. For dry, well-drained
soil in warm position. Hardy to −20°C perhaps.

PENSTEMON

Penstemon ovatus Dougl. ex Hook. Native of S British Columbia, Washington and N Oregon, growing on limestone rocks and in open woods below 1000m, flowering in May–June. Stems 30–100cm, from a rosette of stalked, leathery leaves. Flowers glandular outside, 15–22mm; staminode bearded. For good, well-drained soil. Hardy to −15°C, perhaps.

Penstemon palmeri Gray Native of California in the mountains west of Death Valley at up to 1800m, and in S Utah and Arizona, growing in dry, rocky places, by roadsides and in seasonal stream-beds, flowering in March–September. Stems several to 120cm, from a tufted rootstock. Leaves spiny-toothed, the lower lanceolate-ovate, amplexicaul, the upper perfoliate. Flowers scented, 22–35mm long, to 12mm wide; staminode exserted, shaggy-bearded. For dry, well-drained soil. Hardy to −15°C if dry.

Penstemon rostriflorus syn. *P. bridgesii* Gray Native of E California, to Arizona, SW Colorado and W New Mexico, growing on dry, open, stony hillsides at 1500–3300m and among pinyon and *Pondorosa* pines, flowering in May–September. Plant with several stems to 1m from a slightly woody base. Leaves linear oblanceolate at the base, linear above, not glaucous. Calyx and pedicel glandular. Flowers 22–35mm long, the lower lip reflexed. Staminode glabrous. For well-drained soil in warm position in full sun. Hardy to −15°C.

Penstemon strictus Benth. Native of S Wyoming and Utah, and south to NE Arizona and N New Mexico, growing in canyons and mountains at up to 3000m, among sagebush, flowering in June–July. Stems to 60cm. Leaves oblanceolate, deep green. Inflorescence not glandular. Pedicels appressed to the stem. Flowers deep blue, with a short tube and a swollen throat, 2-lipped at the mouth.

Penstemon superbus A. Nelson Native of SE Arizona and New Mexico (Chihuahua), growing in rocky canyons, along seasonal streams, in sandy or gravelly places, at 1000–1700m, flowering in April–May. Stems to 2m, often many from a stout rootstock. Stem leaves oblong-ovate, blackening on drying. Flowers 20–25mm long, with 7 equal rounded, spreading lobes and stalked glands. Staminode bearded. For well-drained soil in full sun. Hardy to −15°C perhaps, if kept dry in winter.

Penstemon venustus Dougl. ex Lindl. Native of Idaho, Washington and Oregon, growing in open rocky slopes and dry river channels, flowering in May–August. Stems to 80cm high, shrubby at the base, from a stout taproot. Leaves sessile, lanceolate, serrate, 4–10cm long, 1–3cm wide. Flowers lavender to purple or violet, 2.5–3.8cm long, c.1cm wide at the mouth; staminode with a long white beard near the tip. For well-drained soil in full sun. Hardy to −15°C.

Penstemon whippleanus A. Gray Native of Montana, Wyoming, E Idaho to Utah, New Mexico and Arizona, growing in dry, grassy places, scrub or open woods, into the alpine zone, flowering in July–August. Stems 20–60cm from a branching rootstock. Leaves entire, sessile, oblong or lanceolate. Inflorescence and outside of flowers glandular. Flowers blue or violet to deep purplish black, sometimes cream. Staminode bearded at the tip. For good well-drained soil in full sun. Hardy to −20°C or less.

Penstemon whippleanus at Edington, Wiltshire

Penstemon ovatus

Penstemon venustus

Penstemon centranthifolius

Penstemon rostriflorus

Penstemon palmeri

Penstemon alluviorum

Penstemon kunthii
(Keith Rushforth 637)

'Garnet'

'Rubicunda'

*Penstemon
isophyllus*

'Snowstorm'

'Schonholzeri'

'Evelyn'

'Burford Purple'

'Hidcote Pink'

'King George V'

Specimens from the Savill Gardens, Windsor, 28 July. ⅓ life size

Penstemon 'Stapleford Gem' with *Lychnis coronaria* 'Alba'

Penstemon 'Burford Purple'

Penstemon 'Flame'

Penstemon 'Catherine de la Mare'

Penstemon 'Thorn'

Penstemon × gloxiniodes hort.
(*Scrophulariaceae*)   This is the name given to
the large-flowered hybrids between *P. hartwegii*
and *P. cobaea*. Many were raised by the 1840s,
soon after *P. hartwegii* was introduced from
Mexico. They flower from July–September or
the first hard frost. They vary in hardiness, but
all are killed by temperatures of *c.* −15°C, and
often die in warmer winters, probably because
they rot at the root. Cuttings should be taken in
August and wintered under glass.

Penstemon 'Catherine de la Mare'   A low
plant to 30cm, with narrow, toothed leaves and
small, blue-purple flowers. Close to *P.
heterophyllus*, a native of California. 'Blue
Bedder' is rather similar, too.

Penstemon 'Evelyn'   A bushy, pink form or
hybrid of the blue-purple *P. campanulatus*
Willd., native throughout the mountains of
Mexico, in meadows and rocky places. Differs
from *P. kunthii* in flower colour and in its
corolla being abruptly expanded towards the
mouth. Hybrids between the two species are
frequent in the wild. 'Evelyn' is very free-
flowering from June onwards in S England.

Penstemon 'Hidcote Pink'   A hybrid (possibly
between *P. campanulatus* and *P. hartwegii*)
raised at Hidcote. Stems to 75cm. Flowers
produced from July–September.

Penstemon isophyllus Robson   Native of
Mexico. Stems to 2m, subshrubby at the base.
Leaves rather thick and fleshy. Flowers pale in
the throat, with dark lines, *c.* 5cm long. Hardy
to −15°C, perhaps, in a dry position.

Penstemon kunthii G. Don   Native of S & W
Mexico, growing in disturbed ground and by
roadsides in the mountains at 1500–2000m,
flowering in summer. Stems *c.* 60cm. Flowers
red, the corolla narrowly tubular to gradually
ampliate. Hardy to −10°C.

Penstemon 'Stapleford Gem'   A rather small-
flowered plant, with lilac and cream flowers,
close to *P. hirsutus* (L.) Willd., a native of NE
North America, from Quebec and Ontario, to
Wisconsin, Virginia, Kentucky and N
Tennessee. Sometimes incorrectly labelled
'Sour Grapes'. For well-drained soil in full sun.

'Alice Hindley' syn. 'Gentianoides'   A tall
plant to 120cm, with pale bluish-lilac flowers
about 4.4cm long. The leaves are undamaged by
−10°C. Flowering usually from mid-July.
Raised by Forbes of Hawick in 1931.
'Burford Purple' syn. 'Burgundy'   Close
to 'Garnet' but more purple.
'Flame'   A good red, with a dark throat.
'Garnet'   A rich purplish-red.
'King George V'   Height to 80cm. Flowers
from July–October. Raised by Forbes in 1911.
'Rubicunda'   Raised at Lyme Park, Cheshire,
in 1906. Height and width 60cm. The large
flowers are produced in July–September.
'Schonholzeri' syns. 'Ruby', 'Firebird'   A
vigorous plant, up to 1m. Flowers 4cm long,
from early July. Hardy in warm areas only.
'Snowstorm'   Stems to 65cm. Leaves darkish
green. Flowers pure white, with a slightly cream
tube, *c.*4cm long and dark anthers. Flowers
from late July.
'Thorn'   Flowers *c.*4cm long. 'Peace' is
similar. 'Beech Park' is larger.

Penstemon 'Alice Hindley'

Linaria repens in Harry Hay's garden, Surrey

Linaria purpurea 'Canon Went'

Linaria triornithophora

Verbascum bugulifolium

Alonsoa warscewiczii Regel
(*Scrophulariaceae*)   Native of Peru, flowering in
late summer. Plant with several branched
upright stems to 60cm. Leaves ovate, short-
stalked. Flowers intense scarlet, *c*.2.5cm across.
There is also a pale-orange-pink form, 'Peachy-
Keen', found in gardens. Hardy to −5°C
perhaps, but often self-seeding if killed by cold.

Linaria dalmatica (L.) Mill. syn. *L. genistifolia*
(L.) Mill. subsp. *dalmatica* (L.) Maire & Petit
(*Scrophulariaceae*)   Native of S Italy, Romania,
Yugoslavia to Greece, C Turkey and S Russia,
growing in sandy and stony places and
roadsides, flowering in June–August.
Naturalized in Kashmir and North America.
Plant forming patches of decumbent or upright
stems to 100cm. Leaves up to 4cm wide, ovate
to lanceolate (narrower in *L. genistifolia*).
Flowers 2–5cm long. For well-drained soil and
sun in a warm position. Hardy to −20°C.
Linaria grandiflora Desf., which is found
scattered throughout Turkey, has rather shorter
stems, ovate, thick, glaucous leaves and
deflexed bracts; the pedicels are short and stout.

Linaria purpurea (L.) Mill. **'Canon Went'**
Native of C & S Italy and Sicily, but naturalized
in England and Ireland, growing on grassy
roadsides, flowering in June–August. Stems to
90cm, erect from a tufted rootstock. Leaves
linear, alternate above, verticillate below,
glaucous. Flowers in a slender raceme,
9–12mm, usually purple, but in 'Canon Went'
(shown here) pink, and white in 'Springside
White'. For any good soil in sun. Hardy to
−20°C or less.

Linaria repens (L.) Mill.   Native of S Europe,
from N Spain to NW Italy and NW Germany,
but widely naturalized elsewhere in Europe,
including England, and in NE North America,
growing in grassy places, on roadsides and waste
ground, flowering in June–August. Plant with
creeping underground rhizomes, forming
spreading patches. Stems to 120cm, erect, much
branched. Leaves linear. Flowers 8–15mm,
white to pale lilac. Hardy to −20°C. *L.×dominii*
Druce, the hybrid between *L. repens* and *L.
purpurea*, has a longer flowering season and lilac
or pinkish flowers.

Linaria triornithophora (L.) Willd.   Native of
Spain and Portugal, except the south, growing
in hedges and scrub, flowering in June–August.
Plant with several upright stems to 130cm, often
branched. Leaves lanceolate to ovate-lanceolate,
to 7.5cm long, in whorls of 3–4. Flowers in
whorls of 3–4, 35–55mm long, purplish or
pinkish, marked with yellow. For well-drained
soil in sun in a warm position. Hardy to −15°C.

Verbascum blattaria L. (*Scrophulariaceae*)
Native of S Europe and North Africa, east to
Afghanistan and Siberia, and naturalized in
England and North America, growing in waste
places, by roads, in dry scrub and on sand
dunes, flowering in May–July. A biennial or
short-lived perennial, with a rosette of lower
leaves, pinnate with rounded lobes. Stems to
150cm, glabrous below, glandular above.
Flowers 20–30mm across, with a slender
pedicels longer than the bracts. Filaments with
purple hairs; stamens 5. For well-drained,
rather dry soil in full sun. Hardy to −20°C. A
very elegant and dainty plant.

Verbascum bugulifolium Lam. syn. *Celsia
bugulifolia* (Lam.) Jaub. & Spach   Native of S
Bulgaria and extreme NW Turkey, growing in
open woods, scrub and waste places at up to
450m, flowering in April–June. Plant very
glandular with usually simple stems to 75cm.
Basal leaves with a long petiole and ovate
lamina. Inflorescence rather few flowered.
Flowers yellowish or bluish green, 2–3.5cm
across. An unusual species, for a sunny or partly
shady, well-drained, warm position. Hardy to
−15°C.

Verbascum hybrids   Most of the larger
Verbascum species are biennials, but a large
group of hybrids has been raised by crossing the
perennial purple *V. phoeniceum* with a yellow
species. They are not long lived, and should be
propagated regularly by root cuttings. They
flower in June–August. Shown here are:
'Cotswold Beauty'   Stems to 130cm.
'Cotswold Queen'   Stems to 120cm.
'Helen Johnson'   Stems to 120cm.
All are best in well-drained, warm soil, and
grow well on chalk. Hardy to −20°C. 'Mont
Blanc' (not shown) has white flowers.

Linaria dalmatica

Verbascum 'Helen Johnson' at Kew

Verbascum blattaria from Turkey

Verbascum 'Cotswold Queen'

Alonsoa warscewiczii at Edington, Wiltshire

Verbascum 'Cotswold Beauty'

Glumicalyx goseloides at Sellindge, Kent *Zaluzianskya microsiphon* near Cathedral Peak, Natal

Diascia anastrepta Hilliard & Burtt
(*Scrophulariaceae*) Native of the Drakensberg
in Natal, Transkei and Lesotho, growing in
moist, grassy places below cliffs of basalt or
among boulders by streams at 1800–3000m,
flowering in December–March. Plant with long,
slender stems up to 40cm. Leaves ovate,
subcordate or cuneate at the base, 10–25cm
long, on stalks up to 8mm long. Flowers with
corolla *c*.25mm across, the lowest lobe *c*.12mm
× 12mm with dark glands in a loose patch
across its base, with two stamens pointing
upwards and two downwards. Spurs 6–7mm
long, curving outwards. Easily grown in moist
soil. Hardy to −10°C perhaps.

Diascia megathura Hilliard & Burtt Native of
the S Drakensberg in Natal and Lesotho,
growing in short, moist grassland or on stony
slopes at 1800–2400m, flowering in December–
February. Plant with spreading, ascending and
very glandular stems to 45cm, rooting at the
base. Leaves 15–30mm × 11–20mm, ovate,
obtuse, cuneate at base, sometimes shallowly
toothed. Flowers slightly nodding, in loose
racemes, on stalks 15–20mm. Corolla 20mm
across, the lowest lobe 9mm × 11mm, the other
lobes much smaller, with 2 patches of dark
glands on either side of the style and stamens;
yellow patch elongated. Spurs 6–8mm,
spreading, with dark glands inside. 2 stamens ±
sterile, pointing upwards; 2 fertile stamens
pointing downwards with green pollen. Easily
grown in well-drained but moist, sandy soil.
Hardy to −10°C perhaps.

Diascia patens (Thunb.) Fourcade Native of
South Africa, in Cape Province, on the
Rooiberg and the hills near Willowmore,

growing on rocky slopes and by streams and
waterfalls, at *c*.800m, flowering in March–
August. Plant bushy, and sometimes
scrambling through shrubs. Leaves linear to
lanceolate. Flowers 17mm across, deep red to
orange; spurs 4–5mm long, straight, diverging.
Hardy to −10°C, perhaps. An attractive, almost
shrubby species with a long flowering period, in
autumn and early spring.

Diascia purpurea N. E. Br. Native of the N
Drakensberg around Mont-aux-Sources and
south to the upper Loteni valley, growing on
bare patches in moist grassland at 2350–2440m,
flowering in January–April. Plant with rather
few creeping shoots and upright flowering stems
to 45cm. Leaves deep purple beneath, ovate,
obtuse, cuneate at base, margins smooth or
slightly crenate, on stalks to 2mm long. Flowers
nodding in a loose spike-like raceme on
ascending stalks 13–25mm long. Corolla 18–
20mm long, with the lower lobe very short
(*c*.2.5mm), the two upper lobes forming an
elongated upper lip *c*.13mm × 16mm, so that
the flower appears upside down. Spurs curved,
short, 3–4mm long, white; 2 ± sterile stamens
erect; 2 projecting forwards, fertile, with green
pollen. This species is more difficult to grow,
requiring moist, well-drained soil, and high
humidity in summer. Hardy to −15°C perhaps.

Glumicalyx goseloides (Diels) Hilliard & Burtt
(*Scrophulariaceae*) Native of the Drakensberg
in Natal and Lesotho, growing in damp, rocky
grassland and by streams at 1800–2800m,
flowering in December–January. Plant aromatic
with creeping leafy stems and ascending
flowering shoots to 40cm. Leaves 3–4cm long,
obtuse, tongue-shaped, sessile. Flowers in

dense nodding heads with overlapping, leafy
bracts. Corolla 25mm, buff outside, bright
orange inside. Easily grown in well-drained soil;
hardy to −10°C, flowering in late spring and
until late summer if dead-headed and watered.
Source: CD&R 228, from Sani Pass area, Natal.

Nemesia caerulea Hiern (*Scrophulariaceae*)
Native of the Drakensberg, in Natal, Transkei
and Lesotho, growing on grassy slopes, by
roadsides and among rocks at 1800–2900m,
flowering in December–February. Plant with
glandular-hairy creeping and ascending stems to
30cm. Leaves ovate-lanceolate, toothed on
short, 1–3mm stalks. Flowers bluish with a
white, red-edged patch in the throat and a single
downward-pointing spur with 2 yellow furry
bosses almost blocking its throat. Corolla
15mm. *Nemesia fruticans* (Thunb.) Benth.
syn. *N. foetens* Vent. is very similar, but does
not have furry bosses in the throat. Both are
easily grown in ordinary, well-drained soil.
Hardy to −10°C perhaps. Photographed on the
Sani Pass, C Natal. *Nemesia* species are
commonly grown as annuals, most of the
cultivars being derived from *N. strumosa*
Benth., but of the 65 or so species in S Africa
many are perennials.

Sutera breviflora (Schltr.) Hiern
(*Scrophulariaceae*) Native of the Drakensberg
in Natal and Lesotho and on high ground in C
Natal, growing on grassy slopes and ridges at
1800–2800m, flowering in January–March.
Plant with sprawling stems to 30cm from a thin
rootstock. Flowers *c*.1.5cm across, bright red.
Forms hybrids in the wild with *S. pristisepala*.
For well-drained but not dry soil in full sun.
Hardy to −15°C perhaps.

Sutera breviflora

Sutera pristisepala

Diascia anastrepta

Diascia patens at Kew

Diascia purpurea near Mont-aux-Sources

Diascia megathura

Nemesia fruticans at Green Farm Plants

Sutera pristisepala Hiern Native of the
Drakensberg in Natal, NE Cape Province,
Lesotho and Transvaal, at 1980–2900m,
growing on cliffs, rocky slopes and screes,
flowering in December–February. Plant
spreading and almost shrubby at the base to
80cm high and across, glistening glandular-
hairy and strongly aromatic. Leaves silvery,
pinnate with toothed lobes, c.3cm long. Flowers
with a yellow, red-edged spot in the throat,
12mm across, with a bent tube 1cm long. An
attractive silvery plant for a well-drained, warm,
sunny position. Easily grown from cuttings in
late summer. Hardy to −10°C perhaps.

Zaluzianskya microsiphon (O. Kuntze) K.
Schum. (*Scrophulariaceae*) Native of the
Drakensberg in Natal, Transkei, Lesotho and
the NE Cape Province, growing in stony
grassland at 1800–2750m, flowering in January–
March. Plant with few upright stems to 30cm.
Inflorescence elongated, with overlapping,
appressed bracts; corolla tube 15–50mm reddish
outside, whitish on the inside of the limb which
opens in sunlight.

Nemesia caerulea on the Sani Pass in the Natal Drakensberg, South Africa

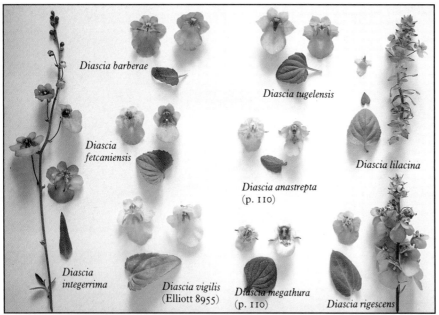

Specimens from Wisley, 5 September. ½ life size

Diascia barberae

Diascia tugelensis

Diascia fetcaniensis

Diascia lilacina

Diascia anastrepta (p. 110)

Diascia integerrima

Diascia vigilis (Elliott 8955)

Diascia megathura (p. 110)

Diascia rigescens

Diascia (*Scrophulariaceae*) These have recently become popular garden plants as they are easily propagated and flower throughout the summer if dead-headed and kept moist. There are altogether around 50 species, mostly annuals, in the summer-dry Cape region of South Africa, but about 18 from the summer-rainfall area of the Drakensberg are perennials. Most of these will tolerate up to $c. -10°C$, especially if protected from wet in winter, but are easily overwintered as rooted cuttings kept in a frame or cold greenhouse. All species are easy to propagate from basal shoots taken off in the autumn or spring and kept moist until rooted. The species are rather similar in general appearance, but differ in details of the flower structure. Hilliard & Burtt (1984).

Diascia barberae Hook. fil. Native of the mountains of Lesotho, and of one or two valleys in C Drakensberg, growing in wet, stony or silty places among rocks in the beds of streams, or in marshy ground at 1980–2000m, flowering in January–February. Plant with low spreading stems to 45cm. Leaves 10–25mm × 5–20mm, ovate or ovate-lanceolate, subcordate, rounded or almost truncate at base. Flowers in very loose racemes. Corolla 23–27mm × 20–24mm, lowest lobe 11–13mm × 13–16mm, with a white patch at the base and 2 patches of dark glands on either side. Spurs 7–8mm long, pointing outwards and downwards, tips slightly incurved with dark glands inside. 'Ruby Field' is a commonly grown and richly coloured clone of *D. barberae*, though it is often listed as *D. barberae × cordata*. *D. barberae* itself has been long cultivated since Mrs Barber sent seeds to Kew in 1870.

Diascia fetcaniensis Hilliard & Burtt syn. *D. felthamii* hort. Native of the S Drakensberg, in the NE Cape, in Lesotho and in Transkei, at 1675–3000m, growing in damp, grassy places below cliffs and by streams, often in shade, flowering in January–March. Plant with many creeping glandular stems to 40cm. Leaves ovate, cordate, rounded or obtuse at apex, 15–24mm long. Corolla 20–24mm × 15–21mm, mid-pink; lowest lobe with a patch of dark glands across the base. Spurs curved downwards and inwards. One of the easiest and hardiest species.

Diascia integerrima Benth. syn. *D. moltenensis* Hiern Native of Lesotho and South Africa, in Natal, Orange Free State, Transkei and NE Cape Province, growing on cliffs, in rock crevices, in loose, gritty soil and by streams, at 1800–3000m, flowering in November–March. Plant forming clumps of thin, wiry stems and far spreading underground by long stolons. Stems up to 1m, but usually $c.30$cm unsupported. Leaves linear to oblong lanceolate, sometimes with a few shallow teeth. Flowers in loose spike-like racemes, 17–24mm × 15–24mm, the lowest lobe 7–11mm × 9–15mm, with a zone of dark glands towards the base and on a shallow keel. Spurs 4–6mm, directed downwards, the tips incurved. More tolerant of dry conditions and hardier than other species, to $-15°C$ perhaps.

Diascia lilacina Hilliard & Burtt Native of NE Cape Province, at Saalboom Nek pass near Barkly East, growing on cliffs at $c.2000$m, flowering in January. Plant softly glandular-hairy, with stems to 30cm. Leaves ovate, $c.15$mm in diameter. Flowers $c.12$mm across, without spurs, but with the 'window' forming a cone $c.3$mm long. For moist, well-drained soil.

Diascia 'Ruby Field' at Edinburgh

Diascia integerrima on Sani Pass

Diascia barberae from Sani Pass

Diascia integerrima at Carlyle's Hoek, NE Cape

Diascia tugelensis

Diascia rigescens Benth.   Native of South
Africa, in S Natal, the Transkei and the E Cape
west to the Great Winterberg, growing in moist
places, especially along the edges of forest and
in grassland at 100–1525m, flowering in
November–April. Plant forming dense mats.
Stems up to 1.3m, usually c.30cm in gardens.
Leaves sessile, usually crowded, opposite or
alternate above, 15–60mm × 10–35mm,
broadly ovate. Flowers crowded into spike-like
racemes. Corolla 11–18mm across, the lowest
lobes 5–8mm × 7.5–11mm with stalked yellow
glands on a keel. Spurs c.3mm long, directed
downwards and inwards. Hardy to −10°C.

Diascia tugelensis Hilliard & Burtt   Native of
the NE corner of the Drakensberg mountains,
around Mont-aux-Sources, growing in rocky
stream beds, in rock crevices and on wet basalt
cliffs, at 1800–3000m, flowering in January–
March (June–August in northern gardens).
Plant forming spreading mats with long, thin
stems ascending to 45cm, with stolons. Leaves
mostly at the base, 8–25mm × 6–15mm, ovate-
cordate, apex subacute, serrate. Flowers in very
loose racemes 20–23mm × 18–20mm, the
lowest lobe 9–11mm × 10–11mm with a pale
patch beneath the projecting stamens. The
yellow and maroon patch on the upper lobe is
Y-shaped and sunken. Spurs 5–7mm directed
downwards and outwards, with swollen ends,
with dark-greyish glands wide. Hardy to −10°C
perhaps.

Diascia vigilis Hilliard & Burtt   Native of the
NE Drakensberg around Mont-aux-Sources,
south to Cathedral Peak, on the Platberg near
Harrismith and in W Lesotho, growing in low
scrub and among rocks in moist places, at 1800–
3000m, flowering in December–March. Plant
with many creeping and ascending stems to
50cm. Leaves ovate or ovate-lanceolate,
subacute, rounded at the base. Flowers usually
pale pink in loose racemes. Calyx lobes not
reflexed. Corolla 22–28mm × 17–23mm, with a
patch of black glands in the centre of the lowest
lobe. Spurs 7–9mm long, curved downwards
and slightly inwards. Elliott 8955 is a good,
large form.

Diascia rigescens at Aldington, Kent

Diascia fetcaniensis

Diascia vigilis

Phygelius capensis in a typical streamside habitat at Naude's Nek, NE Cape Province

Phygelius aequalis Harvey ex Hiern
(*Scrophulariaceae*)   Native of the Drakensberg,
the mountains of C Natal, e.g. Ngeli mountain,
northwards to the NE Transvaal
(Zoutpansberg), growing in grassland on the
margins of streams and on wet rocks, at 1200–
2200m, flowering in October–April. Plant with
stems to 1.5cm, shrubby only at base. Leaves
triangular, cuneate at the base, the blade around
10cm long, 6cm across. Inflorescence
cylindrical. Corolla *c*.4cm long, pale brownish
red, or dusky pink, the tube curved slightly
downwards, or straight, the lobes spreading but
not deflexed; visited by sunbirds. For any good
moist soil in full sun, requiring ample water in
summer. Hardy to −10°C, perhaps less.
'Yellow Trumpet' syns. 'Cream Delight',
'Alba'   This distinct, pale-yellow form was
discovered on Mawahqua mountain, between
Underberg and Bulwer in Natal, and introduced
by B. L. Burtt and Harold Hillier. Yellow forms
have been seen in other areas also.

Phygelius capensis E. Meyer ex Benth.
Native of the Drakensberg in Lesotho and NE
Cape Province, to Orange Free State, more
rarely in Natal, from Mont-aux-Sources
southwards to the Boschberg, and
Koudeveldberg, growing on rocks by mountain
streams, and on moist slopes at above 2000m,
flowering in October–April. Plant with
subshrubby stems to 2m and underground
stolons. Leaves rounded at the base.
Inflorescence pyramidal. Corolla 3.75cm long,
orange or red, yellow on the lobes inside, the
mouth facing downwards, the tube curved
forwards and the lobes reflexed; visited by
sunbirds. A yellow form is recorded from the
Mokhotlong valley in Lesotho at 2100m, but is
probably not in cultivation. For any good soil in
full sun. Hardy to −15°C or less with protection
for the roots.

Phygelius × rectus Coombes   A group of
hybrids between *P. aequalis* and *P. capensis*,
mostly raised by Peter Dummer, the chief
propagator at Hillier Nurseries in around 1985.
They combine the hardiness of *P. capensis* with
the more compact inflorescence of *P. aequalis*.
Five cultivars have been named, as follows:
'African Queen' (not shown)   Raised by John
May in 1969 from *P. aequalis* × *P. capensis*
'Coccineus'.

'Devil's Tears' ('Winchester Fanfare' × *P.
capensis* 'Coccineus')   Stems *c*.1.2m. Panicle
c.45cm.

'Moonraker' ('Yellow Trumpet' × 'Winchester
Fanfare')   Stems to 95cm. Panicle *c*.25cm.
Flowers all round the stem.

'Pink Elf' (not shown) ('Yellow Trumpet' ×
'Winchester Fanfare')   Has shorter stems to
75cm; panicle *c*.15cm. Flowers with the tube
pale pink and lobes deep crimson.

'Salmon Leap' (not shown)   Has corolla tube
orange, with deeper lobes. Stems *c*.1.2m.
Panicle 45cm, open.

'Winchester Fanfare' syn. 'Winton Fanfare'
('Yellow Trumpet' × *P. capensis* 'Coccineus')
Stems *c*.1m. Panicle *c*.30cm.

Phygelius aequalis 'Yellow Trumpet'

Phygelius aequalis at Cathedral Peak

Phygelius 'Moonraker' at Wisley

Phygelius 'Winchester Fanfare'

Phygelius capensis

Phygelius 'Devil's Tears'

Mimulus 'Wisley Red'

Mimulus 'Magnifique'

Mimulus cardinalis

Mimulus 'Western Hills'

Mimulus lewisii in Oregon

Mimulus 'Fire Dragon'

Mimulus lewisii from Kelways' Nurseries

Mimulus moschatus at Kew

Mimulus 'Andean Nymph' at Kew

Mimulus luteus by a chalk spring in Sussex

Mimulus guttatus

Mimulus 'Andean Nymph' (*Scrophulariaceae*) An attractive plant introduced from Chile by John Watson, forming spreading mats of softly hairy stems to 50cm or more across and 10cm high. The pink and yellow flowers are freely produced in June–August. For moist soil in sun or partial shade. Hardy to −15°C perhaps.

Mimulus cardinalis Dougl. ex Benth. Native of Oregon to California, east to Nevada and Arizona and south to Mexico, growing along streams and in wet places, often in shade, at up to 2500m, flowering in March–October, but usually June–August in gardens, and again if cut down after the first flowering. Stems to 80cm glandular-hairy, from a creeping stock. Flowers 4–5cm long, the upper lip arched upwards, the lower reflexed. Pollinated by hummingbirds. For moist but not waterlogged soil in sun or partial shade. Hardy to −15°C.

Mimulus guttatus DC. Native of Alaska south to Mexico and east to Montana, and widely naturalized in Europe and E North America, growing in streams and wet places below 3000m, flowering in March–August. Plant with creeping and rooting stems and ascending inflorescence to 100cm, usually *c*.50cm. Leaves 1–8cm long, toothed. Inflorescence pubescent and glandular. Flowers yellow, spotted red, the throat nearly closed by

hairy ridges. For wet soil or shallow running water in sun or partial shade. Hardy to −20°C or less.

Mimulus × hybridus These are mainly selected from crosses between *M. luteus*, *M. guttatus* and *M. cupreus* Regel from S Chile. **'Fire Dragon'** Stems to 30cm. Flowers large. **'Magnifique'** Stems to 30cm. Flowers large, *c*.60cm across. **'Wisley Red'** Possibly a form or hybrid of *M. cupreus*, raised at Wisley. Stems *c*.15cm tall, flowering in June–August. 'Whitecroft Scarlet' is an older, very similar cultivar. 'Malibu' (not shown) is a vigorous seed strain, with stems to 15cm and deep-orange flowers.

Mimulus lewisii Pursh Native of W North America, from Alaska south to California (Tulare Co.) in the Sierra Nevada, and east to Colorado, growing by streams at 1200–3000m, flowering in June–September. Plant with erect, glandular-hairy stems to 80cm from a creeping rootstock. Leaves oblong-elliptic, 2–7cm long, with wavy teeth. Flowers pink, often blotched maroon, 3–5cm long. Graham Thomas mentions a beautiful white form which I have never seen. For moist or wet soil in sun or partial shade. Hardy to −15°C.

Mimulus luteus L. Native of Chile, and naturalized in Scotland, growing in streams and

wet places, flowering in December–March. Very similar to *M. guttatus* from NW North America, and commonly hybridizing where the two species are naturalized, but with calyx and pedicels glabrous, and flowers with an open throat and large red blotches and patches of colour. Flowers usually yellow, but sometimes creamy or pinkish in the wild as well as in selected cultivars. Hardy to −20°C.

Mimulus moschatus Dougl. ex. Lindl. **Musk** Native of North America, from Alaska to C California eastwards to Newfoundland, south to North Carolina and West Virginia, but probably introduced in much of E North America, growing in damp places and by streams, flowering in June–September. Plant softly glandular and sticky. Flowers 18–25mm long. This plant was valued in the past for its musky smell, but plants in cultivation are scentless. There is no mention of the scent in Munz's *Flora of California*, and Fernald's edition of *Gray's Manual of Botany* says: 'Plant only rarely with musky odour.' The scented plant should be sought in the wild.

Mimulus 'Western Hills' A presumed hybrid between *M. cardinalis* and *M. lewisii*, with stems to 1m and vermilion flowers more open than those of *M. cardinalis* and with less-reflexed corolla lobes.

Digitalis grandiflora

Digitalis grandiflora, naturalized in Kashmir

Digitalis lamarkii from NE Turkey

Digitalis laevigata

Digitalis ferruginea

Digitalis purpurea subsp. *heywoodii*

Digitalis obscura

Digitalis × *purpurascens* at Kew

Digitalis purpurea in Wales

Digitalis ferruginea L. (*Scrophulariaceae*)
Native of Europe, from Italy eastwards to
Romania, Turkey, the S Caucasus and
Lebanon, growing in woods, grassy clearings
and scrub, and on rocky slopes and roadsides at
up to 2700m in Turkey, flowering in June–
September. Plant short-lived or sometimes
biennial; flowering stems to 1m, unbranched.
Stem leaves oblong to linear; sepals glabrous
with a scarious border. Flowers 18–34mm long,
the lower lip *c*.8mm broad. For well-drained,
dry soil in sun or partial shade. Hardy to
−15°C.

Digitalis grandiflora Mill.   Native of C
Europe, from Belgium eastwards to Siberia and
the Altai, south to Turkey in Europe and
naturalized in Kashmir, growing in open woods
and grassy places by streams, flowering in June–
July. Stems often several, to 100cm. Leaves to
25cm × 6cm, ovate-lanceolate. Sepals
lanceolate, acute, glandular-pubescent. Flowers
4–5cm long. For any good soil in partial shade.
Hardy to −20°C or less. In around 1925 the
hybrid *D. purpurea* × *D. grandiflora* was treated
with colchicine and formed the new hybrid
tetraploid species *D.* × *mertonensis* Buxton &
Darlington. It is a short-lived perennial with
rather hairier leaves than *D. grandiflora* and
large pinkish-buff flowers, raised at the John
Innes Horticultural Institution, then at Merton,
Surrey.

Digitalis laevigata Waldst. & Kit.   Native of
SE Europe in Yugoslavia, Albania, Bulgaria and
Greece, growing in woods and scrub, flowering
in June–August. Stems several from a tufted
rootstock to 100cm, glabrous. Leaves oblong-
lanceolate to lanceolate. Sepals ovate, acute or
acuminate. Flowers 15–35mm long, over 25mm
in the north of its range, less than 25mm in the
south (subsp. *graeca* (Ivan.) Werner), from
Thessaloniki southwards. For well-drained soil
in partial shade or sun; and a warm position.
Hardy to −15°C.

Digitalis lamarkii Ivan. syn. *D. orientalis*
Lam.   Native of Turkey, mainly in dry valleys
in the north and north-east, growing on dry,
rocky slopes, in open forest and scrub or in
steppe, at up to 1500m, flowering in May–
August. Plant forming tufts of rosettes of linear
leaves to 20cm long, 8mm wide from a rather
woody rootstock. Stem leaves to 1cm wide.
Sepals mucronate, glandular-pubescent.
Flowers 25–30mm long, hairy outside. For a
dry position in poor, well-drained soil. Very
susceptible to warm damp in winter. Hardy to
−20°C if dry.

Digitalis obscura L.   Native of E & S Spain
and of North Africa, growing in dry open
woods, often on limestone, flowering in May–
July. Plant with branched shrubby stems to 1m.
Inflorescence to 50cm, with narrowly oblong to
lanceolate, entire or toothed evergreen leaves.
Flowers orange-yellow to brownish red, 2–3cm
long. For a warm position in dry soil in sun or
partial shade. Hardy to −10°C perhaps.

Digitalis × **purpurascens** Roth.   This hybrid
between *D. lutea* L. and *D. purpurea* is reported
occasionally where the parents grow together,
i.e. from Belgium to Germany and in Spain.
Stems to *c*.100cm, much branched. Flowers
c.3.5cm long in June–August. Hardy to −20°C.

'Glory of Rounday' is similar, with slightly
larger flowers, and is possibly *D. lutea* × *D.*
×*mertonensis*.

Digitalis purpurea L. **Foxglove**   Native of
W Europe, from Ireland south to Spain and
Morocco, east to Finland, Czechoslovakia and
in Corsica and Sardinia, widely naturalized
elsewhere in Europe, in North America and on
mountains in North Africa, growing in woods and
on rocky slopes, usually on acid soils, flowering
in June–September. Plant usually biennial, but
often perennial in SW Europe and Corsica.
Stems to 180cm. Flowers 40–55mm long,
purplish, pink or white. For any soil except pure
limestone in partial shade. Hardy to −25°C.

Digitalis purpurea subsp. **heywoodii** P. & M.
Silva   Native of S Portugal, around Reguengos
de Monsaraz, growing on granite rocks,
flowering in June. Plant with rosettes of very
woolly, white leaves, the lowest ovate-lanceolate
to lanceolate, tapered into the petiole.
Flowering stems to 75cm. Flowers creamy
white, sometimes yellowish or pinkish, sparsely
hairy outside. A beautiful plant for well-drained
soil in sun or partial shade, not too dry at the
root. Susceptible to warm damp in winter.
Hardy to −15°C. Subsp. *mariana* (Boiss.) Rivas
Goday (not shown) has white woolly leaves but
purplish-pink flowers, glabrous outside. It is
native of SC Spain and NE Portugal, growing
on rocky slopes and plains, flowering in June–
August. *Digitalis thapsi* L. from E Portugal and
C & W Spain is rather similar: covered with
yellowish glandular hairs and the inflorescence
is branched. The purplish-pink flowers are
pubescent outside.

Acanthus spinosus at Nymans, Sussex

Acanthus hungaricus

Acanthus dioscoridis Willd. (*Acanthaceae*)
Native of Turkey, from Kastamonu southwards
and eastwards, of Lebanon, N Iraq and W Iran,
growing on dry hillsides, steppes, rocky slopes
and abandoned fields at up to 2200m, flowering
in May–August. Plant with creeping
underground rhizomes and rosettes of leaves,
narrowly lanceolate and unlobed in var.
dioscoridis, to pinnatifid with spiny lobes in var.
perringii (Siehe) E. Hossain. Flowering stem to
40cm, but only 10–15cm in var. *brevicaulis*
(Freyn) E. Hossain from Kastamonu. Bracts
green; corolla pink or purplish. For dry, well-
drained soil in full sun. Hardy to −15°C.

Acanthus hirsutus Boiss.   Native of Turkey,
from the Mediterranean islands eastwards to
Sivas, at up to 1800m, growing on bare steppes,
on banks between cornfields and in pine forest,
often on non-limy soils, flowering in May–July.
Plant with deep, fleshy roots, without long
underground stolons. Leaves in a basal rosette,
spiny, deeply lobed, lanceolate in outline.
Flowering stems 10–35cm, densely hairy.
Bracts hairy, delicately spiny, 7–13 veined.
Corolla pale yellow or whitish, rarely pink. For
well-drained, sandy soil in full sun in a dry,
warm position. Hardy to −15°C, perhaps less.

Acanthus hungaricus (Borbas) Baenitz syns. *A.
balcanicus* Heywood & Richardson, *A.
longifolius* Host   Native of Yugoslavia,
Romania, southwards to Greece, growing in
woods, scrub and on rocky hills, flowering in
June–July. Plant forming dense clumps. Leaves
not spiny, lanceolate in outline with deep lobes
narrowed at the base and with only broadly
winged midrib between the central lobes.
Flowering stems to 150cm, usually *c.*60cm, with
flowers often in 4 rows. Bracts purplish, corolla
white. For well-drained soil in full sun. Hardy
to −15°C.

Acanthus mollis L.   Native of S & SW
Europe, from Portugal to Italy, Sicily and
Yugoslavia, and in NW Africa, growing in
rocky woods and beneath old walls, flowering in
June–August. Leaves dark green, shining
above, lobed or pinnatisect, but not spiny; the
broadest form, var. *latifolius* (hort. ex Goeze),
which appears to be native of Spain and
Portugal, has shallowly lobed leaves to 20cm
wide, ovate in outline. Flowering stems up to
2m, usually suffused with purple. Corolla
white, sometimes with pinkish veins. For a
deep, well-drained soil in a warm position in full
sun. This plant always looks best associated
with old stone or brickwork. Hardy to −15°C.

Acanthus mollis var. *latifolius* at Kew

Acanthus hirsutus at Wisley

Acanthus syriacus near Gaziantep, S Turkey, photographed by Brian Mathew

Acanthus dioscoridis from Hakkari

Strobilanthes atropurpureus

Acanthus spinosissimus at Kew

Acanthus spinosissimus Desf. This is now considered merely a form of *A. spinosus* L., but it is distinct enough to be worth illustrating separately. Native of the E Mediterranean in SW Turkey, Rhodes and possibly Crete, growing in dry scrub, on roadsides and in pine forest at up to 600m, flowering in May–June, Plant with a tufted rootstock, forming clumps. Leaves ovate in outline to 40cm long, and 30cm broad, deeply dissected to the midrib, with stiff white spines on all edges. Flowering stems to 1.2m with a very long, dense inflorescence. Bracts greenish, tipped with purple. For a hot, dry position in well-drained soil. Hardy to −15°C. Not free-flowering even in S England, except in hot summers.

Acanthus spinosus L. Native of the E Mediterranean area, from Italy and Yugoslavia southwards, growing in scrub and grassy places, flowering in May–July. Plant forming dense clumps. Leaves lanceolate in outline, dissected to the midrib, with scattered, rather soft spines, flowering stem to 1.5m, not very dense; bracts purple; corolla white. For well-drained soil in full sun. Hardy to −15°C and free-flowering.

Acanthus syriacus Boiss. syn. *A. hirsutus* subsp. *syriacus* (Boiss.) Brummitt Native of SE Turkey from Adana to Urfa, W Syria, Lebanon and Palestine, growing in abandoned fields, scrub and on rocky limestone slopes at 500–1900m, flowering in April–June. Plant with creeping underground rhizomes. Leaves to 32cm long, lanceolate in outline, very spiny, deeply dissected and hairy. Flowering stems to 60cm, with a short and rather compact inflorescence. Bracts deep purple, 7–11 veined. Corolla white. For dry, well-drained soil in full sun. Hardy to −15°C perhaps. *A. caroli-alexandri* Hausskn., from N Greece, is very similar, but usually taller.

Strobilanthes atropurpureus Nees syn. *Pteracanthus urticifolius* (Kuntz.) Bremek (*Acanthaceae*) Native of the Himalayas, from Kashmir to C Nepal, growing in forests and scrub at 1200–2700m, flowering in July–October. Plant forming a large clump of upright stems to 2m. Leaves ovate, toothed and strongly veined, acuminate. Inflorescence glandular; bracts soon withering. Flowers *c*.3.5cm long, blue to purplish. For any good soil in partial shade. Hardy to −20°C.

Centranthus ruber at Cockermouth Castle, Cumbria

Phuopsis stylosa

Triosteum pinnatifidum at Kew

Valeriana phu 'Aurea' in spring

Valeriana pyrenaica

Asperula taurina L. subsp. **caucasica** (Pobed.)
Ehrend. syn. *A. caucasica* Pobed. (*Rubiaceae*)
Native of the Caucasus, N Turkey and N Iran,
with subsp. *taurina* in SE Europe and N
Turkey, growing in woods, scrub and on rough
banks at 550–2100m, flowering in April–
August. Plant suckering to form loose patches.
Leaves hairy on both surfaces, 3–8cm long.
Flowers 8–14mm long, pale lilac to bluish, or
usually white or very pale in subsp. *taurina*. For
leafy soil in partial shade. Hardy to −20°C.

Centranthus ruber (L.) DC. (*Valerianaceae*)
Red Spur Valerian   Native of the
Mediterranean region, but widely naturalized
further north, growing in rocky places, old walls
and on coastal shingle, flowering in May–
August. Plant with a tough, woody rootstock
and stems to 80cm. Flowers 9–10mm, with a
spur 5–7mm long, red, pinkish or white. For a
very well-drained position. Hardy to −15°C.

Galium odoratum (L.) Scop. syn. *Asperula
odorata* L. (*Rubiaceae*) **Sweet Woodruff**
Native of Europe, but rare in the south, and of
North Africa and W Asia to S Turkey, east to E
Siberia, Korea and N Japan, growing in rich
deciduous woods and hedges, flowering in May–
July. Plant with wiry, creeping, underground
rhizomes and upright stems to 45cm, usually
*c.*20cm. Leaves 2.5–4cm, in whorls of 6.
Flowers 4–6mm long. For a shady position in
good not very acid soil. Hardy to −25°C or less.

Patrinia triloba Miq. var. **palmata** (Maxim.)
Hara (*Valerianaceae*)   Native of Japan, in W
Honshu and Kyushu, growing in grassy places
in the mountains, flowering in July–August.
Plant with shortly creeping stolons. Stems 20–

Asperula taurina subsp. caucasica at Sellindge, Kent

Valeriana phu in flower

Galium odoratum

Thladiantha dubia at Kew

Patrinia triloba var. palmata

60cm. Leaves orbicular, 5-angled, palmate, 4–8cm long. Flowers 7–8mm across, spurred at the base. For moist soil in a cool position. Hardy to −15°C, perhaps less.

Phuopsis stylosa (Trin.) B. D. Jackson (*Rubiaceae*)   Native of the Caucasus and N Iran, in the Elburz near Chalus, flowering in June–September. Plant with a characteristic pungent scent, forming spreading patches. Stems to 30cm from an underground branching and creeping rootstock. Flowers pale pinkish, deeper purplish-pink in 'Purpurea', with a tube *c*.1cm long. For moist, sandy soil in sun or partial shade. Hardy to −20°C or less.

Thladiantha dubia Bunge (*Curcubitaceae*) Native of Korea and N China and naturalized in C Japan, growing in scrub and rocks flowering in June–July. Plant with a large tuberous rootstock and climbing stems to 3m, with simple tendrils. Leaves ovate-cordate. Flowers 6–7mm across; the males solitary in the leaf axils. For any soil in a sheltered position with protection for the young shoots. Hardy to −20°C or less.

Thladiantha olivieri cogn. ex Oliv.   Native of SW China, in Hubei and Sichuan, growing in hedges and on rock ledges by streams, flowering in May–June. Plant with a stout rootstock and climbing or hanging stems to 4m or more. Leaves to 25cm long on a stalk to 10cm long. Tendrils branched. Flowers *c*.5cm across. For a warm, sheltered position moist in summer. Hardy to −15°C perhaps.

Triosteum pinnatifidum Maxim. (*Caprifoliaceae*)   Native of N China and Japan

(where it is very rare), growing in scrub, flowering in July–August. Stems few, 45–60cm, from a stout rootstock. Leaves slightly hairy, glandular. Flowers *c*.10mm long; fruit a white berry, *c*.8mm across. For well-drained but humus-rich soil in sun or partial shade. Hardy to −20°C, perhaps less. The genus is interesting as one of the few herbaceous genera in the Honeysuckle family. *T. perfoliatum* L., the Feverwort, with orange fruit in the leaf axils, is native of E North America, and *T. himalayanum* Wall., with red fruit, is found in dry scrub and forest W China to N India.

Valeriana phu L. '**Aurea**' (*Valerianaceae*) Native of Europe (perhaps) and Turkey (one record) (but native distribution uncertain because it was widely grown for the drug 'Valerian'), growing on rocky slopes flowering in July–August. Plant with a thick, woody rhizome. Basal leaves golden when young in the commonly grown 'Aurea', simple or compound. Stem leaves amplexicaul, the upper pinnatifid. Stems to 1.5m. Flowers white, with a tube 4mm long. For good soil in sun or partial shade. Hardy to −20°C or less.

Valeriana pyrenaica L.   Native of the Pyrenees in France and Spain, and in the Cantabrian mountains, growing in damp woods and subalpine meadows; flowering in May–July. Sometimes also found naturalized in Scotland and Ireland. Plant with a short, stout rhizome and upright stems to 110cm. Basal leaves ovate-cordate, toothed. Flowers 5–6mm long. For moist, peaty soil or a rich border in partial shade. *V. alliarifolia* Adams, from Euboea, the Caucasus and N Turkey, is similar but has all leaves simple, the upper ovate or lanceolate.

Thladiantha olivieri near Baoxing, Sichuan

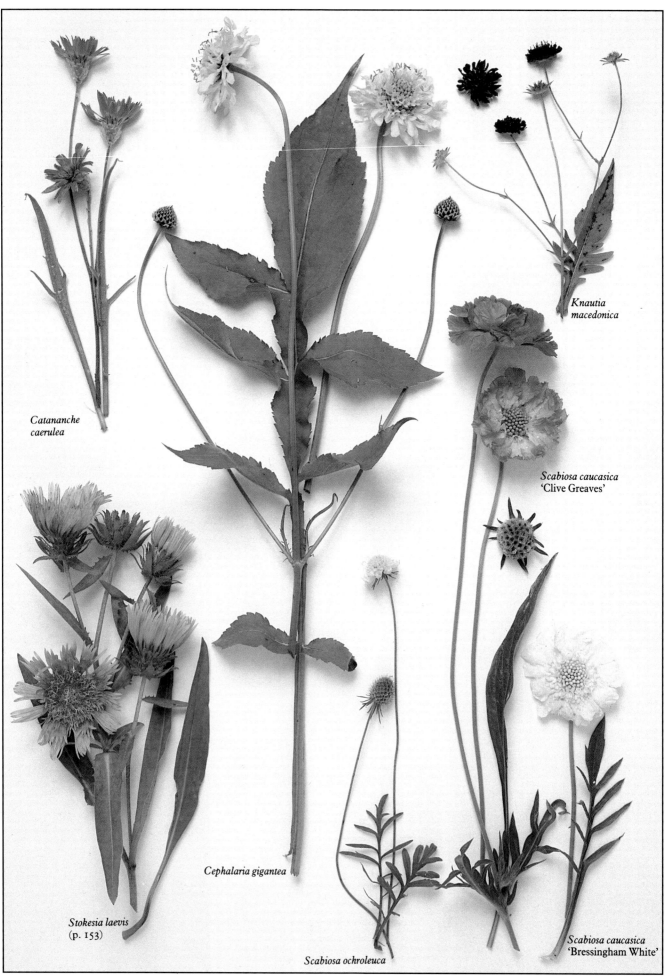

Catananche
caerulea

Knautia
macedonica

Scabiosa caucasica
'Clive Greaves'

Stokesia laevis
(p. 153)

Cephalaria gigantea

Scabiosa ochroleuca

Scabiosa caucasica
'Bressingham White'

Specimens from Beth Chatto, 17 August. ½ life size

Catananche caerulea L. (*Compositae*)   Native
of SW Europe, from Spain to France and Italy,
and North Africa, growing in dry, grassy places,
flowering in June–August. Plant with many
wiry upright stems to 45cm from a compact
rootstock. Leaves linear, entire or with up to 4
narrow teeth. Flowers 3cm across, with
transparent, papery, overlapping bracts, usually
bluish, sometimes white, with a dark centre.
For sandy soil in full sun. Hardy to −15°C.

Cephalaria alpina (L.) Roem. & Schult.
(*Dipsacaceae*)   Native of the SW & C Alps,
Jura and N Apennines, from France to Austria
and Italy, growing in rocky meadows at up to
1800m, flowering in June–July. Stems to 2m,
usually *c*.1.2m. Leaves pinnate or lyrate with
3–8 pairs of leaflets. Flower-heads *c*.2cm across.
Flowers *c*.12mm long. Receptacular scales
spiny. For any well-drained, moist soil in sun or
partial shade. Hardy to −20°C or less.

Cephalaria gigantea (Ledeb.) Bobrov. syn.
Scabiosa tartarica M. Bieb.   Native of the
Caucasus and N Turkey, growing by streams, in
wet meadows and on rocky slopes at 1350–
2600m, flowering in July–August. A huge
perennial with stems to 3.5m. Lower leaves to
40cm long, lyrate or pinnatisect. Flower-heads
4–6cm across. Flowers 15–18mm long.
Receptacular scales acuminate, not spiny. For
any rich, moist soil in sun or partial shade.
Hardy to −20°C or less.

Knautia arvensis (L.) Coult. (*Dipsacaceae*)
Field Scabious   Native of Europe eastwards to
the Caucasus and W Siberia, growing in
meadows, and on grassy hills, especially on
limestone, flowering in July–September. Plant
with a deep taproot and branched stems to
100cm. Leaves oblanceolate or pinnatifid at the
base; stem leaves pinnatifid. Flower-heads
3–4cm across, bluish. For any well-drained soil
and good for meadow garden. Hardy to −25°C
or less.

Knautia macedonica Griseb. syn. *Scabiosa
rumelica* hort.   Native of Yugoslavia to
Albania, Bulgaria and SE Romania, growing in
scrub and open woods, flowering in July–
August. Sometimes biennial, but usually
perennial. Basal leaves undivided, but withered
by flowering time. Upper leaves pinnate with an
ovate, serrate terminal lobe. Flower-heads
1.5–3cm across, dark red, but sometimes lilac;
the unusual dark-red colour is also found in the
annual or biennial *Scabiosa atropurpurea* L. For
well-drained soil in a warm position. Hardy to
−20°C or less.

Scabiosa caucasica M. Bieb. (*Dipsacaceae*)
Native of the Caucasus, N Iran and NE Turkey,
growing in subalpine meadows and sunny,
rocky slopes at 1900–2900m in Turkey,
flowering in July–August. Plant with simple
stems to 60cm, sometimes with a few branches.
Lower leaves lanceolate, entire, upper
pinnatsect. Flower-heads 4–6cm across, bluish-
lavender, the outer flowers with finely toothed
petals. Two cultivars are shown here.
'Bressingham White', raised by Alan Bloom;
'Loddon White' and 'Miss Willmott' are also
white. 'Clive Greaves', raised in 1929, is
lavender-blue. 'Moonbeam Blue' is darker. For
well-drained, chalky or limy soil in full sun.
Hardy to −20°C or less, but short-lived on acid
or wet soils. Easily raised from seed.

Scabiosa ochroleuca L. syn. *S. columbaria* L.
var. *ochroleuca* (L.) Coulter   Native of C and S
Europe, W Russia, North Africa, Lebanon to

Turkey, the Caucasus and Siberia, growing in
dry meadows and rocky slopes, flowering in
May–September. Basal leaves obovate-
lanceolate, crenate. Stem leaves lyrate or 1-
pinnatisect. Flower heads 15–25mm across. For
well-drained soil in full sun. Hardy to −20°C or
less.

Succisa pratensis Moench. (*Dipsacaceae*)
Devil's Bit Scabious   Native of most of
Europe, and of North Africa, eastwards to W
Siberia, the Caucasus and N Turkey, growing in
wet, heathy, grassy places among heather and in
open forest, flowering in June–October. Plant
with few stems from a short rootstock. Leaves
5–30cm in a basal rosette, obovate-lanceolate.
Flowering stems to 100cm. Flower-heads
1.5–3cm across, purplish blue, rarely pink or
white (even rarer). For moist, preferably peaty
soil in sun or partial shade. Hardy to −20°C.

Catananche caerulea

Catananche caerulea

Succisa pratensis

Cephalaria alpina

Knautia arvensis

Knautia macedonica

Morina coulteriana near Gadsar, Kashmir

Acanthocalyx delavayi (Franch.) Cannon syns. *Morina bulleyana* Forrest & Diels, *M. delavayi* Franch. (*Morinaceae*)   Native of SW China, especially Yunnan, growing on rock ledges and grassy, stony places on limestone at *c*.3000m, flowering in May–June. Plant with rosettes of barely spiny, linear leaves to 10cm long. Stems to 15cm. Flowers in a loose head, with a curved tube *c*.2cm long. For well-drained soil in sun or partial shade. Hardy to −20°C. *A. nepalensis* (D. Don) Cannon syn. *Morina nepalensis* D. Don is very similar, but appears to be taller, with narrow leaves, with a margin of 2 rows of stiff hairs.

Morina coulteriana Royle (*Morinaceae*) Native of Pakistan to NW India and Xizang, and locally abundant in Kashmir, growing on steep grassy slopes in rather dry valleys, at 2400–3600m, flowering in June–August. Plant with several stems to 90cm, from a deep, fleshy rootstock. Leaves to 15cm, with slender spines on the edges. Flowers with a tube 2cm long, and lobes 8mm long, sweetly scented. A long-lived perennial, for well-drained but rich, deep, sandy soil in full sun. It resents disturbance, so is best established from seedling plants. Hardy to −20°C or less.

Morina kokanica Regel   Native of C Asia, in the region of Kokand and Ferghana, growing in conifer forests, flowering in May–June. Stems several, upright, to 1.2m, from a fleshy rootstock. Leaves narrowly lanceolate, smooth and spineless. Inflorescence with spines only on the bracts. Flowers *c*.3cm long, opening white, becoming pale pink with a red blotch. For good, well-drained soil in full sun. Hardy to −15°C, perhaps less. *M. subinermis* Boiss., recorded once from W Turkey, is similar in being spineless, except on the inflorescence.

Morina longifolia Wall. ex DC.   Native of the Himalayas, from Kashmir, where it is common, to Bhutan, growing on moist but steep slopes, on open hillsides or in clearings in woodland, at 3000–4000m, flowering in June–September. Plant with few stems to 1m, from a deep, fleshy root. Leaves spicily aromatic, to 20cm long, with short, rather weak spines on the toothed edges. Flowers with a tube 2.5cm long, and lobes 6mm long, opening white, becoming pink at maturity. A beautiful plant for a moist but well-drained border, not difficult to grow but often short-lived. Hardy to −15°C, but liable to rot in cold, damp conditions.

Morina persica L.   Native of Greece, Turkey and the Lebanon, eastwards to C Asia, growing in dry steppes, on rocky slopes and roadsides, and on screes at 300–2750m in Turkey, flowering in May–August. Plant with several stiff, upright stems to 1.5m. Leaves very spiny, lanceolate. Flowers scented, white, becoming pink or reddish. For a very dry position in well-drained, poor soil. Hardy to −20°C, but likely to die of damp in winter. This species is not often grown; I have collected seed several times, but never succeeded in germinating it.

Stellera chamaejasme L. (*Thymelaeaceae*) Native of the Himalayas from N India to Nepal, Bhutan and N & W China in Yunnan and Xizang, growing on stony slopes and plains, and on abandoned fields, at 2700–4300m, flowering

Morina coulteriana at Edington, Wiltshire

Morina kokanica in Tashkent BG

Acanthocalyx delavayi at Lijiang

Morina persica near Kayseri, Turkey

Morina longifolia

Stellera chamaejasme at Branklyn

Stellera chamaejasme near Lijiang, Yunnan

in May–July. A herbaceous relative of *Daphne*. Plant with several simple leafy stems from a very stout, long-lived rootstock. Flowers 1–1.5cm long in a terminal head, either white, pink in bud (in the Himalayas) or yellow (in Yunnan). For very well-drained soil in full sun. This plant is very rare in gardens because it is so hard to propagate except from seed. Very old plants are found in gardens in E Scotland, e.g. in Branklyn in Perth, and in the Royal Botanic Garden, Edinburgh. Hardy to −20°C.

Morina longifolia near Vishensar, Kashmir

Campanula latiloba at Hidcote Manor, Gloucestershire

Campanula carpatica Jacq. (*Campanulaceae*)
Native of the Carpathians, in Poland,
Czechoslovakia, Romania and W Russia,
growing on mountain rocks, flowering in June–
August. Plant with a tuft of thin, white
rhizomes and many stems to 45cm. Basal leaves
rounded, cordate, the upper rather narrower.
Flowers solitary on 10–15cm stalks, *c.*3cm wide
in 'Chewton Joy', a good blue with a pale
centre, white in 'Hannah', or deep blue in
'Isabel', among numerous named forms. For a
well-drained position in full sun but moist soil.
Hardy to −25°C or less.

Campanula lactiflora M. Bieb.   Native of the
Caucasus, NE Turkey and NW Iran (and
naturalized in Scotland), growing in forests,
scrub and subalpine meadows at 600–2400m,
flowering in July–October. Stems several, to
1.5m or more in gardens, from a stout
rootstock. Leaves numerous up the stem, ovate-
oblong or oblong. Flowers 1.5–2.5cm long,
bluish purple, pale blue or white, pinkish in cv.
'Loddon Anna'. For moist, rich soil in sun or
partial shade. Hardy to −20°C or less. 'Pouffe'
and 'White Pouffe' are dwarf forms which lack
the good points of the normal form. 'Prichard's
Variety' has dark purple flowers and is rather
shorter (*c.*75cm) than the normal type.

Campanula latiloba DC. syn. *C. persicifolia* L.
subsp. *sessiliflora* (K. Koch) Velen. ex W.
Greuter & Burdet   Native of N Turkey, from
Ulu Daǧ, near Bursa, east to Samsun, growing
in meadows at 200–1200m, flowering in June–
August. Stems thicker than *C. persicifolia*, 10–
15mm thick, to 100cm tall, stiff. Stem leaves
broadly lanceolate, acute, attenuate. Flowers
sessile, 2–3 in each axil, shallower and wider
open than *C. persicifolia*, bluish or in 'Hidcote
Amethyst' pinkish mauve. Other cultivars
include 'Alba' and 'Percy Piper', a dwarf
variety. For any good soil in sun or partial
shade. Hardy to −20°C or less.

Campanula persicifolia L.   Native of most of
Europe from Belgium and Holland eastwards,
to C & S Russia, and NW Turkey, growing in
meadows, open woods and on the edges of forest
at up to 2000m in Turkey, flowering in June–
August. Plant forming rosettes of narrow leaves
from shortly running rhizomes. Stems 40–
70cm, glabrous with scattered narrow leaves.
Flowers horizontal or slightly drooping, 4–5cm
long, 5cm across the mouth. Numerous
varieties of this species are cultivated, including
whites, pinks, semi-doubles, doubles and a
'cup-and-saucer' white, 'Hetty'; 'Hampstead
White' is similar, if not the same. For any good
garden soil; easy and very long-lived. Hardy to
−25°C or less.

Campanula rhomboidalis L.   Native of
Europe in the Jura, SW & C Alps, from France
to Switzerland and Italy and naturalized in
Belgium, Holland, Germany and Austria,
growing in alpine and subalpine meadows,
flowering in July–September. Plant with a

Campanula persicifolia 'Alba'

Campanula rhomboidalis in the Valais

Campanula lactiflora above Trabzon

Campanula lactiflora at Withersdane Hall, Wye, Kent

Campanula carpatica

Campanula trachelium near Wye, Kent

Campanula trachelium 'Alba'

stout, deep taproot and upright stems to 60cm. Stem leaves ovate to broadly lanceolate, acute, toothed. Buds erect. Flowers *c*.2cm long, few, in a loose raceme. For any good, well-drained soil in full sun. Hardy to −20°C or less.

Campanula sarmatica Ker-Gawl. Native of the Caucasus, growing on dry cliffs and on rocky slopes at up to 1800m, flowering in June–July. Plant with a deep, branching taproot and roughly hairy, narrowly ovate, cordate basal leaves. Flowering stems several, spreading, to 30cm. Flowers pale blue, *c*.20mm long. A long-lived plant for a very well-drained, rather dry position. Hardy to −20°C or less.

Campanula trachelium L. **Nettle-leaved bell-flower** Native of most of Europe, including England, North Africa, Turkey and West Syria, N Iran and W Siberia, growing on wood margins, in hedges and in forests, often on chalky soils, flowering in July–September. Stem to 100cm or more. Leaves ovate, cordate, sharply toothed. Flowers 2.5–3.5cm long, usually mid-blue to mauve, short-stalked, or sessile in subsp. *athoa* from Greece and Turkey. For any good soil in sun or partial shade and tolerant of dry shade. The white form, 'Alba', is very beautiful; there is also a double white in cultivation. Hardy to −20°C or less.

Campanula latiloba 'Hidcote Amethyst'

Campanula sarmatica from the N Caucasus

Campanula ossetica at Washfield Nurseries

Campanula glomerata 'Superba' at La Vesterival, near Dieppe

Campanula alliarifolia at the Royal Botanic Garden, Edinburgh

Campanula crispa near Erzurum

Campanula alliarifolia Willd.
(*Campanulaceae*) Native of the Caucasus and
N Turkey, from Ordu eastwards, growing on
wet cliffs and steep banks in Spruce forest, and
in scrub, at up to 1830m, flowering in June–
September. Plant with several simple or
branched stems to 70cm from a tufted
rootstock. Leaves roughly hairy, broadly
triangular-cordate, obtuse or acute. Flowers
nodding in a one-sided stem, *c.*20mm long,
always white. For a moist position in sun or
partial shade, but does well amongst shrubs in a
border. Hardy to −20°C perhaps.

Campanula 'Burghaltii' Probably a hybrid
between *C. punctata* and *C. latifolia*, with *C.
punctata* on the seed parent. Rhizome not
creeping. Stems to 60cm spreading. Flowers
greyish mauve, 7–10cm long. Calyx lobes
declined and spreading.

Campanula crispa Lam. Native of of NE
Turkey and adjacent Soviet Armenia and
Azerbaijan, growing on dry rocks and low cliffs,
at 1500–2500m, flowering in June–August.
Stems upright to 50cm from a fleshy rootstock,
sometimes monocarpic. Leaves glabrous, shiny.
Flowers white or blue, deeply 5-lobed, to 3cm
across. An unusual species, rather like a
Michauxia in appearance. For a dry, well-
drained position. Hardy to −25°C, or less if dry.

Campanula glomerata L. Native of most of
Europe, from England, where it is frequent on
chalk downs, south to Spain and east to Siberia

and SW Asia, growing in scrub and mountain
meadows, flowering in May–September. Plant
suckering to form spreading clumps. Stems 30–
60mm. Flowers in clusters in the axils of leafy
bracts, and in a terminal head, 15–20mm long,
dark purplish blue. For any good, well-drained
soil in sun or partial shade. 'Superba', raised by
G. Arends, is a large form, similar to that shown
here. There are also several named white forms.
Hardy to −25°C.

Campanula latifolia L. Native of most of
Europe, including England, where it is
commonest in the north-west, the Caucasus, N
Turkey, N & C Iran and W Siberia, growing in
hedges, scrub, forests and meadows often on
limestone, at up to 2600m in Turkey, flowering
in June–August. Plant with a compact, tufted
rootstock with upright stems to 100cm. Lower
leaves ovate, cordate, doubly serrate. Flowers
40–55cm, with lobes, pale to deep blue; rarely, a
beautiful pure white in 'Alba'. Var. *macrantha*
DC. is a coarser plant with long, *c.*55mm,
mauve-blue crowded flowers, which is
sometimes cultivated: it lacks the charm of the
ordinary variety. For any heavy soil in shade or
partial shade. Hardy to −25°C or less.

Campanula ossetica M. Bieb. Native of the
Caucasus, growing on rocks and in ravines,
flowering in June–July. Plant with trailing or
almost climbing stems to 60cm. Basal leaves
cordate, double-toothed. Flowers *c.*3cm long.
Calyx teeth narrowly lanceolate. Introduced to
cultivation by Bill Baker. Hardy to −20°C.

Campanula punctata Lam. **'Rubra'** Native of
Japan, in all the islands, growing on grassy
slopes at low altitudes and in foothills, flowering
in June. Plant with creeping underground
rhizomes, sometimes with stolons. Lowest
leaves ovate-cordate. Flowering stems 40–80cm,
usually simple. Flowers *c.*5cm long, reddish,
sometimes very pale, spotted and long-hairy
inside. For moist, leafy soil in sun or part shade;
it may require protection from slugs. Hardy to
−15°C, perhaps less.

Campanula takesimana Nakai Native of
Korea and of Ullung-Do, an island off the east
coast of Korea, growing in grassy places,
flowering in July–September. Plant with
creeping rhizomes and rosettes of leaves, with a
blade *c.*8cm long. Stems to 36cm, leafy. Flowers
*c.*5cm long, pale blue to pink, spotted inside.
For moist, leafy soil in part shade. Hardy to
−20°C perhaps. The fleshy rhizomes are liable
to attack by cockchafer grubs or slugs, but
otherwise the plant appears easy to grow.

Campanula 'Van Houttei' Probably a hybrid
between *C. latifolia* and *C. punctata*, of
uncertain origin before 1878. Stems to 45cm.
Flowers mauve or greyish blue, 10cm long, but
also variously described as deep indigo or
lavender. Calyx lobes spreading and reflexed,
closer to *C. latifolia*, which is said to be the seed
parent. Both these hybrids will grow in an
ordinary, rather moist border, or among shrubs.
Hardy to −20°C perhaps.

Campanula 'Van Houttei'

Campanula takesimana

Campanula punctata 'Rubra'

Campanula latifolia seedlings with the leaves of *Diphylleia*

Campanula 'Burghaltii'

Campanula latifolia var. *macrantha*

Codonopsis lanceolata near Kyoto, Japan

Codonopsis lanceolata

Codonopsis tangshen at Windsor

Codonopsis ovata in Kashmir, with the leaves of *Bergenia stracheyi* behind

Adenophora triphylla in Hokkaido

Wahlenbergia undulata on Ngeli Mountain, Natal

Platycodon grandiflorus

Adenophora triphylla (Thunb.) A. DC. var. **japonica** (Regel) Hara (*Campanulaceae*)
Native of Japan, in all the islands, growing in grassy places in lowlands and mountains, and on the edges of woods, flowering in July–October. Plant with deep, thick roots and stems to 90cm, usually *c*.50cm. Leaves in whorls of 4, oblong or ovate-elliptic. Flowers 13–22mm long, arranged in whorls on the inflorescence. For moist, peaty soil in sun or partial shade. Hardy to −20°C. *Adenophora* differs from *Campanula* in having a tubular or cup-shaped disc around the base of the style. *A. confusa* Nannfeldt has broader leaves and short-stalked flowers scattered up a tall inflorescence.

Codonopsis lanceolata (Sieb. & Zucc.) Trautv. (*Campanulaceae*)   Native of Japan, in all the islands, with var. *emaculata* Honda in E Siberia, Korea and N China, growing in scrub, bamboo, on the edges of woods and in clearings on low mountains and hills, flowering in August–October. Plant with large, fleshy tuberous roots. Stems climbing, to 2m or more. Leaves narrowly oblong to ovate, glabrous, glaucous beneath. Flowers 3–3.5cm long, 6–10mm wide; calyx lobes acuminate, 2–2.5 cm long. Seeds white, winged on one side (var. *emaculata* has flowers without spots inside). Pollinated by large wasps. For moist, leafy soil among shrubs. Hardy to −20°C, possibly less.

Codonopsis ovata Benth.   Native of the Himalayas, from Pakistan to Kashmir, where it is common, growing on rocky, grassy slopes at 3000–4200m, flowering in July–August, often in June in gardens. Plant with fleshy roots and few to several upright stems to 20cm. Leaves 1–3cm long, tubular campanulate often expanded at the mouth with spreading calyx lobes. For moist but well-drained soil in full sun, but not easy to grow. Hardy to −20°C or less. *C. clematidea* (Schrenk) C. B. Clarke, from C Asia to N India, is found in similar habitats, but is taller, to 60cm, and has rounded bells, narrow at the mouth, and recurved calyx lobes. Easier to grow.

Codonopsis tangshen Oliver   Native of W China, growing in scrub, flowering in August– September. Plant with long, fleshy roots and climbing stems to 2m or more. Leaves ovate to ovate-lanceolate. Calyx lobes ovate, 5–6mm long. Flowers to 3.5cm long, veined inside towards the base of the bell. For loose, peaty soil in sun or partial shade. Hardy to −20°C perhaps.

Ostrowskia magnifica Regel (*Campanulaceae*)
Native of C Asia, in the Pamir-Alai, growing on rocky hillsides, flowering in May–June. Stems few, to 1.5m, from a tuberous rootstock. Leaves in whorls of 4 or 5, ovate-lanceolate, 10–15cm long. Flowers 12–15cm across, rather few at the top of the stems. For well-drained, sandy, leafy soil in full sun, dry in late summer and with protection from excess wet in winter. Hardy to −20°C or less.

Platycodon grandiflorus (Jacq.) A. DC. (*Campanulaceae*)   Native of Japan, in all the islands, of Korea, N China and E Siberia, growing on grassy slopes in hills and mountains, flowering in August–September. Plant with a tufted rootstock and thick roots. Stems 40– 100cm, usually *c*.20cm in the commonly cultivated 'Apoyama'. Flowers 4–5cm across, blue, or, in 'Mother-of-Pearl', pale pink. For any good, moist, sandy soil in sun or partial shade. Hardy to −20°C or less.

Wahlenbergia undulata (Thunb.) A. DC. (*Campanulaceae*)   Native of South Africa, from E Cape Province northwards to Natal, growing in dry places among rocks at up to 1800m in Natal, flowering in November–March. Plant with branched stolons from a tufted rootstock, forming many-stemmed clumps, often flowering in a year from seed. Stems to 40cm. Leaves wavy-edged, obtuse. Flowers *c*.3cm across, pale blue, mauve or white. Hardy to −15°C, perhaps less if dry in winter.

Ostrowskia magnifica in Tashkent

Lobelia siphilitica near New York

Lobelia × *speciosa* 'Queen Victoria' at the Savill Gardens, Windsor

Lobelia × *gerardii* 'Vedrariensis'

Lobelia cardinalis

Lobelia 'Russian Princess' at Wisley

Lobelia tupa (detail)

Lobelia tupa in SE Chile, photographed by Martin Gardiner

Lobelia laxiflora var. *angustifolia*

Lobelia × *speciosa* 'Cherry Ripe'

Lobelia cardinalis L. (*Campanulaceae*)
Cardinal Flower Native of North America, from New Brunswick, S Quebec and Minnesota, south to Florida and E Texas, with subsp. *graminea* (Lam.) McVaugh syn. *L. splendens* Willd. from Arizona to California and southwards to Mexico and C America, growing by lakes, in damp meadows and along streams, flowering in June–October. Plant with a tufted rhizome and stems to 1.8m; leaves lanceolate to ovate-lanceolate, or narrow-lanceolate to linear in subsp. *graminea*. Flowers 3–4.5cm long. For good soil in sun or partial shade, by water or in a moist border. Hardy to −25°C and less.

***Lobelia* × *gerardii* 'Vedrariensis'** A hybrid between *L. cardinalis* and *L. siphilitica*, known in the wild. Several colour forms are in cultivation: 'Vedrariensis' is rich purple; 'Tania' is redder, described as crimson-purple, 'Blauzauber', presumably more blue.

Lobelia laxiflora H., B. & K. var. **angustifolia** DC. Native of S Arizona, Mexico and much of C America, growing in oak woodland at *c*.1500m in Arizona, flowering in May. Var. *angustifolia* is the plant found in Arizona. Plant forming spreading clumps of stems to 60cm. Leaves linear-lanceolate, *c*.7cm long. Flowers *c*.3.5cm long, red and yellow or pure yellow. For well-drained, sandy but moist soil in a warm position. Hardy to −10°C, or less for short periods.

Lobelia siphilitica L. Native of E North America, from Maine and South Dakota, southwards to Missouri and east Kansas and Texas, growing in moist woods and marshes, flowering in August–September. Plant with a tufted rootstock and stems to 1.3m. Leaves ovate, thin. Flowers 2.3–3.5cm long, usually blue, rarely white. For moist soil in sun or partial shade. Hardy to −25°C or less.

Lobelia* × *speciosa Sweet A hybrid race derived from *L. cardinalis*, *L. fulgens* Willd. from Mexico and *L. siphilitica*. All require rich, moist, peaty soil in sun or partial shade. Best with protection from cold, wet winters, and well mulched.
'Cherry Ripe' Leaves green; flowers cherry-red.
'Queen Victoria' An old variety, with deep-red leaves and stems. Flowers intense red. Stems to 1m.
'Russian Princess' Leaves purple; flowers red-purple. Stems to 80cm, with a rather elegant habit.

Lobelia tupa L. Native of Chile, growing on sandy hills near the sea, flowering in December–April, or July–October in the north. Plant with a large tufted rootstock and numerous stems to 2.5m. Leaves softly hairy to 20cm. Flowers thick and fleshy, *c*.6cm long, doubtless pollinated by hummingbirds. For really well-drained but good soil, kept moist in summer. Hardy to −10°C, and lower if the rootstock is protected against wet and frost in winter. Grows well along the west coasts of Europe and North America.

Anthemis tinctoria 'E. C. Buxton'

Echinacea purpurea

Anthemis tinctoria

Anthemis tinctoria L. (*Compositae*)   Native of most of Europe, Turkey, the Caucasus, W Syria and Iran and naturalized in the British Isles and North America, growing on roadsides, steppes, waste places and in scrub, flowering in May–July. Plant with several branching upright stems to 45cm. Leaves 2–3 pinnatisect, oblanceolate to obovate in outline, 1–5cm long. Flowers 2.5–4.5cm across, yellow or white or cream in var. *pallida* DC., pale yellow in 'E. C. Buxton', paler still in 'Wargrave'. For well-drained soil in full sun; good on chalk. Hardy to −25°C, perhaps less.

Arnica montana L. (*Compositae*)   Native of most of Europe from Belgium and Holland eastwards to Russia, and south to S Portugal, C Italy and Yugoslavia, growing in meadows, heaths and subalpine meadows, mainly on acid soils, at up to 2500m in the Alps, flowering in June–August. Plant with short rhizomes and stems 25–60cm tall. Basal leaves obovate to oblanceolate, glandular-pubescent. Stem leaves in pairs, linear-lanceolate. Flowers 5–6.5cm across, 1–3 per stalk. For well-drained, sandy or peaty soil in full sun. Hardy to −25°C.

Coreopsis verticillata L. (*Compositae*)   Native of E North America, from Florida to Alabama and Arkansas, north to Maryland and Virginia, growing in open woods and clearings in rather dry soil, flowering in June–July. Plant bushy with short rhizomes and much-branched stems to 110cm, usually *c*.60cm in gardens. Leaves with hair-like segments, 0.3–1.5mm wide. Flowers 4–6cm across, usually bright yellow, but a beautiful pale lemon yellow in 'Moonbeam'. For well-drained soil in sun or partial shade. Hardy to −25°C or less.

Echinacea purpurea (L.) Moench (*Compositae*)   Native of Virginia west to Ohio, Michigan, Illinois and Iowa, and south to Georgia and Louisiana, growing in prairies and dry, open woods, flowering in June–October. Plant with a short, spreading rootstock and stems to 1.2m. Leaves rough, the lowest ovate, the rest ovate-lanceolate. Flowers purplish, rarely white, to 12cm across. Several (*c*.8) named cultivars are available: 'White Lustre', raised in America, is said to have drooping petals. 'Robert Bloom' is a rich mauve-crimson; this is now usually sold as seedlings or

Arnica montana

Echinacea tennesseensis

Leucanthemum × *superbum* 'Wirral Supreme'

Leucanthemum × *superbum* 'Everest'

Senecio doronicum in Switzerland

'Bressingham hybrids'. For good, light soil in a border, where it makes a bold feature. Hardy to −20°C, perhaps less.

Echinacea tennesseensis (Beadle) Small   A rare plant found in Tennessee and Arkansas, in the Interior and Ozark plateaux, growing on gravelly hillsides. Differs from *E. purpurea* in its vertical, not spreading, rootstock, linear leaves, and smaller 'petals', to 2.5cm long.

Eriophyllum lanatum (Pursh) Forbes (*Compositae*) **Golden Yarrow**   Native of S California, north to British Columbia and the Rockies, growing in dry scrub at up to 3000m, flowering in April–August. A variable plant with stems up to 80cm, usually *c*.50cm. Leaves usually toothed, often woolly. Flowers with 8–13 petals, *c*.2.5cm across. For a dry position in full sun. Hardy to −25°C, if introduced from a cold area.

Leucanthemum × **superbum** Bergman ex Ingram syn. *Chrysanthemum maximum* hort. (*Compositae*)   The large garden Shasta daisies formerly listed under *L. maximum* (Rem.) DC., a Pyrenean species, are now considered hybrids between *L. maximum* and *L. lacustre* (Brot.) Samp., from the Estremadura in WC Portugal, a very similar but slightly smaller-flowered species. Numerous cultivars have been raised and named, and 48 are listed in Trehane's *Index Hortensis*. Shown here are 'Everest', large-flowered to 10cm across, on stems around 90cm, and 'Wirral Supreme', a double with stems again *c*.90cm. 'Snowcap' is a short-stemmed single, *c*.50cm tall. 'Phyllis Smith' has the petals interestingly recurved and twisted, on stems to 90cm. 'Cobham Gold' has pale-yellow flowers, and stems 60cm, but is now very rare. All flower in late summer, in June–September.

Senecio doronicum L. (*Compositae*)   Native of C & S Europe, from Spain and France to Greece and Romania, growing in grassy and rocky places in the mountains at 1500–2700m, usually on limestone, flowering in June–August. Plant variable, but stems usually *c*.30cm. Leaves thick, usually white and cottony beneath. Stem leaves few, alternate, lanceolate. Flowers orange-yellow, 3–6cm across, 1–3 per stem. For well-drained soil in sun or partial shade. Similar in general appearance to *Arnica*, but that has stem leaves in pairs. Hardy to −20°C or less.

Coreopsis verticillata

Eriophyllum lanatum

Coreopsis verticillata 'Moonbeam'

137

Achillea 'Coronation Gold'

Tanacetum ptarmicifolium 'Silver Feather' in the White Garden at Sissinghurst Castle

Achillea tomentosa

Achillea filipendulina 'Gold Plate'

Achillea 'Taygetea'

Achillea decolorans 'W. B. Child'

Achillea ptarmica

Achillea 'Cerise Queen'

Achillea 'Galaxy hybrids'

Achillea 'Paprika'

Achillea 'Coronation Gold' (*Compositae*)   A hybrid between *A. clypeolata* and *A. filipendulina*, a chance seedling in the garden of Miss R. B. Pole. Stems *c*.90cm. Leaves greyish, flower-heads looser than those of *A. filipendulina*. Hardy to −25°C or less.

Achillea decolorans Schrad. **'W. B. Child'**   A plant of uncertain origin but probably a hybrid between *A. ptarmica* and *A. macrocephala*, both of which occur in the Alps where *A. decolorans* is said to have originated. Plant forming spreading patches of lax stems to 60cm. Leaves sharply toothed with long, curved teeth. Flowers in loose heads, *c*.8mm across. For a moist border in sun or partial shade. Hardy to −20°C or less.

Achillea filipendulina Lam. **'Gold Plate'**   Native of the Caucasus and SE Turkey to Iran, C Asia and Afghanistan, growing in wet meadows, by streams or lakes and on rocky slopes, flowering in June–August. Plant forming dense clumps of upright stems to 120cm. Leaves green, densely hairy, 10–20cm long 3–7mm wide, oblong, deeply divided. Flower-heads 4–10cm or more across; flowers 2.5–3.5mm across, rich golden yellow. For any good soil in full sun and in cool climates, tolerant of summer drought. Hardy to −25°C. *A. clypeolata* Sm., from Greece and European Turkey to Romania, has woolly, narrower leaves to 4cm wide and smaller heads of flowers.

Achillea 'Galaxy hybrids'   A group of hybrids between *A. millefolium* and the yellow-flowered *A.* 'Taygetea' (itself a hybrid between *A. clypeolata* and *A. millefolium*), raised by A.

Kikillus in Germany and introduced by Blooms of Bressingham. The main named colour forms are as follows:
'Apfelblute' ('Apple Blossom')   Flowers pink; *c*.90cm.
'Hoffnung' ('Great Expectations')   Sulphur-yellow *c*.60cm.
'Lachsschoenheit' ('Salmon Beauty')   Pale salmon-pink, fading to cream.
'Fanal' ('The Beacon')   Bright red, *c*.75cm.
'Paprika'   *c*.60cm, appears to be of similar parentage.
All are easily grown in full sun and tolerate poor soil. Hardy to −25°C or less.

Achillea millefolium L.   Native of most of Europe and W Asia east to the Himalayas and naturalized in North America, Australia and New Zealand, growing in meadows and dry, grassy places, flowering in June–September. Plant forming spreading mats of rosettes of deeply divided leaves and erect flowering stems to 60cm. Middle stem leaves 2-pinnatisect, lanceolate in outline. Flowers usually white, sometimes pale pink, deep pink or crimson; there are many named forms, including 'Cerise Queen', bright pinkish-red; all have petals (ligules) 1–2.5mm long. Pale-pink flowers and very hairy leaves are common in subsp. *sudetica* (Opiz) Weiss, from the mountains of central Europe. A drought-resistant plant for a sunny border, and common in old lawns where it stays green after the grass has gone brown. Hardy to −25°C and less. *A. asplenifolia* Vent., closely related to *A. millefolium*, is a tall plant, to 100cm, found in wet meadows in SE Europe, from Austria to Romania. It has glabrous, finely cut leaves and pink or purplish-red flowers.

Achillea ptarmica L.   Native of N Europe to N Spain, N Italy and SW Romania, eastwards to Siberia and naturalized in North America, growing in wet meadows, marshes and heaths, flowering in July–September. Plant with a creeping rhizome, forming loose patches. Leaves 1.5–8cm long, linear-lanceolate, finely toothed. Stems floppy, 20–60cm. Flowers 12–18mm across, rather dirty white, but pure white and perfectly double in 'Boule de Neige', syns. 'The Pearl' and 'Schneeball', which is commonly cultivated. For a moist, rich border in sun or partial shade. Hardy to −25°C or less.

Achillea 'Taygetea'   A hybrid of uncertain origin, probably between *A. millefolium* and *A. clypeolata*. Leaves green, flatter and less divided than *A. millefolium*. Stems *c*.60cm tall. Flowers pale yellow. *A. ochroleuca* Ehrh, from Czechoslovakia to the Ukraine, appears very similar. *A. taygetea* Boiss. & Held., from S Greece, is greyish-hairy, has yellow flowers and is considered in *Flora Europaea* to be synonymous with *A. aegyptiaca* L.

Achillea tomentosa L.   Native of SW Europe, from C France and C Italy to Spain, growing on dry hills and waste ground, flowering in May–June. Plant forming mats of woolly or silky leaves with linear lobes, with flowering stems to 40cm. Flowers *c*.3mm across. Petals 2mm. For dry soil in full sun. Hardy to −15°C.

Tanacetum ptarmicifolium (Webb & Berth.) Schulz-Bip (*Compositae*)   **Silver Feather** Native of Gran Canaria, where it is very rare, growing on rocks and cliffs in the mountains. Often grown as an annual for bedding.

'Foerster's Liebling'

'Quakeress'

'Felicity'

'Dignity'

'Amity'

'Prosperity'

'Adria'

Erigeron specimens from Kelways' Nurseries, 24 June. ¼ life size

***Erigeron* cultivars**   These have been raised from the American species *E. speciosus* (Lindl.) DC., crossed with *E. speciosus* var. *macranthus* (Nutt.) Cronquist, *E. glaucus* (q.v.) and *E. aurantiacus* Regel, with orange-yellow flowers. About 50 named cultivars are now extant. Shown here are:
'Adria'   Lavender-blue; stems *c.*75cm, raised by H. Goetz in 1954.
'Amity'   Lilac-pink; stems *c.*60cm, raised by Alan Bloom.
'Dunkelste Aller'   syn. 'Darkest of All'   Deep purplish blue, stems to 60cm, raised by Benary in 1951.
'Dignity'   Violet-blue; stems to 45cm, raised by Alan Bloom.
'Felicity'   Bright pink; stems to 60cm, raised by Alan Bloom.
'Foerster's Liebling'   Deep reddish pink; stems to 45cm, raised in Germany in 1951.
'Prosperity'   Lilac; stems to 45cm, raised by Alan Bloom.
'Quakeress'   Pale lilac-pink; stems to 45cm, an old variety.
All flower in late June–July and require good, well-drained soil in full sun. Hardy to −25°C or less.

Erigeron glaucus Ker-Gawl. (*Compositae*)
Native of California, from San Luis Obispo north to Oregon and naturalized in Europe, especially by the sea, growing on coastal bluffs and cliffs, sand dunes and on beaches, flowering in April–August. Plant forming wide, spreading mats of obovate to oblanceolate, obtuse leaves. Stems glandular-hairy, 10–40cm tall. Flowers 4–6cm across, usually pale purplish, but pinkish in 'Roseus'. 'Elstead Pink' is possibly a hybrid. For sandy, dry soil in full sun. Hardy to −10°C, perhaps less. Common in gardens near the coast.

Osteospermum jucundum (E. P. Phill.) T. Norl. syn. *Dimorphotheca jucunda* E. P. Phill. (*Compositae*)   Native of South Africa, from the Transvaal south to Lesotho and Natal, growing on rocks and in moist grassland at up to 3200m, flowering in December–February, or July–September in the north. Plant forming mats of narrowly oblanceolate leaves. Flowering stems to 30cm. Flowers *c.*6cm across. For well-drained sandy, peaty soil, moist in summer, dry in winter. This should be the hardiest *Osteospermum*, as it comes from such high altitudes in the Drakensberg. Hardy to −10°C, or less if dry.

***Tanacetum* cultivars**   The garden Pyrethrums are selections of *Tanacetum coccineum* (Willd.) Grierson, syns. *Pyrethrum roseum* (Adams) M. Bieb., *Chrysanthemum roseum* Adams, a native of subalpine meadows in the Caucasus. In the wild it has pale-pink flowers and stems *c.*60cm tall. The garden selections have brighter flowers, often double or semi-double. They do best in well-drained, slightly acid, sandy soil in an open, sunny position, and flower in June–July. Shown here are:
'Brenda'   Bright cerise-pink, stems *c.*60cm.
'Eileen May Robinson'   Pale pink, stems *c.*60cm.
'Mont Blanc'   White double, stems *c.*60cm.

Osteospermum jucundum

Erigeron 'Dunkelste Aller'

Erigeron glaucus

Pyrethrums in a Cambridgeshire garden

Tanacetum coccineum 'Brenda'

Tanacetum coccineum 'Eileen May Robinson'

Tanacetum coccineum 'Mont Blanc' at Bridge of Alford, Aberdeenshire

Cicerbita alpina

Syneilesis aconitifolia

Cicerbita alpina at Edington, Wiltshire

Adenostyles alpina near Samaden, Switzerland

Lactuca perennis at St Luc, the Valais

Liatris spicata 'Alba'

Hieraceum lanatum at Wisley

Adenostyles alpina (L.) Bluff & Fingerh. (*Compositae*)   Native of the Jura, the Alps, Apennines and Corsica (subsp. *briquetii*) eastwards to Yugoslavia, growing in woods, by streams, in alder scrub and on damp, rocky slopes usually north-facing, usually on limestone at up to 2400m, flowering in June–September. Plant with large, rounded basal leaves *c*.15cm across and few upright stems to 50cm. Flowers in a loose, flat-topped inflorescence. For a cool, rich position in shade or partial shade. Hardy to −20°C or less. *A. alliariae* (Gouan) A. Kerner has more branched, woolly flowering stems and usually sessile upper-stem leaves. It has darker purplish-pink flowers.

Cicerbita alpina (L.) Wallr. (*Compositae*) Native of Europe, from Scotland (where it is *very* rare) and Norway to the Alps, the Pyrenees and Carpathians, eastwards to Russia and Bulgaria, growing on shady, moist cliffs and in alder scrub flowering in July–September. Plant with few simple or branched stems to 250cm. Lower leaves to 25cm, with a large, triangular terminal lobe and a few pairs of small lateral lobes. Upper leaves clasping the stem. Flowers in a rounded, then elongated head, *c*.2cm across. For moist, rich soil in partial shade. Hardy to −20°C or less.

Cicerbita bourgaei (Boiss.) Beauv.   Native of NE Turkey, from Giresun eastwards, and of Soviet Georgia, growing in forest clearings, by

streams and in hazel scrub at 1050–1820m, flowering in August–September. Plant forming clumps of erect stems to 3m from a tufted rootstock. Leaves elliptic, unlobed or with 2–4 rounded lateral lobes. Flowers 1.7–1.9cm long. For moist, rich soil in sun or partial shade. Hardy to −25°C or less. *C. macrophylla* (Willd.) Wallr. from C Russia and the Caucasus south to the Talysh has a far-creeping rhizome and is naturalized in N & C Europe. It often persists as a roadside weed after it has been thrown out of a nearby garden. It has stems to 180cm and flowers to 3cm across in a loose, rather flat-topped inflorescence.

Hieraceum lanatum Vill. (*Compositae*)   Native of France and N Italy, in the Alps and the Jura, growing on limestone rocks and cliffs at 300–2100m, flowering in May–July. Plant with a rosette of densely white-felted leaves, the blade to 10cm long, ovate, elliptical or lanceolate, usually ovate in cultivated plants. Flowers with the involucre 12–15mm long. For a very well-drained, sunny position such as on this old wall. Hardy to −20°C, perhaps less.

Lactuca perennis L. (*Compositae*)   Native of Europe, from Spain to France, Germany and Belgium east to Romania, growing on sunny banks and among dry rocks in the hills, usually on limestone, flowering in June–August. Plant with a rosette of pinnatifid or pinnatisect rather glaucous leaves, with lanceolate segments. Stems several, to 80cm, much branched.

Flowers *c*.2.5cm across, blue to lilac. For dry, well-drained soil in full sun. Hardy to −25°C perhaps. A delicate and attractive garden plant.

Liatris spicata (L.) Willd. (*Compositae*) Native of E North America, from Pennsylvania and New Jersey west to Michigan and Wisconsin, and south to Florida and Louisiana, growing in damp meadows, the edges of marshes and in savannahs, flowering in July–September. Plant with stiff, upright stems to 1.8m, from corm-like rhizomes. Leaves glabrous, linear to linear-lanceolate, to 40cm long, 2cm wide. Involucral bracts with appressed tips (tips spreading in *L. pycnostachya* and *L. scariosa*). For good, moist soil in full sun. Hardy to −25°C or less. Various colour forms are cultivated in shades of bluish purple, violet and white.

Syneilesis aconitifolia (Bunge) Maxim. (*Compositae*)   Native of N Honshu and NE China, north of Beijing, where it is common, growing in dry woods and scrub in low hills, flowering in August–October. Plant with a tufted rootstock. Leaves silky when young, on upright stalks to 60cm, peltate, deeply divided and with jaggedly toothed lobes to 30cm across. Flowering stems to 1m or more, with pinkish flowers without rays. For sun or partial shade in leafy soil. Hardy to −25°C or less. The leaves are exciting, the flowers a disappointment.

143

Ligularia 'Gregynog Gold' in the stream garden at Leeds Castle, Kent

Ligularia 'Zepter' in the Savill Garden, Windsor

Ligularia stenocephala 'The Rocket' in the Wild Garden at Wisley

Ligularia macrophylla at Kew

Ligularia dentata (A. Gray) Hara syn. *L. clivorum* Maxim. (*Compositae*)   Native of China, from W Sichuan eastwards, and in Japan in Honshu, growing in scrub, forest clearings, by ditches and in mountain meadows, flowering in July–August to October in the wild. Plant with a tufted rootstock and long-stemmed leaves to 30cm long, 38cm wide, cordate. Stem leaves usually 2; stems to 1.2m; flower-heads *c*.11cm across. For moist, rich soil in shade or partial shade. Hardy to −25°C or less. Several cultivars have been named: 'Othello' (1915) was the earliest of the purple-leaved cultivars; 'Moorblut' is said to have even darker leaves; 'Desdemona', surprisingly, is similar to 'Othello'. These purple-leaved forms come more or less true from seed.

Ligularia 'Gregynog Gold'   A hybrid between *L. dentata* and *L. veitchiana*, raised by Hess in 1950. This is one of the finest of the *Ligularias*, with large flowers, rich orange-yellow, the lowest *c*.10cm across, in a loose spike. Stems to 1.8m. For rich, moist or boggy soil in sun or partial shade. Hardy to −20°C.

Ligularia macrophylla (Ledeb.) DC.   Native of C Asia, in Kazakstan and NW China in Sinjiang, growing on dry but fertile hillsides, flowering in July–August. Leaves very glaucous, upright from a deep rootstock, the blades broadly ovate, finely toothed. Inflorescence to 1.5m, of numerous small flowers 3–5cm across. For deep, rich but well-drained soil in full sun. This requires moisture in spring but can be dry in the latter part of the summer. Hardy to −25°C or less. Very rare in gardens but the fine clump in the order beds at Kew shown here is often illustrated, e.g. in Graham Thomas' *Perennial Garden Plants* and elsewhere. It covers the foothills of the Tien Shan above Alma Ata and in NW China.

Ligularia × palmatiloba Hesse syn. *L. × yoshizoeana* (Mak.) Kitam., the hybrid between *L. dentata* and *L. japonica*, has fewer deeply lobed leaves, but better flowers than *L. japonica*, *c*.7cm across. *L. japonica* (Thunb.) Less. itself is a native of W China in Hubei and Sichuan and in Korea, Taiwan and in Japan, in W Honshu, Shikoku and Kyushu, growing in rich, moist meadows and clearings in the mountains, flowering in June–August. Plant with a stout rootstock and large, orbicular

Ligularia veitchiana

Ligularia sibirica by a forest stream near Kyoto, Japan

Ligularia × *palmatiloba*

Ligularia dentata at Wallington, Northumberland

cordate lobed leaves, the lobes variably lobed or jaggedly deeply toothed. Inflorescence to 1.5m rather flat-topped, corymbose with flower stalks 2.5–20cm long. Flower-heads 2–8, about 10cm across. Both need moist, deep soil in shade or partial shade. Hardy to −20°C, perhaps less.

Ligularia sibirica (L.) Cass.   Native of Europe, from C France and Bulgaria eastwards to the Caucasus, Siberia, China and Japan (var. *speciosa* DC.), growing in wet woods, meadows and scrub by streams, flowering in July–October. Plant forming a large clump of rounded cordate leaves to *c*.32cm long and wide, sometimes densely hairy beneath. Flowering stems to 2m tall, usually *c*.1.5m. Flower-heads 4–5cm across, with 7–11 'petals'.

Ligularia stenocephala (Maxim.) Matsum. & Koidz. **'The Rocket'**   Native of Japan in all the islands except Hokkaido, N China and Taiwan, growing in wet places in the mountains, flowering in June–September. Plant forming large clumps of triangular leaves with narrow, elongated points and fine, irregular teeth to 24cm long, 20cm wide. Flowering stems often blackish, tall and slender to 1.2m. Flower-heads with 1–3 'petals', each 2–2.5cm long. For moist, rich soil in partial shade. Hardy to −25°C or less. *Ligularia przewalskii* (Maxim.) Diels has jagged, deeply toothed and lobed leaves, with a rather similar inflorescence. It is native of NW China.

Ligularia veitchiana (Hemsl.) Greenman Native of W China, in Hubei growing in wet

places at 1100–1800m, flowering in July–September. Plant forming a large clump of soft, rounded leaves to 60cm across with solid stalks. (Leaf stalks hollow in the similar *L. wilsoniana* (Hemsl.) Greenm.). Inflorescence to 1.8m, of numerous flower-heads *c*.6cm across, with broad bracts. For rich, moist soil in partial shade and shelter. Hardy to −20°C or less.

Ligularia 'Zepter'   This is the hybrid between *L. veitchiana* and, it is said, *L. przewalskii*, raised by K. Partsch in 1975. A striking plant for rich, moist soil in partial shade. If 'The Rocket' was the parent instead of the true *L. przewalskii* then the plant shown here would be a likely outcome. The leaves show no lobing; the black stalk takes after 'The Rocket'.

Telekia speciosa with *Myrrhis odorata*

Inula racemosa at the Savill Garden, Windsor

Inula hookeri

Inula royleana in Kashmir

Inula hookeri C. B. Clarke (*Compositae*)
Native of the Himalayas, from C Nepal east to
Burma and SW China, growing in scrub at
2400–3600m, flowering in August–October.
Plant forming spreading patches with numerous
slender, rather lax leafy stems to 75cm tall.
Leaves elliptic-lanceolate, 8–15cm long, hairy.
Buds covered with shaggy hairs. Flower-heads
3.5–6cm across. For moist but well-drained soil
in sun or partial shade. Hardy to −20°C,
perhaps less.

Inula racemosa Hook. fil.   Native of NW
China and Afghanistan to C Nepal, usually
growing near habitations, at 2000–3200m,
flowering in July–September. It is cultivated
because its roots are used for medicine. Stems to
2m or more from a stout rootstock. Lower
leaves elliptic-lanceolate, to 45cm long. Flower-
heads 4–8cm across. For deep, rich soil in sun
or partial shade. Hardy to −25°C or less.

Inula royleana C. B. Clarke   Native of the W
Himalayas, from Pakistan to Kashmir, where it
is common, growing in scrub and grassy
clearings in forest at 2100–4000m, flowering in
July–September. Plant with few, rather stout,
upright stems to 60cm. Leaves few, large,
elliptic-lanceolate. Flower-heads 10–12.5cm
across, usually solitary. For moist but well-
drained soil in sun or partial shade. Hardy to
−20°C or less.

Senecio bicolor (Willd.) Tod. subsp. *cineraria*
(DC.) Chater (*Compositae*)   Native of the W
Mediterranean region, Portugal and North
Africa, and naturalized in the British Isles,

growing in rocky and sandy places by the sea,
flowering in July–August. Plant with leafy,
cottony stems to 50cm, somewhat shrubby at
the base. Leaves ovate to ovate-lanceolate in
outline, deeply divided, with the ultimate lobe
longer than wide, subacute. In subsp. *bicolor*,
from the E Mediterranean, the leaves are ovate,
often lyrate, with the ultimate lobe as wide as
long and obtuse. Flower-heads on short
peduncles, with very short 'petals'. For well-
drained, sandy soil in full sun. Hardy to −10°C,
perhaps less in some cultivars.

Senecio doria L. syn. *S. macrophyllus* M.
Bieb.   Native of most of Europe from France,
Spain and North Africa, east to Bulgaria and the
Caucasus growing in wet meadows and marshes,
flowering in June–July. Plant with several
upright stems to 1m from a tufted rootstock.
Lower leaves linear-elliptical to oblong-obovate,
usually 3–7cm wide, dentate or entire. Flower-
heads small, 12–25mm across with 5–6 'petals'.
For moist or wet soil in full sun. Hardy to
−25°C. This species has been sold in error
under the name *Ligularia macrophylla*!

Senecio jacquemontianus (Decne.) Benth. ex
Hook.   Native of the W Himalayas, from
Pakistan to Kashmir, where it is locally
common, growing in alpine meadows at 3000–
4000m, flowering in July. Plant with thick,
upright stems and *Ligularia*-like habit. Basal
leaves heart-shaped, to 20cm across. Stem
leaves with a sheathing stalk. Flower-heads to
4cm across with rather few (12–15) 'petals',
c.1.5cm long. For moist soil in full sun or partial
shade. Hardy to −20°C or less.

Senecio pseudoarnica

Senecio pseudoarnica on the coast of Hokkaido

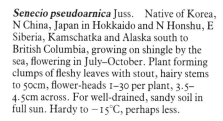

Senecio tanguticus at Inverewe

Senecio jacquemontianus in Kashmir

Senecio doria in Kent

Senecio pseudoarnica Juss.   Native of Korea, N China, Japan in Hokkaido and N Honshu, E Siberia, Kamschatka and Alaska south to British Columbia, growing on shingle by the sea, flowering in July–October. Plant forming clumps of fleshy leaves with stout, hairy stems to 50cm, flower-heads 1–30 per plant, 3.5–4.5cm across. For well-drained, sandy soil in full sun. Hardy to −15°C, perhaps less.

Senecio tanguticus Maxim.   Native of NW China in Gansu, growing in meadows, flowering in August–October. Plant with tall, black stems to 3m. Leaves 12–18cm, ovate in outline, deeply cut into jaggedly toothed lobes. Flower-heads very small, with 3–4 ray florets and 3–4 disc florets. For moist, peaty soil in shade or partial shade. Hardy to −25°C or less.

Telekia speciosa (Schreb.) Baumg. syn. *Bupthalmum speciosum* Schreb. (*Compositae*) Native of of C Europe, from Poland and Yugoslavia east to the Caucasus and Turkey, and naturalized elsewhere in NW Europe, growing in clearings in forest and by streams in scrub, at 300–1700m, flowering in July–September. Plant with a stout, shortly spreading rhizome and upright stems to 2m. Basal leaves ovate, on long stalks, rather thin, aromatic. Flower-heads 7.5–10cm across. For deep, moist soil in partial shade. Hardy to −25°C or less. A bold, tough plant with large *Hosta*-like leaves.

Senecio bicolor subsp. *cineraria*

Rudbeckia 'Goldquelle'

Rudbeckia laciniata

Rudbeckia hirta

Grindelia maritima at Santa Barbara

Rudbeckia fulgida var. *speciosa*

Rudbeckia 'Goldsturm'

Rudbeckia laciniata in Arizona

Grindelia maritima (Greene) Steyerm.
(*Compositae*) **Gum Weed**   Native of California,
on the coast around San Francisco, growing in
scrub and on rocky bluffs by the sea, flowering
in August–September. Plant woody at the base,
to 80cm. Leaves rather thick, the lowest
narrowly oblanceolate, to 18cm long. Flower-
heads 2.5–4cm across, excluding the 'petals'
which are 10–13mm long. Bracts with green,
mostly erect tips (recurved tips are found in
other species including *G. squarrosa* (Pursh)
Dunal from the Great Plains). For well-drained
soil in full sun. Hardy to −10°C, perhaps less.
G. chiloensis (Corn.) Cabr. is rather similar to
the above. The white gum on the buds is
characteristic of *Grindelia*, of which there are 11
species in California.

Ratibida columnaris (Pursh) D. Don f.
pulcherrima (DC.) Fern. syn. *Lepachys
columnaris* (Pursh) Torrey & Gray (*Compositae*)
Mexican Hat   Native of North America, from
Alberta south to Mexico east to Manitoba,
Minnesota, Illinois, Arkansas and Texas,
growing in prairies, dry, grassy valleys and
gorges usually on limestone, flowering in June–
September. Plant with stems to 80cm,
branching from the base. Leaves pinnate, with
5–9 oblong, narrowly linear leaflets. Flower-
heads with the column 3–6cm high; 'petals'
rather few, 1.3–2cm long, yellow or reddish-
brown in f. *pulcherrima*. For dry, well-drained
soil in full sun. Hardy to −25°C or less.

Ratibida pinnata (Vent.) Barnh. syn. *Lepachis
pinnata* (Vent.) Torr. & Gray   Native of E
North America, from S Ontario and New York
west to Minnesota and Nebraska, south to
Georgia and Oklahoma, growing in dry places,

flowering in June–September. Column *c.*2cm
high. 'Petals' drooping, *c.*5cm long, pale yellow.

Rudbeckia fulgida Ait. var. **speciosa** (Wend.)
Perdue syn. *R. newmannii* Loud. (*Compositae*)
Native of E North America from New York to
Georgia, Alabama and Missouri, growing in
woods and marshy valleys, flowering in late
July–September. Stems to 1m from an
elongated rhizome. Basal leaves ovate, with a
long stalk; stem-leaves lanceolate, deeply
toothed; 'Goldsturm' is the common garden
clone of this variety and has stems usually
*c.*60cm. Flowers 5–9cm across. For any soil in
full sun. Hardy to −25°C or less.

Rudbeckia hirta L.   Native of E North
America, from Massachusetts to Illinois, south
to Georgia and Alabama, growing in open
woods, scrub and rough meadows, flowering in
June–October. Plant with several stems to 1m,
from spreading rhizomes. Basal leaves ovate, to
7cm across. Stem leaves ovate, coarsely toothed.
Flower-heads orange-yellow, 5–8cm across. For
any good soil in full sun. Hardy to −25°C.

Rudbeckia laciniata L. **Cut-leaved
Coneflower**   Native of North America, from
Quebec west to Montana and south to N
Florida, Texas and through the Rockies to
Arizona, growing in moist meadows in valleys
and on grassy hills, flowering in July–October.
Plant forming loose clumps of stems 60–120cm
tall. Leaves deeply lobed into 3–7 pointed and
toothed segments. Flowers 7.5–15cm wide,
with a conical centre, or double in 'Goldquelle',
a common garden form with stems to 1.2m. For
any good soil in full sun. Hardy to −25°C.

Ratibida columnaris f. *pulcherrima*

Ratibida pinnata

Artemisia stelleriana on the coast of Hokkaido, near Shari

Artemisia ludoviciana with *Salvia aethiopis* at the Royal Botanic Garden, Edinburgh

Anaphalis margaritacea in Hokkaido

Artemisia lactiflora, a bit too dry

Anaphalis margaritacea

Anaphalis triplinervis

Artemisia schmidtiana

Artemisia 'Canescens'

Helichrysum 'Schwefellicht'

Anaphalis margaritacea (L.) Benth. & Hook. syn. *A. cinnamomea* DC. (*Compositae*) **Pearly Everlasting**   Native of North America, from Newfoundland to Alaska and in the mountains, and the Himalayas, growing on sand dunes, dry, stony lake shores, dry meadows and subalpine slopes, flowering in July–September. Plant with spreading rhizomes, forming dense patches. Stems 10–90cm, usually *c*.40cm, white, woolly. Leaves very variable, 3–20mm wide, variably hairy; green or greyish above, white beneath. Bracts rounded, erect at flowering. Shown here are: a wild form from Japan, probably var. *margaritacea*, the broadest-leaved variety; and an old garden variety, close to the American var. *subalpina* Gray, which has leaves hairy above, rather blunt at the apex. For any well-drained soil in full sun, not too dry in summer. Hardy to −25°C.

Anaphalis triplinervis (Sims) Sims ex. C. B. Clarke   Native of the Himalayas, from Afghanistan to SW China, growing in meadows and clearings in forest at 1800–3300m, flowering in July–October. Var. *intermedia* (DC.) Airy Shaw is found at higher altitudes, at 2900–4100m. Plant forming spreading clumps of rather lax stems 30–60cm tall, with leaves green above, 5–10cm long. Bracts spreading, acute. Var. *intermedia* has shorter (*c*.3cm) woolly leaves on shorter stems to 30cm. In gardens two named varieties are 'Silberregen' and 'Sommerschnee' (syn. 'Summersnow'), a dwarfer variety which seems to fall between *intermedia* and *triplinervis*. This is perhaps the same as *A*. 'Nubigena' of gardens. All need well-drained soil in full sun, but not too dry in summer. Hardy to −25°C or less.

Artemisia absinthium L. (*Compositae*) **Wormwood**   Native of Europe eastwards to W Asia and Siberia, and of North Africa, growing in grassy places by streams, in steppes, dry fields and by roadsides, flowering in June–September. Plant somewhat shrubby at the base. Flower-heads 3–5mm across in a branched, narrow or broad inflorescence up to 1m tall. 'Lambrook Giant', selected by Margery Fish, is a tall form; 'Lambrook Silver', a smaller one with stems to 75cm. For any dry soil in full sun.

Artemisia 'Canescens' syn. *A. armeniaca* hort.   A garden plant of uncertain origin, but distinct in its very fine curling leaf segments which join at right angles, giving the shoots a characteristic spiky look. Flowering stems narrow, to 45cm. Flower-heads globose, 6mm wide. For any well-drained soil in full sun.

Artemisia lactiflora Wall. ex DC.   Native of W China, in Sichuan, and recorded by Roy Lancaster on Omei Shan, growing in scrub and forest clearings, flowering in August–October. Plant forming large clumps of graceful stems to 1.8m. Leaves green, coarsely toothed. Flowers creamy yellow. For moist, peaty soil in sun or partial shade. Hardy to −20°C, perhaps less.

Artemisia ludoviciana Nutt. **Western Mugwort**   Native of North America, from Michigan to Washington south to Texas and Mexico, and naturalized further east, growing in prairies, dry, open ground or light woodland, flowering in July–September. Plant spreading by long, thin stolons to form loose patches. Stems 30–100cm. Leaves variable, green or white above, often with a few large teeth, but extra white in cultivar 'Silver Queen', which has stems to 75cm, and lanceolate leaves.

Artemisia
'Powys Castle'

Artemisia ludoviciana
'Silver Queen'

Artemisia
ludoviciana

Artemisia
absinthium
'Lambrook Silver'

Artemisia pontica

Artemisia stelleriana
'Mori's Form'

Specimens from the Savill Garden, Windsor, 28th August. ¼ life size

Artemisia pontica L.   Native from Germany and Austria eastwards to Russia, Bulgaria and C Asia, growing on dry, grassy and rocky hills, flowering in May–July. Plant forming clumps of stems 40–80cm. Flower-heads in a very narrow inflorescence, nodding, *c*.2.5mm across. For any soil in full sun. Hardy to −25°C or less.

Artemisia 'Powys Castle'   This is probably a hybrid between *A. absinthium* and the shrubby *A. aborescens*, which has finely divided leaves with segments to 2mm wide. 'Powys Castle' can form a shrub, as can be seen in the picture of the original plants in *Shrubs*, p. 160, but is also a quick-growing perennial, often killed by hard winters, but very easily raised from cuttings. Longest-lived when planted in the poorest soil.

Artemisia schmidtiana Maxim.   Native of Japan, in Hokkaido and N Honshu, and of Sakhalin and the S Kurile Islands, growing in bare soil in the mountains, and by the sea, flowering in August–October. Plant with creeping vegetative shoots forming hummocks or mats of soft, silvery, hair-like leaves.

Flowering stems to 30cm, usually *c*.15cm. Flower-heads nodding, *c*.8mm across. For well-drained, sandy soil in full sun. Hardy to −20°C or less. Usually called 'Nana', but all *A. schmidtiana* are dwarf.

Artemisia stelleriana Bess.   Native of E Siberia, N Japan, in Hokkaido and N Honshu, Korea, Sakhalin and the Kurile Islands, and widely naturalized in North America on the east coast, growing on sand dunes and on coastal cliffs, flowering in July–October. Plant with stolons and more or less prostrate vegetative shoots. Flowering stems to 65cm. Leaves thick, ovate to oblong, greyish or white with obtuse lobes. Flower-heads 8–10mm wide. For sandy soil in full sun. 'Mori's Form' syn. 'Boughton Silver' is an extra-white and more prostrate form introduced from Japan by Kazno Mori.

Helichrysum 'Schwefellicht' syn. 'Sulphur Light' (*Compositae*)   Raised by H. Klose. A tufted plant with upright stems 20–30cm tall, and softly woolly leaves. Hardy to −15°C, perhaps less.

151

Centaurea argentea

Centaurea macrocephala

Centaurea montana 'Alba'

Centaurea montana

Centaurea dealbata 'Steenbergii'

Centaurea atropurpurea

Centaurea argentea L. (*Compositae*)   Native of
Crete and Kithira, growing on mountain rocks,
and in gorges, flowering in June–July. Leaves
silvery, lyrate. Flower-heads 5–7mm across,
solitary on stalks 10–45cm high. For a dry,
sunny position on a wall or in some crevice.
Hardy to −15°C perhaps.

Centaurea atropurpurea Waldst. & Kit.
Native of Yugoslavia, Albania and Romania,
growing on rocky slopes in the mountains,
flowering in June–July. Stems to 150cm,
branched above. Flowers dark reddish purple,
above 4cm across. For well-drained soil in full
sun. Hardy to −20°C perhaps. This species is
striking mainly for its colour, like that of
Cirsium rivulare 'Atropurpureum' or *Knautia
macedonica* (see pp. 155 and 125).

Centaurea cuneifolia Sm. subsp. **pallida**
(Friv.) Hayek syn. *C.* 'Pulchra Major'
perhaps   Native of SE Europe, from
Yugoslavia and Romania to Turkey as far south
as Balikeşir, growing in forests and on sand
dunes, flowering in May–July. Plant forming
many-stemmed clumps to 80cm tall. Leaves
greyish white, hairy, the lowest lyrate-pinnatifid
with an oblong terminal segment. Flower-heads
6–8mm across at the base; bracts with brown,
papery appendages. For any dry, well-drained
soil in full sun. Hardy to −20°C or less. *C.
rhapontica* L. syn. *Leuzea rhapontica* (L.) J.
Hulub is a much larger plant with red or purple
flowers and flower-heads to 11cm across, and
appendages *c.*10mm wide.

Centaurea dealbata Willd.   Native of the
Caucasus to NE Turkey, growing in subalpine
meadows and on rocky slopes, flowering in
June–August. Plant forming clumps of green
leaves, pinnatisect with lobed or pinnatifid
segments, greyish beneath. Stems *c.*50cm, but
can grow up to 100cm. Flowering stems leafy,
often with leaves surrounding the pinkish
flower. 'Steenbergii' syn. 'Skanbergii' has deep-
reddish-purple flowers, and stems *c.*30cm. For
well-drained soil, in full sun. Hardy to −25°C or
less. *C. hypoleuca* DC., from the S Caucasus,
NW Iran and N Turkey, is very similar, but, in
the commonly cultivated form 'John Coutts', has

Centaurea declinata

Stokesia laevis 'Wyoming'

Centaurea cuneifolia subsp. *pallida*

slender, branched stems with lanceolate upper leaves with perhaps 1 or 2 lobes near the base, flowers bright pink, with a pale centre, *c*.6cm across, and dark-brown appendages with whitish hairs on the margins.

Centaurea declinata M. Bieb.   Native of the Caucasus and the Crimea, growing in dry, rocky subalpine meadows and subalpine woods, flowering in June–July. Plant forming mats of leaves, greyish above and below, with rounded segments. Flowering stems 10–30cm. Flower-heads *c*.5cm across, short and thick, bracts with spreading, pointed appendages. For well-drained soil in full sun, or a crevice on a wall. Hardy to −25°C or less.

Centaurea macrocephala Muss.-Puschk. ex Willd.   Native of the Caucasus and extreme NE of Turkey, growing in subalpine meadows at 2000–2300m, flowering in July–August. Plant with several stout, upright stems to 1m. Stems densely leafy. Flowers yellow, the flower-heads 4.5–5.5cm across, with large, to 2cm broad, rounded papery appendages on the bracts. For rich soil in full sun, moist in summer. Hardy to −20°C.

Centaurea montana L.   Native of Europe, from the Ardennes in Belgium south to the Pyrenees in Spain and east to Poland and C Yugoslavia, growing in subalpine meadows and open woods, flowering in May–July. Plant with creeping rhizomes forming spreading patches. Stems to 60cm usually simple. Leaves undivided, softly silky beneath. Flowering *c*.5cm across, blue or sometimes white in 'Alba', pink in 'Carnea' and mauve in 'Violetta'; three colour forms grown in gardens. For moist but well-drained soil in sun or partial shade. Hardy to −20°C or less.

Centaurea simplicaulis Boiss. & Huet   Native of NE Turkey and S Caucasia, growing in rock crevices and on screes at 400–2600m in Turkey, flowering in May–June. Plant forming mats of pinnatisect leaves, green above, whitish beneath, but variable in shape. Flowering stem 5–35cm, usually *c*.20cm in gardens. Flower-heads *c*.5cm across, rather long and slender with

Centaurea simplicaulis at Coldham, Kent

characteristic white-tipped appendages on the bracts. For a well-drained position in full sun, at the front of a border or on a wall. Hardy to −25°C or less.

Stokesia laevis (Hill) E. Greene (*Compositae*) Native of SE North America, from Florida and Louisiana to South Carolina, growing in moist pinelands on acid soil, flowering in April–July. Stems to 50cm, usually woolly. Lower leaves elliptic or narrowly lanceolate. Flowers purplish blue or white. For sandy soil in full sun. Hardy to −15°C, perhaps less.

Centaurea hypoleuca 'John Coutts' at Wisley

Berkheya purpurea with *Eucomis*

Senecio smithii in the Royal Botanic Garden, Edinburgh

Cirsium falconeri in Kashmir

Echinops exaltatus

Echinops ritro

Cirsium rivulare 'Atropurpureum'

Carlina acaulis at Powys Castle

Cynara scolymus with *Crambe maritima*

Cynara cardunculus in the long border at Great Dixter

Berkheya purpurea (DC.) Masters (*Compositae*)   Native of South Africa, in the Drakensberg, Natal and NE Cape Province (Winterberg), growing on moist, rocky, grassy slopes at 1800–2800m, flowering in December–February. Plant with few upright, thistle-like stems to 80cm. Basal leaves to 45cm long, white cottony beneath. Flower-heads *c*.7.5cm across, purple to white. For moist, peaty but well-drained soil in full sun. Hardy to −15°C.

Carlina acaulis L. (*Compositae*)   Native of Europe from C France and C Spain to Poland, W Russia and Greece, growing in rather dry alpine and subalpine meadows at up to 2500m, flowering in July–August. Plant usually short-lived or monocarpic, with rosettes of thistle-like leaves to 60cm across. Flowering stems variable in height: in subsp. *acaulis* usually stemless, but if grown in rich soil or partial shade with a short stem, to 15cm or so; in subsp. *simplex* (Waldst. & Kit.) Nyman, with an often branched stem up to 60cm, with up to 6 flowers. Flower-heads 8–12cm across, with silvery-white or pale-pink shining bracts. Hardy to −20°C.

Cirsium falconeri (Hook. fil.) Petrak (*Compositae*)   Native of the Himalayas, from Pakistan to SE Xizang (Tibet), growing in grassy places and clearings in forest at 2700–4300m, flowering in July–September. Plant with few upright stems to 1.5m. Whole plant covered with whitish spines. Flower-heads nodding, 7–8.5cm across in Kashmir as shown here; upright and purple-flowered in Nepal to SE Xizang. For moist but well-drained soil in sun or partial shade. Hardy to −20°C or less.

Cirsium rivulare (Jacq.) All. **'Atropurpureum'** Native of C Europe, from the Pyrenees in Spain and France eastwards to Yugoslavia and W Russia, growing in damp meadows usually on acid soils, flowering in June–July. Plant forming spreading clumps by shortly creeping rhizomes. Stems to 120cm or more in gardens. Flower-heads in clusters, *c*.3cm across, purple or deep crimson-purple in commonly cultivated 'Atropurpureum'. For a moist, sandy border in sun or partial shade. Hardy to −20°C or less.

Cynara cardunculus L. (*Compositae*) **Cardoon**   Native of SW Europe, from Portugal to S France, Italy, Greece and North Africa, growing on stony slopes and in dry grassy places, flowering in June–August. Stems to 100cm, in the wild, to 2m or more in gardens. Leaves greyish, to 1m long, deeply dissected, usually with some spines. Flower-heads 5–8cm across, with spiny, spreading bracts. For deep, well-drained soil in full sun. Hardy to −10°C or less with protection. *C. hystrix* Ball, from North Africa is sometimes grown in gardens. It has very spiny, narrow leaves and stems *c*.100cm; flower-heads with reddish-purple bracts.

Cynara scolymus L. **Artichoke**   The cultivated Artichoke is usually grown as a vegetable, but makes a handsome plant for a border if it is allowed to flower. It is unknown in the wild, and is almost certainly a form of the Cardoon (see above), long cultivated for its edible flower-head, which in a good cultivar may be 12cm or more across.

Echinops exaltatus Schrad. syn. *E. commutatus* Jur. (*Compositae*)   Native of Europe, from Italy and Poland, eastwards to W Russia and Bulgaria, growing in grassy places and scrub, flowering in August–September. Plant forming huge clumps of upright stems to 2m. Leaves ovate to elliptical in outline, green above, hairy beneath; segments triangular with few slender spines and a very rough margin. Flower-heads white or greyish, 3.5–6cm across. For good soil in full sun or partial shade. Hardy to −20°C or less. *E. sphaerocephalus* L. is a similar huge, white-flowered plant, but has leaves with smooth margin.

Echinops ritro L. incl. *E. ruthenicus* M. Bieb. **Globe Thistle**   Native of Europe from S France and Spain eastwards to Siberia and C Asia, growing in scrub, on rocky slopes and in bare, stony places, flowering in July–October. Plant with a tufted rootstock and several white-hairy stems 30–60cm. Leaves stiff, leathery, very spiny, green above, white beneath, pinnatifid, with segments 4mm wide or more at the base; leaves more finely divided and segments less than 2mm wide in subsp. *ruthenicus* (M. Bieb.) Nyman. Flower-heads blue, 3.5–4.5cm across. For well-drained, dry soil in full sun. Hardy to −20°C or less. Another dwarf species worth growing is *Echinops emiliae* O. Schw. from limestone screes in SW Turkey. It has stems to 60cm, but huge pale jade-green flower-heads to 15cm across. It was discovered by Peter Davis in 1947, but still awaits introduction!

Senecio smithii DC. (*Compositae*)   Native of W Argentina north to 46°S and S Chile north to 43°S, growing in marshes, wet grassy places, along the coast and by streams crossing shingle beaches, flowering in December–April, or July–August in the north, where it is naturalized in Shetland, and other parts of W Scotland, growing by streams across bogs. Plant forming large clumps of stalked leaves with blade 8–25cm long, white-hairy beneath. Flowering stems to 120cm. Flower-heads 3–5cm across. For wet, peaty soil or shallow water in sun or partial shade. Hardy to −25°C, perhaps less. Often damaged by slugs.

Veratrum nigrum with *Cimicifuga racemosa* in Kent

Veratrum mengtzeanum at Windsor

Amianthium muscaetoxicum (Walt.) A. Gray (*Liliaceae-Melanthiaceae*) **Fly-poison** Native of E North America, from Long Island and E Pennsylvania, south to Florida, Missouri and Oklahoma, growing in open, sandy woods, bogs and wet, sandy fields, flowering in May–July. Plant with a slender, bulbous rootstock and linear basal leaves to 3cm wide. Stems 45–120cm tall, not branched. Flowers 5–7mm across, without nectaries. Hardy to −20°C.

Stenanthium gramineum (Ker-Gawl.) Morong. (*Liliaceae-Melanthiaceae*) Native of E North America, from Virginia to Kentucky, south to Missouri, Florida and E Texas, at up to 1800m in North Carolina, growing in dry, open woods in the mountains, in scrub and on the edges of swamps (var. *robustum* (S. Wats.) Fern.), flowering in mid-June–September. Plant with a slightly bulbous rootstock and upright stems to 1.9m. Leaves numerous, to 3cm broad, rather lax. Inflorescence with a spike-like terminal branch, and several, usually nodding, side branches, but ascending and more densely flowered in var. *robustum*. Flowers usually whitish, but sometimes greenish or bronze-purple. Rare in cultivation, but grows well in the Royal Botanic Garden, Edinburgh.

Veratrum album L. incl. *V. lobelianum* Bernh., *V. oxysepalum* Turcz. and *V. grandiflorum* (Maxim.) Loes. (*Liliaceae-Melanthiaceae*) Native of Europe, from Norway, France and Spain, eastwards to the Caucasus, Siberia, China, Japan and Alaska, growing in moist, grassy, subalpine meadows and open woods, flowering in June–July. Plant with a short, stout rootstock and upright stems to 2m. Leaves hairless above, hairy beneath on the veins. Flowers 1.5–2.5cm across, whitish, yellowish or green. The distinction between green forms of this species and the E American *V. viride* Ait. is not clear. *V. viride* is said to have leaves hairy beneath, and more drooping side branches to the inflorescence. It grows in wetter places than are usual for *V. album*.

Veratrum mengtzeanum Loes. fil. syn. *V. wilsonii* C. M. Wright Native of W China, in Yunnan, Sichuan and Guizhou, growing in stony pastures, scrub and forest, flowering in June–September. Stems to 1.5m. Leaves linear

Stenanthium gramineum

Stenanthium gramineum at Edinburgh

Veratrum leaves with *Phalaris arundinacea* 'Picta'

Veratrum album (green form)

Veratrum album at Wisley

or linear-lanceolate to 50cm long, 1.5–3.5cm wide, hairless. Flowers 1.5–2.5cm across, on long, 7–15mm, pedicels; with 2 conspicuous nectaries on each petal. For moist, peaty soil in partial shade. Hardy to −20°C perhaps.

Veratrum nigrum L. fil. syn. *V. ussuriense* (Loes. fil.) Nakai   Native of Europe, from France and Poland eastwards to Siberia, N China and Korea, growing in subalpine meadows, scrub and openings in woods, flowering in June–August. Plant with short, stout rootstock and stems to 130cm. Leaves glabrous on both sides, pleated when young. Flowers 9–15mm across, blackish purple to reddish brown, smelling of rotten fruit and visited by flies. For any good, moist soil in sun or partial shade. Hardy to −25°C or less.

Veratrum taliense Loes. fil.   Native of W China, in Yunnan and Sichuan, growing in alpine meadows, flowering in June–July (to September in gardens). Stems to 1.5m. Leaves narrowly lanceolate, acuminate, 30–50cm long, to 2.5cm wide. Flowers 1.5–2.2cm across, glabrous inside and out, with a small 2-lobed nectary. Introduced by Roy Lancaster from the mountains near Dali, Yunnan.

Xerophyllum tenax (Pursh) Nutt. (*Liliaceae-Melanthiaceae*) **Indian Basket Grass**   Native of W North America, from California, in Monterey Co., north to British Columbia, and in the Rockies in Idaho and Montana, growing on dry, sunny hills and in open woods, flowering in May–August. Plant with a short, thick, rootstock and solitary upright stems to 150cm. Basal leaves to 4mm wide, with numerous narrower stem leaves. Raceme 10–60cm long. Flowers 12–20mm across. For well-drained soil in full sun. Hardy to −20°C.

Zigadenus elegans Pursh syn. *Anticlea elegans* (Pursh) Rydb. (*Liliaceae-Melanthiaceae*) Native of E North America, from New Brunswick to Vermont, New York and Missouri and in the Rockies south to New Mexico and Arizona, growing in pine woods, and moist places at up to 3000m, flowering June–August. Plant with slender bulb, forming small clumps. Stems to 90cm. Flowers 16–20mm across, with an obcordate nectary.

Veratrum taliense at Edinburgh

Xerophyllum tenax

Zigadenus elegans at Wisley

Amianthium muscaetoxicum at Harry Hay's

Paradisea liliastrum near St Luc, the Valais

Paradisea lusitanica at Sellindge, Kent

Anthericum ramosum in NW Italy

Paradisea liliastrum

Paradisea lusitanica

Anthericum ramosum L. (*Liliaceae-Asphodelaceae*)   Native of S Sweden and N France south to the Pyrenees, C Italy, Bulgaria, the Crimea and NW Turkey, growing in dry sunny meadows and open scrub, flowering in May–July. Stems to 90cm. Flowers starry, on a branched stem; petals 10–14mm long. *A. liliago* L., from Europe and S Turkey, and especially the clone 'Major', have larger petals to 22mm long, on usually unbranched stems, like a smaller-flowered *Paradisea*. Both species are easy to grow in well-drained soil in a sunny position.

Asphodeline liburnica (Scop.) Reichb. (*Asphodelaceae*)   Native of Austria and Italy east to Greece, Crete and Turkey-in-Europe, growing in dry scrub and open woods, flowering

in June–July. Stems to 100cm, few , upright, from fleshy roots. Leaves mostly on the lower half of the stem. Inflorescence simple or with 1 or 2 branches; flowers 5–6cm across. For dry, well-drained soil in full sun. Hardy to −15°C.

Asphodeline lutea (L.) Reichb.   Native of the Mediterranean area, from C Italy to Romania, Greece and Turkey east to Trabzon (and North Africa?), growing on rocky slopes and in scrub, usually on limestone, at up to 1650m in Turkey, flowering in March–June. Stems to 150cm, covered with narrow, grassy leaves. Bracts *c.*10mm wide. Flowers numerous, 20–30mm long. This is the commonest species in cultivation. For well-drained soil in full sun, and a warm position. Hardy to −15°C perhaps.

Asphodeline taurica (Pall.) Kunth   Native of Greece, the Crimea, the Caucasus, Turkey and W Syria, growing on rocky hills, in dry meadows and in open woods, at 500–2500m, flowering in May–July. Stems to 80cm, glaucous, leafy throughout. Flowers white, 2.5–3cm across. For dry, well-drained soil in full sun. Hardy to −15°C.

Asphodelus albus Mill. (*Asphodelaceae*)   Native of S & W Europe, from NW France and Portugal to Hungary and North Africa, growing in rocky places, scrub, open woods and heathland, flowering in April and May. Roots swollen and fleshy. Leaves 1–2cm wide, flat. Stems 30–100cm, usually not branched. Bracts dark brown in subsp. *albus*, whitish and papery in subsp. *villarsii*. Petals 15–20mm long. *A.*

Asphodeline liburnica

Asphodeline taurica in the Tauros Mountains, south of Kayseri, Turkey

ramosus L. is rather similar but has much-branched candelabra-like flowering stems and roots tuberous towards their ends. It is common from Spain, Portugal and North Africa, east to Greece and NW Turkey. Hardy to −15°C. *A. aestivusa* Brot. syn. *A. microcarpus* Viv. is like *A. ramosus* but fruits are obovoid, smaller, with lateral branches shorter. Tubera narrowing to a point.

Bulbinella hookeri (Colenso ex Hook.) Cheeseman syn. *Chrysobactron hookeri* Colenso ex Hook. (*Asphodelaceae*) Native of New Zealand, in North and South Islands, from Lake Taupo and Mount Egmont southwards, growing in subalpine grassland, flowering in October–January. This has become much more common in the wild because it is not grazed and can survive burning. Leaves many in a tuft, from a clump of fleshy, edible roots. Stem 25–45cm. Flowers 6–8mm across. For moist, peaty soil in full sun. Hardy to −5°C, possibly less.

Paradisea liliastrum (L.) Bertol. (*Asphodelaceae*) **St Bruno's Lily** Native of the Alps, Jura, Pyrenees and N & C Apennines, from Spain to Italy and Yugoslavia, growing in subalpine meadows, flowering in June–July. Plant forming small clumps. Leaves to 5mm wide. Stems 30–60cm, with usually 4–10 flowers, each 30–50mm long. Not easy to grow; moist but well-drained soil and a sunny position. Photographed near St Luc, in the Valais, S Switzerland. 'Major' or 'Magnificum' is a large clone or selection.

Paradisea lusitanica (Cout.) Samp. Native of N Portugal and adjacent parts of Spain, growing in woods, marshes and damp meadows, flowering in May–June. Plant forming clumps to 50cm across. Leaves to 2cm wide; stems 50–150cm, with 20–25 flowers, each 20–35mm long and 40mm across. Easily grown in rich, moist soil in sun or partial shade. Hardy to −10°C and below? This elegant species has been distributed by Dr J. Smart from his garden at Barnstaple, N Devon.

Bulbinella hookeri with meadowsweet

Asphodeline lutea at Kew

Asphodelus albus on limestone rocks near Ronda

Kniphofia caulescens at 2800m on Carlyle's Hoek, above Rhodes, NE Cape Province

Kniphofia rooperi

Kniphofia breviflora Harv. ex Baker (*Liliaceae-Asphodelaceae*) Native of South Africa in Natal and Orange Free State, in the foothills and slopes of the Drakensberg, at 1800–1900m, growing singly in thick mountain grassland, flowering in January–March. Flowers normally a uniform clear yellow, but a form with white flowers is found in Natal. *K. buchananii* Baker also has white flowers and is similar to *K. breviflora*, but with shorter flowers 3–7mm long (7–11mm in *K. breviflora*). Hardy to −15°C.

Kniphofia caulescens Baker Native of South Africa, from NE Cape Province, E Orange Free State, Lesotho and the crest of Natal Drakensberg at 1800–3000m, growing often in colonies on peaty soil overlying rock along

Kniphofia rooperi at Wisley, in autumn

Kniphofia linearifolia

Kniphofia linearifolia in a marsh at the foot of the Sani Pass, Natal

Kniphofia northiae on Bustervoedpad, NE Cape Province

Kniphofia breviflora at Mont-aux-Sources

seepage lines, flowering in January–March. This species produces short, almost woody stems, often branching. The glaucous leaves with serrulate margins and bicolorous flowers on an inflorescence 60cm tall make it easily identifiable. It is hardy to −20°C

Kniphofia linearifolia Baker syn. *K. uvaria* var. *maxima* Baker   Native of South Africa, Swaziland and Zimbabwe, this is the most widespread of all *Kniphofias* and is closely related to several other robust 'Red-hot Pokers'. From it are raised some well-known garden cultivars. It is found in large clumps in damp grassland. Flower colour is usually bright pinkish red in bud, opening to orange or yellow. The bright inflorescence is large, elongate or rhomboid in shape as opposed to globose in *K.*

uvaria (L.) Hook., and the plant is larger with stiffer leaves. *K. praecox* Baker is also similar but has narrow bracts with an acuminate tip. Hardiness variable, to −10°C perhaps, in the hardiest forms.

Kniphofia northiae Baker.   Native of South Africa in NE Cape Province, Natal and Lesotho, growing in steep, grassy gullies in wet, peaty soil, sometimes in large colonies at 1600–3000m, flowering in November–February. This is a solitary non-clump-forming species which produces thick stems. These can be more than 1m tall and are crowned by a rosette of wide, evergreen, strap-shaped leaves, up to 1.5m long × 5–10cm wide. Most forms of *K. northiae* have a U- rather than V-shaped keel as the section of the leaf. Inflorescence ovoid, dense with

pinkish-red buds, opening whitish or yellow, flowering in December–February. Hardy to −10°C.

Kniphofia rooperi (Moore) Lem.   Native of E Cape Province and S Natal, growing in marshy places near the coast, flowering in June–September, but at other times of year in gardens. Plant robust, with broad acuminate leaves. Inflorescence large and globose. Flowers 32–44mm long. *K. uvaria* is similar, but usually less robust, often with a more cylindrical inflorescence. Intermediates are found in the wild, but *K. uvaria* is commonest in the S & W Cape, flowering at any time of year. Hardy to −15°C perhaps.

Kniphofia thodei on Ngeli Mountain

Kniphofia thodei near Mont-aux-Sources

Kniphofia triangularis in Natal

Kniphofia porphyrantha

Kniphofia ritualis near Mont-aux-Sources

Kniphofia rufa (yellow form)

Kniphofia thomsonii var. *snowdenii* at Beth Chatto's

Kniphofia laxiflora Kunth (*Liliaceae-Asphodelaceae*)   Native of South Africa, mainly in Natal and Transvaal. This clump-forming species is found from sea level to 2400m on the Natal Drakensberg. It is a variable species and plants known as *K. natalensis* Baker are now included in *K. laxiflora*. Flower colour varies from yellow, yellow-green, orange, salmon and orange-red. Some plants are found on grassy slopes, others among rocks flowering in February–May.

Kniphofia parviflora Kunth   Native of South Africa, from the coast of Transkei to the mountains of Natal. A solitary species growing in marshy ground and wet grassland up to

Kniphofia laxiflora near Himeville, Natal

Kniphofia parviflora on Ngeli Mountain

1800m, flowering in January–March. Unique in South African species is the second inflorescence (flowers borne on one side of the stem only). Inflorescence narrow, 6–28cm long, with many small greenish flowers. Difficult to discern on the landscape but for its delicious fragrance, not dissimilar from that of carnations. There are a few other fragrant, small-flowered species, the most spectacular of which is *K. typhoides* Codd. This has a tall, narrow inflorescence up to 30cm long, with many fragrant purple-brown flowers. Hardy to −10°C perhaps.

Kniphofia porphyrantha Baker   Native of South Africa in NW Natal, E Orange Free State, S Transvaal and W Swaziland. This clump-forming species is usually found growing in groups in grassland at 1000m–2500m in the Orange Free State Drakensberg. The inflorescence is shortly cylindrical, almost globose, with reddish buds opening to yellow flowers tinted with pale yellowish green. A most attractive small species. Leaves smooth-margined. Flowering October–December, but later higher up in the mountains. Hardy to −15°C.

Kniphofia ritualis Codd   Native of South Africa in Orange Free State, Natal and Lesotho, and in N Transvaal on the Wolkberg, usually at 2100–3000m on the Drakensberg escarpment and outlying sandstone hills, growing in clumps in damp grassland, flowering in January–

March. Leaves strongly serrulate, flower buds orange-red, becoming greenish yellow as they open. *K. sarmentosa* (Andr.) Kunth is similar, but has orange-red flowers and leaves with smooth margins. Hardy to −10°C.

Kniphofia rufa Baker   Native of South Africa mainly along the Natal Drakensberg, growing beside mountain streams and in wet grassland at up to 2100m, flowering from November until early April. There are three distinct colour forms; coral red, white and yellow. The yellow form resembles the closely related *K. ichopensis* Baker ex Schinz. which is generally larger with longer flowers 3–4.2cm long (1.9–3cm in *K. rufa*). Both species have characteristically lax inflorescences with the individual flowers hanging down gracefully. Hardy to −15°C perhaps.

Kniphofia thodei Baker   Native of South Africa in E Orange Free State, Natal, Transkei and Lesotho, growing as solitary plants in moist grassland at 1500m–2800m, flowering in January–February. The typical form is bicolorous with reddish buds opening into waxy white flowers in a short globular inflorescence. Another form on Ngeli mountain has narrow, red, tubular flowers with a white rim at the end of the tube. Hardy to −15°C perhaps.

Kniphofia thomsonii Baker var. **snowdenii** (C. H. Wright) Marais   Native of C Africa, in Uganda and Kenya. A solitary species found in

wet grassland at 1800m–3900m, flowering in November–April. The tall, lax inflorescences carry pendulous flowers which are yellow, orange or red. This is one of several species found on the slopes of the high Central African mountains. Now considered a variety of *K. thomsonii*, var. *snowdenii* has hairs in the lower part of the flower tube whereas var. *thomsonii* is quite smooth. This plant is grown outside in sheltered areas of Britain with fair success provided the soil is not wet and cold in winter. It has the great advantage of sending up a succession of flowers from midsummer until the frost. Hardy to −10°C perhaps.

Kniphofia triangularis Kunth   Native of South Africa, from E Cape Province, E Orange Free State, C & S Natal, in the Drakensberg, and Lesotho, growing in moist, peaty grassland at 1800–2000m, flowering in January–April. A variable species with red concolorous inflorescences which now includes plants previously known as *K. nelsonii* Mast. and *K. macowanii* Baker. Plants with narrow leaves 1–3mm wide, with serrulate margins come under subsp. *triangularis*, whilst plants with broader leaves 3–10mm wide with smooth margins come under subsp. *obtusiloba* (Berger) Codd. One of the hardiest species, forming small clumps, which flowers very freely with adequate summer rain. Hardy to −15°C perhaps.

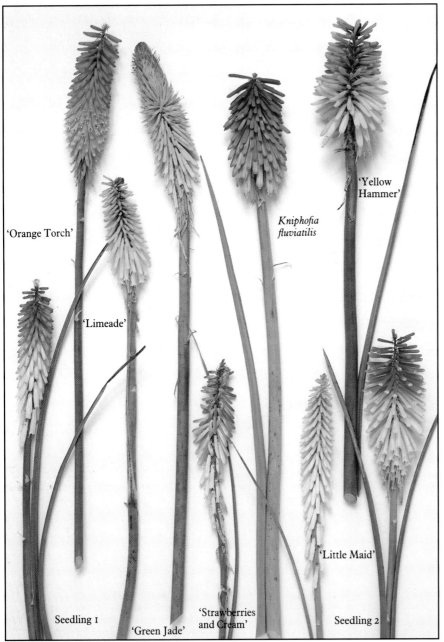

'Orange Torch'

'Limeade'

'Yellow Hammer'

Kniphofia fluviatilis

'Little Maid'

Seedling 1

'Green Jade'

'Strawberries and Cream'

Seedling 2

Specimens from Beth Chatto, 17 August. ¼ life size

Kniphofia cultivars or 'Red-hot Pokers' Most species of *Kniphofia* cross very easily and numerous garden hybrids have been raised and named. The following is a selection mostly of the smaller hybrids. All do best in moist, sandy soil in full sun and are hardy to −10°C or less for short periods.

'Brimstone' A late-flowering hybrid, with stems to 1m and a slender inflorescence. Graham Thomas reports that it is of 'imperturbable hardiness'.

'Green Jade' This is a seedling selected from plants in Sir Cedric Morris's Suffolk garden grown at the Beth Chatto Gardens in 1968. Beth Chatto has since raised other green cultivars but regards this original very highly. It is a robust, clump-forming plant producing rich-green spikes of flowers on 120cm-tall stems. Flowering in late summer.

'Ice Queen' This seedling was selected by Alan Bloom. The stems can reach 1.5m, and are produced late in the season, usually in October, until the frost. The flowers are at their palest in cool weather.

'Limeade' A hybrid of medium height, about 1.2m, raised by Beth Chatto; flowers intense green.

'Little Maid' A Beth Chatto favourite, this little *Kniphofia* was selected from her garden in the late 1960s. It is a small, clump-forming plant with narrow, grassy leaves and flower spikes up to 60cm tall. The buds are pale-green, sometimes faintly pink-tinged, opening to clear-white flowers. It flowers from late summer onwards.

'Mount Etna' Previously known as 'Wallenden's Mount Etna', named after a northern breeder. This has *K. linearifolia* in it and makes a large clump-forming plant. Tall stems to 120cm with red buds, flowers creamy; inflorescence long and dense.

'Orange Torch' A tall orange-yellow, raised by Beth Chatto. Stems to 1.5m.

'Painted Lady' A hybrid of medium height, about 1.5m, flowering in late summer. Flowers orange in bud, opening creamy white.

'Spanish Gold' A tall, stout hybrid to 1.5m; flowers green in bud, opening rich yellow.

'Strawberries and Cream' A dwarf, with stems *c.*60cm, raised by Beth Chatto.

'Yellow Hammer' A plant of medium height, *c.*1m, raised by Slieve Donard Nursery in Northern Ireland. A good, rich yellow.

Unnamed seedling 1 Called 'Red and maize yellow'; this is a seedling of medium height, *c.*1.2m.

Unnamed seedling 2 This has stems around 1.2m, with a rather short head of flowers, of clear bicolour, red and yellow.

Kniphofia fluviatilis Codd. (*Liliaceae-Asphodelacieae*) Native of South Africa in Natal, NE Orange Free State, E Transvaal. A clump-forming species usually found with its feet in water (*fluviatilis* = of rivers) growing on streamsides from 1000–2500m in the sandstone foothills and main range of the Drakensberg mountains, flowering in November–January. Inflorescence conical up to 80cm tall. The buds are orange or flame-yellow, with the long tubular flowers apricot or greenish yellow. The flowers may be 4–5cm long, longer than in most species.

Kniphofia 'Ice Queen'

Kniphofia 'Mount Etna'

Kniphofia 'Spanish Gold' at Wisley

Kniphofia 'Painted Lady' at Abbey Dore Court

Kniphofia 'Little Maid' in Beth Chatto's nursery

Kniphofia 'Brimstone' with a *Verbascum*

Kniphofia 'Green Jade' at Wisley

Kniphofia 'Underway'

Kniphofia 'Lord Roberts'

Kniphofia 'Atlanta' (*Liliaceae-Asphodelaceae*)
Found in the garden of Atlanta Hotel, Tintagel,
Cornwall. This is a large clump-forming cultivar
with a bicoloured inflorescence of red and cream
above glaucous foliage. Early summer
flowering, the stems reach 120cm high.

Kniphofia 'Erecta' An oddity in the *Kniphofia*
world with flowers which turn upside down,
giving the inflorescence a curious shape. It was
sent from France in 1903 and has been
cultivated ever since. The strong reddish-pink
colour is constant on spikes 100cm high above
large clumps of leaves.

Kniphofia 'Gold Else' Raised by Wallace in
1906. A dwarf hybrid between the endangered
K. pauciflora Baker and the more robust
globular-headed *K. citrina* Baker. A diminutive
species with small yellow inflorescences to
75cm, making small clumps which flower in
mid-summer.

Kniphofia 'Lord Roberts' A fine, old, clump-
forming cultivar close to, if not synonymous
with, 'John Benary'. The scarlet buds and
flowers create a uniformly coloured elongated
inflorescence, which may reach 120cm in
height, flowering in late summer.

Kniphofia 'Gold Else'

Kniphofia 'Atlanta'

Kniphofia 'Lye End' Flower spikes 100cm,
with long inflorescences consisting of pinkish-
red buds on top of white flowers. Raised by
A. M. Pole in 1976, flowering from July
onwards above large clumps of stiff, green leaves.

Kniphofia 'Royal Standard' Raised by
Prichard in 1921, with stout stems to 100cm
high and bicoloured pokers of scarlet buds
opening to bright-yellow flowers. A handsome
clump-forming plant which flowers in midlate
summer.

Kniphofia 'Samuel's Sensation' Justifiably
one of the best cultivars in recent years. Free-
flowering, bright-scarlet flowers with a hint of
yellow on the oldest flowers near the base. Tall,
uniformly elegant spikes which are elongate in
shape, stems 150cm high above green leaves.
Plants in large clumps, flowering from late
summer onwards.

Kniphofia 'Underway' Raised by the great
gardener Norman Hadden in Somerset between
the World Wars, probably a cultivar of *K.
triangularis*. A grassy-leaved plant which makes
small clumps with slender spikes of pale orange
to 80cm in autumn.

Kniphofia 'Erecta'

Kniphofia 'Lye End' in the monocot borders at Wisley

Kniphofia 'Royal Standard'

Kniphofia 'Samuel's Sensation' in the trial at Wisley

Hosta nakaiana 'Golden'

Hosta longipes

Hosta 'Halcyon'

Hosta rectifolia hybrid (p. 175)

Hosta fortunei 'Freising'

Specimens from Wisley, 17 August. ⅓ life size

Hosta minor

Hosta tardiflora at Washfield Nurseries

Hosta fortunei (Baker) Bailey **'Freising'** (*Liliaceae-Hostaceae*)   Native of Honshu. Leaves green 36cm × 20cm, puckered; plant forming a mound 80cm high; for shade to half-shade; flowers white, in July.

Hosta 'Halcyon'   Leaves blue-grey, 18cm × 10cm. Plant forming a large mound 30cm high. Veins 10–12. Fades in colour if it gets too much sun, so best in full shade. Flowers violet, in August.

Hosta hypoleuca Murata   Native of C Honshu, growing in crevices on damp cliffs. Leaves thin textured, 38cm × 30cm, pale green, with distinctive powdery-white coating on the underside, with 8 pairs of veins. Plant forming a mound 30cm high. For shade to partial shade. Flowers on tall stems almost white, in July.

Hosta longipes (Franch. & Sav.) Matsumura Native of Japan. Leaves dark green, 15cm × 8cm, with 7–8 pairs of veins. Plant forming a mound 15cm high. Flowers and leaf stems with dark-brown spots. For shade to three-quarters sun. Drought-tolerant. Flowers pale lilac and sometimes bluish, in late August–September.

Hosta minor (Baker) Nakai   Native of S Japan and Korea. Leaves 8cm × 5cm, winged, broadly ovate, dark green, with 4 or 5 pairs of veins, petioles winged. For shade to half-shade. Flowers bluish purple.

Hosta nakaiana Maekawa **'Golden'**   Native of Honshu and Kyushu. Leaves heart-shaped, 10cm × 5cm, golden green with wavy edge, 5–6 pairs of veins. Plant forming a mound *c*.46cm high. Shade to three-quarters sun. Flowers pale purple, in August.

Hosta tardiflora (Irving) Stearn   Not known in the wild. Leaves 10–15cm long, 3–4cm wide, tapering into the stalk; deep green, with 4–5 pairs of veins. Flowers late, with a dense head of flowers 4–4.5cm long.

Hosta ventricosa Stearn   Native of China. Leaves 18cm × 12cm, heart-shaped, pointed, dark glossy green, with 8–9 pairs of veins. Plant forming a mound 60cm high. For shade to half shade. Inflorescence tall, to 90cm, rising far above the leaves; without vestigial leaves; flowers dark violet, in August.

Hosta ventricosa 'Aureomaculata' Henson syn. *H. ventricosa* 'Maculata'   Leaves with a yellowish-green centre with a dark-green margin, but the central colour darkens in the summer until the leaves are uniform dark green. For shade to half-shade. Flowers violet, in August.

Hosta ventricosa 'Aureo-marginata'   Leaves 18cm × 15cm, heart-shaped, twisted, with an irregular yellowish margin which matures white. Plant forming a mound 45cm high, and persisting until the first frosts. Shade to three-quarters sun. Flowers mauve, in July.

Hosta ventricosa in the Wild Garden at Wisley

Hosta ventricosa 'Aureomaculata'

Hosta species on a wet cliff in C Honshu

Hosta hypoleuca in Honshu

Hosta ventricosa 'Aureo-marginata'

Hosta 'Halcyon'

Hosta fortunei
'Albo-marginata'

Hosta fortunei
'Spinners'

Hosta fortunei
'Goldbrook'

Hosta fortunei
'Francie'

Hosta
'Northern
Halo'

Hosta sieboldiana
'Frances Williams'

Hosta sieboldiana
'Thomas Hogg'

Hosta crispula

Specimens from Goldbrook Nurseries, 20 August. ⅓ life size

Hosta crispula Maekawa (*Liliaceae-Hostaceae*)   Leaves 10cm × 20cm, oval with a long point often twisted back underneath, dark green with a broad white margin and wavy edges, with 7–8 pairs of veins. Wide mound up to 40cm tall, but subject to damage from cold winds. Flowers 30 or more on a green scape, pale lavender. Shade to half-shade, flowering in late June–July.

Hosta 'Fall Emerald'   Introduced by Alex Summers. Close to *H. sieboldii* with large, bright-green leaves which hold their colour longer. Flowers in June–July.

Hosta fortunei 'Albo-marginata'   Leaves sage green with a white edge. Mound 35cm high. Stays in good condition until the first frost. Shade to three-quarters sun. Flowers lavender, in July.

Hosta fortunei 'Albopicta'   Leaves bright yellow, edged with pale green, gradually fading until the yellow is nearly the same as the edge by mid-summer. Mound 60cm high. Shade to three-quarters sun. Flowers elegant, pale lavender, in July–early August.

Hosta fortunei 'Aureo-marginata'   Leaves with a distinct wide golden edge. Shade to three-quarters sun.

Hosta fortunei 'Francie'   Introduced by Klopping. Leaves 15cm × 13cm, forest-green with white margins. Rapid grower to mound of 30cm high. Shade to three-quarters sun. Flowers lavender in August–early September.

Hosta fortunei 'Goldbrook'   Registered by Mrs S. Bond. Leaves mid-green with a wide creamy white margin and a rather wavy edge. Shade to three-quarters sun. Flowers violet, in July.

Hosta fortunei 'Spinners'   Registered by Peter Chappell. Leaves with a very wide irregular white margin. Shade to three-quarters sun. Flowers violet, in July.

Hosta lancifolia (Thunb.) Engler   Native of Japan. Leaves lance-shaped 15cm × 5cm, dark glossy green, with 4–5 pairs of veins. Mound

Hosta fortunei 'Albopicta'

Hosta fortunei 'Aureo-marginata'

30cm high. Needs shade, or not more than half-shade at most. Flowers purple, in August.

Hosta 'Northern Halo'   Registered by Walters Gardens in 1984. *H. sieboldiana* 'Elegans' sport. Leaves 26cm × 30cm, blue-green with an irregular creamy white margin, slightly cupped upward, with puckering between the 14 pairs of veins. Shade to half-shade. Flowers on one-sided scapes, white with a hint of purple, in late June–July.

Hosta sieboldiana (Hook.) Engler & Prantl Native of Honshu. Leaves large and sumptuous, bluish grey-green 30cm × 35cm, heavily puckered with a lovely bloom at first, forming large mound. Shade to three-quarters sun. Flowers white with just a hint of violet on short stems, in July.

Hosta sieboldiana 'Elegans'   Leaves round, bluish, heavily puckered, 30cm × 35cm, forming a magnificent clump. Shade to half-shade. Flowers white with just a hint of lilac on rather short stems that nestle attractively among the leaves, in July.

Hosta sieboldiana 'Frances Williams' Leaves bluish green with wide irregular yellowish margins 36cm × 20cm, puckered. Forms a magnificent mound 80cm high. Shade to half-shade. Flowers pale lavender, in July.

Hosta sieboldii 'Alba' syn. *H. albomarginata* var. *alba*   The word 'alba' refers to the colour of the flowers which are white. Leaves bright green, 13cm × 4cm, with 3–4 pairs of veins. Mound 30cm high. Shade to half-shade. Flowers white, on rather tall scapes, in August.

Hosta 'Thomas Hogg' syn. *H. undulata* 'Albomarginata'   Leaves lanceolate, green, with an irregular creamy white margin which continues down the stem, 20cm × 8cm. Mound 30cm high. Shade to half-shade. Flowers lilac, on tall scapes in late June–July.

Hosta 'True Blue'   Registered by Paul Aden. Leaves broad, 20cm × 18cm, a good blue-green, puckered, with 11–14 pairs of veins. Keeps its colour well in sun, a quarter to three-quarters sun. Flowers delicate mauve with white edges, in July–early August.

Hosta 'Fall Emerald'

Hosta sieboldiana

Hosta sieboldiana 'Elegans'

Hosta sieboldiana 'Frances Williams'

Specimens from the Savill Gardens, Windsor, 10 July. ⅕ life size

Hosta sieboldii 'Alba'

Hosta 'True Blue'

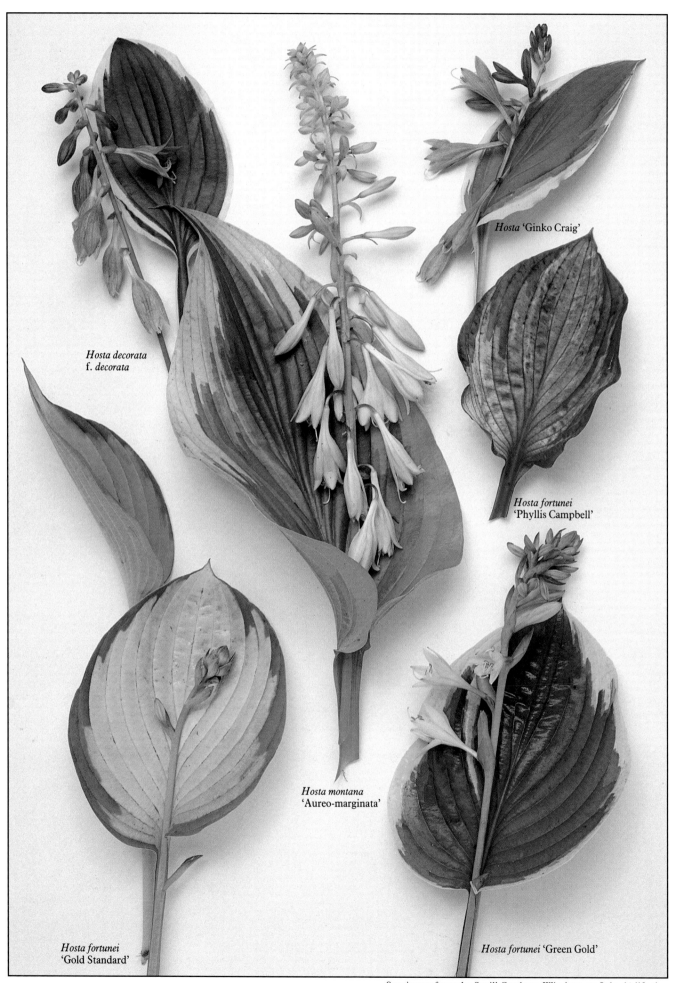

Hosta decorata
f. decorata

Hosta 'Ginko Craig'

Hosta fortunei
'Phyllis Campbell'

Hosta montana
'Aureo-marginata'

Hosta fortunei
'Gold Standard'

Hosta fortunei 'Green Gold'

Specimens from the Savill Gardens, Windsor, 17 July. ½ life size

Hosta montana 'Aureo-marginata' at Wisley

Hosta fortunei 'Gold Standard' at Goldbrook Plants, Suffolk

Hosta 'Zounds' at Goldbrook Plants, Suffolk

Hosta 'Sun and Substance' at Goldbrook Plants, Suffolk

Hosta decorata Bailey f. **decorata** (*Liliaceae-Hostaceae*) Leaves 8cm × 13cm, oval, pointed with a narrow, white, slightly wavy margin, with 5–6 pairs of veins. The variegated form came to Europe before the all-green form, which is called *H. decorata* f. *normalis*. Plant 26cm high. Stem tall with dark-lilac flowers in July–early August; the seed heads are good for flower arranging. Shade to half-sun.

Hosta fortunei '**Gold Standard**' Introduced by Pauline Banyai in 1976. Yellow leaves with green edges or tending to green in the shade, blotched, 18cm × 13cm. Plant 60cm high; a rapid grower which gives the best colour when mature. A quarter to three quarters sun. Flowers pale lavender, in July–early August.

Hosta fortunei '**Green Gold**' Leaves with a satin sheen, heart-shaped, with a gold margin

which fades gradually with age. A quarter to three-quarters sun. Flowers pale lavender, in July–early August.

Hosta fortunei '**Phyllis Campbell**' Leaves green, firm, not wavy edged, splashed with yellow in the centre. Shade to half-sun. Flowers lavender, in July.

Hosta '**Ginko Craig**' Introduced by Alex Craig-Summers, who reputedly found it in a Japanese market. It is named for his Japanese wife. Leaves frosted green with a narrow white edge. Makes an attractive flat rosette even when young, in older plants the leaves are larger. Flowers good, purple on tall stems.

Hosta montana Maekawa '**Aureo-marginata**' Leaves large, 35cm × 26cm, elongated, heart-shaped, rich green with irregular yellow

margins, deeply veined with 13–17 pairs. Plant 65cm tall, 100cm wide. Shade to three-quarters sun. Stems 100cm with densely grouped pale-lavender flowers in July–August.

Hosta '**Sun and Substance**' Registered by Paul Aden in 1980. Leaves strong golden yellow, more greenish if not in strong light, 30cm × 26cm, thick and tough. Plant up to 75cm across, pest-resistant. Flowers lavender, in August–early September.

Hosta '**Zounds**' Introduced by Paul Aden. Leaves golden metallic colour 20cm × 18cm. Plant up to 35cm. A quarter to three-quarters sun. Flowers pale lavender, in July–early August.

HOSTA

Hosta helonioides 'Albo-picta'

Hosta 'Kabitan'

Hosta 'Shiro-Kabitan'

Hosta sieboldii

Hosta kikutii var. polyneura

'Brian Martin'

H. sieboldii 'Emerald Isle'

Hosta sieboldii 'Inaho'

'Gloriosa'

Hosta longissima

Hosta undulata var. univittata

Hosta capitata

Specimens from Goldbrook Plants, 20 August. ⅓ life size

Hosta capitata (Koidzumi) Nakai (*Liliaceae-Hostaceae*)   Heart-shaped green leaves, 13cm × 8cm, with wavy edges, 6–8 pairs of veins, forming a 26cm-high mound. Shade to three-quarters sun. Flowers purple on a purple dotted, ridged stem, in July–August.

Hosta fortunei (Baker) Bailey   Nothing definite is known of its origin and it probably should really be regarded as a hybrid. Leaves green, 18cm × 12cm, with 9–11 pairs of veins, edges rather wavy. A rapid grower to a mound 35cm high. Shade to three-quarters sun. Flowers profuse, violet, in July.

Hosta 'Green Fountain'   Registered by Paul Aden in 1979. A cultivar of *H. kikutii*. Leaves 25cm × 8cm, shiny green in a dense mound 90cm high. Pest-resistant and sun-tolerant. Flowers lavender, in August–September.

Hosta helonioides Maekawa **'Albo-picta'** Leaves elongated, 18cm × 3cm, bright green with a broad, creamy yellow margin, with 3–4 pairs of veins. Plant 26cm high. Flower stems tall, up to 60cm, with horizontal purple-striped flowers. Shade to three-quarters sun, flowering in August-early September. *H.* 'Brian Martin' is very similar, and has broader leaves with broad white or cream margin.

Hosta kikutii Maekawa   Native of Kyushu. Leaves 23cm × 3cm, glossy green, with 8–10 veins, stems short. Plant 30cm high, drought-resistant. Shade to three-quarters sun. The white flowers are on a tall, light-green stem, with bird-head-shaped bracts covering the buds, flowers in August.

Hosta longissima (Honda) Honda   Native of W Honshu. Leaves very narrow, 18cm × 2cm, with 3 pairs of veins, forming an arching mound 15cm high. This is a bog *Hosta*, and is flood-tolerant but not drought-tolerant. Shade to half-sun. Flowers few on each stem, pale violet, in September.

Hosta plantaginea (Lam.) Asch. var. **grandiflora** (Sieb.) A. & G.   Native of China. Leaves 20cm × 30cm, cordate, large without bloom, glossy, bright yellowish green. Flowers white, scented, large with vestigial leaves on a 75cm-high scape, in August. This plant will stand quite a lot of sun. *H. plantaginea* 'Honeybells' has pinkish flower buds and a faint pint flush to the flowers. Flowers late August–September.

Hosta 'Royal Standard' at Wisley

Hosta plantaginea var. grandiflora

***Hosta rectifolia* 'Tallboy'** Named by Sir Eric Savill in 1968, registered in 1983. Possibly *H. rectifolia* × *H. ventricosa*. Leaves 23cm × 41cm, bright green, making a 75cm upright mound. Shade to three-quarters sun. Flowers dark lilac, about 20 on each; 90cm-tall scape, with vestigial leaves, in August–September.

***Hosta* 'Royal Standard'** Registered by Wayside Gardens. Leaves heart-shaped, 26cm × 18cm, rich green, shiny, deeply veined and puckered with wavy edges, forming a mound 60cm high. Flowers, like its parent *H. plantaginea*, are white and fragrant, in August–September.

***Hosta* 'Shade Fanfare'** A sport of *H.* 'Flamboyant', introduced by Paul Aden. Leaves come early and are a good golden green in the centre, with creamy margins 20cm × 15cm. Plant 50cm high. For shade to full sun, but colours best in sun. Rapid grower, pest-resistant. Flowers beautiful lavender, in July–early August.

Hosta sieboldii (Paxton) Ingram syn. *H. albomarginata* (Hook.) Ohwi Leaves 13cm × 4cm, wavy, dark green with a narrow white edge, with 3–4 pairs of veins. Plant 30cm high. Likes wet soils, shade to half-sun. Flowers violet, in August.

***Hosta sieboldii* 'Emerald Isle'** Has more pointed leaves than *sieboldii*. Shade to half-sun. Flowers white, in August.

***Hosta sieboldii* 'Inaho'** syn. *H. tardiva* hort. non Nakai Leaves 13cm × 4cm, moss-green blotched with golden green. Shade to half-sun. Flowers purple, in August.

***Hosta sieboldii* 'Kabitan'** Maekawa Leaves small, yellow with a green margin, lance-shaped, 13cm × 3cm, undulate on the margins. Shade to three-quarters sun. Flowers whitish with purple veins, in August. 'Shiro-Kabitan' has leaves white, with a green margin.

Hosta undulata (O. & D.) Bailey var. **univittata** (Miq.) Hyland. Leaves small, 4cm wide, twisted towards the tip, with a white median stripe surrounded by blue-green, both colours run down the wavy stem wings. Plant 45cm high. Shade to half-sun. Flowers rich lilac, in July.

Hosta fortunei

Hosta plantaginea 'Honeybells'

Hosta rectifolia 'Tallboy' at Wisley

Hosta 'Shade Fanfare'

Hosta 'Green Fountain' at Goldbrook Plants, Suffolk

Pontederia cordata at Wisley

Sagittaria latifolia

Dianella tasmanica

Astelia nervosa Hook. fil. (*Liliaceae-Asteliaceae*)   Native throughout New Zealand, growing in moist places in lowland and subalpine forest, flowering in October–January. Plant forming tussocks of stiff silvery leaves, to 200cm long, usually *c*.60cm in gardens. Flowers on a short, branched inflorescence to 60cm, green or reddish, scented. Fruits berry-like, orange, in yellow cups formed by the persistent petals, but seldom produced in gardens. For moist, peaty or clay soil in shade or partial shade. Hardy to −10°C, but best in moist, coastal gardens in Europe and NW North America.

Commelina tuberosa L. (*Commelinaceae*)   Native of Mexico, flowering in mid-summer. Plant with fleshy, swollen roots. Stems to 75cm. Leaves linear, *c*.2.5cm across; flowers usually closing by evening. For a warm position in full sun. Hardy to −10°C, provided the rootstock is protected from freezing.

Dianella tasmanica Hook. (*Liliaceae-Phorminaceae*)   Native of SE Australia, in New South Wales, Victoria and Tasmania, growing in cool, damp, shady forest, flowering in August–October, fruiting in January–February, or spring and summer in the north. Plant forming clumps of stiff leaves to 120cm tall, 3cm wide, with rough edges. Flowering stems to 150cm. Flowers pale blue; anthers brownish yellow. Berries 1–2cm long.For a sheltered position in shade with a peaty soil. Hardy to −10°C for short periods.

Phormium cookianum Le Jolis syn. *P. colensoi* Hook. fil. (*Phormiaceae*) **Mountain Flax, Wharariki**   Native of New Zealand, and naturalized on the Scilly Isles, growing on coastal rocks and cliffs, and in the mountains at up to 1500m, on rocky outcrops, flowering in December–January. Plant with soft, lax leaves

to 1.6m long, 3.5–6.5cm wide. Flowering stems 1.3–1.6m. Flowers yellowish; fruits hanging and usually twisted. Recommended for coastal planting in exposed sites. Hardy to −10°C perhaps.

Phormium tenax J. R. & G. Forst. **New Zealand Flax, Harakeke**   Native of New Zealand and Norfolk Island, and naturalized in W Ireland, SW England and the Azores, as well as on other Atlantic Islands such as Tristan da Cunha where it has become a pest, growing in lowland marshes and bogs, flowering in November–January, or July–August in the north. Leaves tough and leathery, evergreen, to 3m long, 5–12.5cm wide. Inflorescence to 5m. Flowers 2.5–5cm long. Fruits erect. For any deep soil that does not dry out, but most striking in a warm, wet and sheltered position. Hardy to −10°C or less for short periods.

Phormium cultivars   There are numerous named varieties of *Phormium*, many of hybrid origin between the two species. Most were grown by Duncan and Davis in New Zealand and introduced by them to Europe.
'Dazzler'   A hybrid with particularly brightly coloured leaves, raised by W. B. Brockie in *c*.1940.
'Sundowner'   A colour form of *P. tenax*, with good greyish purple leaves.
Other colour forms available are indicated by their names: 'Cream Delight', 'Apricot Queen', 'Bronze Baby', 'Yellow Wave', etc.

Pontederia cordata L. (*Pontederiaceae*) **Pickerelweed**   Native of E North America, from Prince Edward Island west to S Ontario, south to N Florida, Missouri and Oklahoma, growing in shallow water, flowering in June–November. Plant forming spreading patches by a thick, creeping rhizome. Stems fleshy to 120cm. Leaves varying from broadly ovate to

linear-lanceolate, cordate or truncate at the base, sometimes with submerged, linear leaves only. Flowers 8mm long, blue, in a dense spike. For shallow water by a pond or stream. Hardy to −25°C or less.

Sagittaria latifolia Willd. (*Alismataceae*) **Wapato, Arrowhead**   Native of North America, from New Brunswick to S British Columbia, south to South Carolina, Alabama, Louisiana, Arizona and California, growing in shallow water in lakes and rivers, flowering in July–September. Plant with a tuberous rootstock and upright stems to 150cm. Leaves variable in shape, sagittate, usually with a broad main lobe and smaller, narrower basal lobes. Flowers white, with petals unmarked; stamens yellow. For wet soil or shallow water. Hardy to −20°C or less. This is the common North American Arrowhead; the European differs in its usually narrower leaves, flowers with purple blotches at the base of each petal, and purple anthers.

Tradescantia virginiana L. (*Commelinaceae*) **Spiderwort**   Native of E North America, from Connecticut east to Wisconsin, south to NW Georgia, Tennessee and Missouri, growing in woods, scrub and meadows, flowering in April–July. Stems many, to 35cm, from a tufted rootstock with fleshy roots. Petals 12–18mm long, blue to pink or white, on pedicels 1.5–3.5cm long.

Tradescantia × andersoniana Ludwig & Rohweder   Most of the cultivars are said to belong to this hybrid group, between *T. virginiana* and other species, of which there are ten in E North America. Colours vary from almost blue to magenta, nearly red, pink and white. They all require good, moist soil in sun or light shade and flower from midsummer to autumn. Hardy to −20°C or less.

Phormium 'Sundowner'

Phormium cookianum

Phormium tenax naturalized in Connemara, near Ballynahinch

Phormium 'Dazzler'

Tradescantia virginiana

Commelina tuberosa

Astelia nervosa

Tradescantia × *andersoniana*

Yucca filamentosa 'Ivory'

Yucca filamentosa

Yucca 'Vittorio Emmanuele'

Beschorneria yuccoides

Yucca gloriosa 'Variegata' at Wisley

Beschorneria yuccoides Hook. subsp. **dekosteriana** (C. Koch) Garcia-Mendoza (*Agavaceae*) Native of Mexico, in Hidalgo and Veracruz states, growing in *Liquidambar* and *Alnus* woodland in the mountains, flowering in May–June. Plant forming large clumps. Leaves 60–100cm long, green or glaucous. Inflorescence up to 2.5m, reddish. Flowers 3.5–6cm long, green, tubular. For any good soil in sun or partial shade. Hardy to −5°C.

Yucca filamentosa L. (*Agavaceae*) Native of E North America, from S New Jersey to Florida, growing on dunes, rocky bluffs, sandy fields and dry pine forest along the coastal plain, flowering in June–September. Plant with a short, mostly underground stem. Leaves usually hooded below the spine, oblanceolate, with curled threads on the margins. Inflorescence 1.5–2m. Flowers 5–7cm long. **'Ivory'** A short form with stems to 1.2m, very free-flowering, raised by G. R. Jackman. **'Variegata'** Leaves striped with pink and cream. For dry, well-drained soil in full sun. Hardy to −20°C.

Yucca flaccida Haworth Native of E North America, from North Carolina to Alabama, especially along the Blue Ridge and Appalachian mountains, growing in dry, stony places, flowering in May–July. Plant stemless. Leaves tapering from base to apex, with straight or slightly curled threads. Flowering stem hairy to 1.5m. Flowers 5–8cm long. For well-drained, sandy soil in full sun. Hardy to −15°C.

Yucca gloriosa L. **'Variegata'** Native of SE North America, from South Carolina to NE Florida, growing on sand dunes and stony places by the sea, flowering in July–August. Plant with a sometimes branched woody trunk to 8m, usually up to *c.*1m. Leaves 40–60cm long, 5–7.5cm wide, with a sharp, stiff point. Flowers to 5.5cm long, often tinged purple. For a dry, sunny and sheltered position. Hardy to −25°C perhaps.

Yucca recurvifolia Salisb. Native of E North America, from Georgia to Missouri and E Louisiana, growing on dunes on the coastal plains, flowering in July–September. Stems in clumps, woody, to 5m, usually less than 2m. Leaves soft, recurved towards the apex, *c.*5cm wide. Inflorescence to 120cm. Flowers 5–7cm long. For a warm, dry position in well-drained soil. Hardy to −15°C perhaps.

Yucca 'Vittorio Emmanuele' Close to *Y. gloriosa*, with exceptionally heavily marked flowers. Similar purplish-flowered cultivars have been raised in Tashkent Botanic Garden.

Yucca whipplei Torr. **Our Lord's Candle** Native of S California, north to Monterey Co., and in Baja California, growing on dry, grassy hills and in scrub and chaparral, flowering in April–June. Plant stemless, often monocarpic, with a bulbous base, but in subsp. *percursa* suckering to form young plants, and in subsp. *caespitosa* and subsp. *intermedia* forming clumps of rosettes. Leaves to 100cm long, 10mm wide, with a terminal spine 1–2cm long. Inflorescence 1.5–2.5m, sometimes to 3.5m. Flowers pendent 2.5–3.5cm long, often purplish outside, sweet-scented. For a warm, sunny, sheltered position in full sun. Hardy to −10°C for short periods; has survived to flowering outside at Kew and at Bodnant in North Wales. *Yucca newberryi* McKelvey from NW Arizona is very similar.

Yucca filamentosa 'Variegata'

Yucca whipplei near New Cuyama, California

Yucca flaccida

Yucca recurvifolia

Agapanthus campanulatus subsp. *patens* on Mont-aux-Sources, Orange Free State

Agapanthus campanulatus subsp. *patens*

Agapanthus caulescens

Agapanthus nutans 'Albus'

Agapanthus inapertus subsp. *hollandii*

Agapanthus campanulatus subsp. *patens* F.
M. Leighton (*Liliaceae-Alliaceae*)   See p. 183.

Agapanthus caulescens Spreng.   Native of
Swaziland, with subsp. *angustifolius* in NE
Natal, in the Ubombo area, growing in grassy
places, flowering in January–February. Plant
with distinct leek-like stems to the leaves, with
short, lower leaves to 15cm, and upper leaves,
usually stiff, to 60cm and 4cm or more broad.
Inflorescence to 130cm, with a dense head of
spreading and drooping flowers. Flowers 3–5cm
long, with the tube 1–2cm, and wide-spreading
petals, recurved in subsp. *gracilis* Leighton.
This last is similar to *A. campanulatus*, though
separated in the wild, and usually with larger
flowers in a more crowded umbel. For any good
soil in full sun. Hardy to −10°C perhaps.

Agapanthus dyeri Leighton   Native of the
Transvaal, in the Blaauberg, on the Mohlakeng
plateau, and of S Mozambique, at *c*.1800m
perhaps, flowering in January–February. Plant
clump-forming, with stems to 90cm. Leaves
deciduous, to 1.5cm broad. Flowers in umbels
of *c*.35, ascending in bud, but more or less
hanging when open. The tube 1.3–1.4cm long,
sometimes curved; the segments to 11mm long,
usually rather pale blue. Like *A. inapertus* but
with a shorter tube and more spreading lobes.
For well-drained soil in a warm position. Hardy
to −10°C perhaps, as it survives at Kew.

Agapanthus inapertus Beauv. subsp. **hollandii**
Leighton   Native of the E Transvaal in the
Lydenberg area. This differs from the other
subspecies in its narrower but more wide-
spreading petals, which are generally blue.
Hardy to −10°C perhaps.

Agapanthus inapertus Beauv. subsp.
intermedius Leighton   Native of the Transvaal
and Swaziland, mainly on the periphery of the
area of the other subspecies; flowers 2.5–4.5cm
long, opening at the mouth, with the lobes and
tube about equal. It seems likely that it is the
result of hybridization with other species in the
wild, and the photograph shown here, of a
garden plant, is possibly another such hybrid.

Agapanthus inapertus subsp. **pendulus** (L.
Bol.) Leighton   Native of the E Transvaal in
the Lydenberg, Belfast and Dullstroom areas,
often above 2000m, growing in grassy veldt or
in clearings in forest, flowering in January–
February. Plant forming clumps of rather
upright deciduous leaves, 2–3cm across.
Flowering stems tall, to 180cm. Flowers fleshy,
hanging, 2.5–4cm long, the tube making up ⅔
of the flower, often purplish and sometimes very
dark in colour; the segments are barely open at
the mouth. For any good garden soil. Hardy to
−10°C, or less with protection. The dark-
coloured forms of this species are particularly
fine.

Agapanthus nutans Leighton   Native of
scattered localities in Natal and C Transvaal,
growing on grassy slopes and cliff ledges,
flowering in January–February. Plant forming
clumps; leaves usually erect, often glaucous,
20–50cm long, to 4cm broad. Inflorescence to
90cm, usually not greatly exceeding the leaves.
Umbels few or many-flowered. Flowers blue or
white in 'Albus' (shown here): tube 1.3–2.7cm
long, segments 2.2–3.3cm, spreading gradually
to the mouth, not reflexed. For any good soil in
full sun. Hardy to −15°C, or less with
protection. Generally a rather low plant with
broad leaves and long, slender flowers without
reflexed petals.

Agapanthus nutans

Agapanthus dyeri at Kew

Agapanthus inapertus subsp. *intermedius*

Agapanthus inapertus subsp. *pendulus* in Natal

Agapanthus inapertus subsp. *pendulus*

Agapanthus
'Buckingham Palace'

Agapanthus
'Rosemary'

Agapanthus
'Luly'

Agapanthus
comptoni subsp.
longitubus

Agapanthus
'Diana'

Agapanthus campanulatus
subsp. *campanulatus*

Agapanthus campanulatus
subsp. *patens*

Agapanthus 'Molly Fenwick'

Specimens from the Savill Gardens, Windsor, 28 August. ⅓ life size

Agapanthus 'Ben Hope'

Agapanthus 'Loch Hope' at the Savill Garden, Windsor

Agapanthus campanulatus F. M. Leighton subsp. **campanulatus** (*Liliaceae-Alliaceae*) Native of South Africa, in Natal, and N Cape Province, at no great altitude, growing in grassy and rocky places, often among bracken and in moist, peaty soil, flowering in December–February, or July–August in the northern hemisphere. Plant forming large clumps of thick, fleshy roots in gardens, often more or less solitary in the wild. Leaves deciduous, up to 2.5cm wide, forming a short leek-like stalk. Flowering stems up to 1m or more. Flowers 2–3.5cm long, blue, or white in 'Albus', which is most beautiful. Petals spreading to 45°. For rich, well-drained, sandy soil in full sun, with water in summer. Hardy to −15°C, or less if the rhizomes are protected. *Agapanthus campanulatus* subsp. *patens* F.M. Leighton differs in its more widely spreading petals and short tube. It is found at higher altitudes, up to 2400m, throughout the Drakensberg and north to the Traansvaal. Stems 40–70cm. Probably the hardiest of the species, to −15°C, at least.

Agapanthus comptoni F. M. Leighton subsp. **longitubus** F. M. Leighton   Native of South Africa, in E Cape Province, on the coast around East London, Port Elizabeth, and Grahamstown, flowering in January–February. Plant forming clumps in gardens. Leaves evergreen, to 2cm across. Flowers up to 6.5cm long, with the tube 2–2.5cm, in a few to many-flowered, but not dense, inflorescence, on a stem to 100cm. For well-drained soil, in full sun, with water in summer. Hardy to −10°C, perhaps less.

Agapanthus 'Headbourne Hybrids'   Most hardy (z.6–9) *Agapanthus* are sold under the name 'Headbourne Hybrids'. These were raised by the Hon. Lewis Palmer in his garden at Headbourne Worthy, Hampshire, in the late 1940s from seeds which originated in the *Agapanthus* collection in Kirstenbosch Botanic Gardens in Cape Town. He raised around 300 seedlings, all of which proved to be hybrids, and from these selected the named varieties listed below. The best were sent for trial at Wisley, and judged there over a period of several years, but, good though they are, they are not generally available because they are slow to propagate. Seedlings called 'Headbourne

Agapanthus campanulatus 'Albus'

Agapanthus 'Bressingham Blue'

Hybrids' are usually deciduous like *A. campanulatus*, but with larger flowers. Named varieties shown here were all raised by Lewis Palmer, with the exception of 'Bressingham Blue', which was raised by Alan Bloom.
'Ben Hope'   Height to 1.2m.
'Bressingham Blue'   Height 70–80cm. An exceptionally deep blue, with rather tubular flowers, showing the influence of *A. inapertus* subsp. *pendulus*.
'Buckingham Palace'   Height to 1.8m.
'Delft'   Height to 1m.
'Diana' (AM 1977)   Height to 45cm.
'Loch Hope' (AM 1977)   Height to 1.5m.
'Luly' (FCC 1977)   Height to 75cm.
'Molly Fenwick'   Height to 75cm.
'Rosemary' (AM 1977)   Height to 1.4m.

Agapanthus 'Delft'

Hemerocallis middendorfii

Hemerocallis flava

Hemerocallis minor

Hemerocallis yezoensis

Hemerocallis flava 'Major'

Hemerocallis forrestii

Specimens from Beth Chatto's, 9 June. ¼ life size

Hemerocallis dumortieri at the Royal Botanic Garden, Edinburgh

Hemerocallis altissima Stout (*Liliaceae*)   The plant shown here appears to be close to *H. thunbergii*, with tall stems to 1.5m and pale-yellow, long-tubed flowers, flowering in July–September. Several cultivars have been raised from this, now incorporating different flower colours on strong slender stems up to 1.8m. Examples are 'Autumn Minaret', golden yellow; 'Challenger', brick-red with a yellow throat; and 'Statuesque' with pale-yellow flowers of a good shape.

Hemerocallis citrina Baroni   Native of China, but wild distribution uncertain, flowering in gardens in June–July. Plant forming large clumps of leaves 70–80cm long. Flowering stems longer than the leaves. Many-flowered (20–65 flowers). Flowers 9–12cm long, with narrow, lemon-yellow petals, scented, opening at night; tube ⅓ the length of the flower. For any good soil with ample water in summer. Hardy to −20°C or less.

Hemerocallis dumortieri Morr.   Native of Japan in Hokkaido and N & C Honshu, E Siberia, NE China and Korea, growing in meadows in the mountains, flowering in May–June. Plant forming large clumps of flopping leaves. Flowering stems 25–50cm, as long as, or slightly shorter than, the leaves. Flowers few, ascending, with very short stalks hidden by broad bracts, 5–7cm long with a tube *c*.1cm long. Inner petals less than 2cm, usually *c*.1.2cm wide. For any good, moist soil in sun or partial shade. Hardy to −20°C or less.

Hemerocallis exaltata Stout   Native of Tobishima Island, off the west coast of N Honshu, growing in meadows, flowering in June–July. Plant similar to *H. middendorfii* (q.v.), but with taller stems to 1m or more, and longer pedicels, almost forming an umbel. Flowers orange-yellow. For any good, moist soil. Hardy to −15°C, possibly less.

Hemerocallis flava L.   Native of E Siberia and N China, growing in grassy places, flowering in May–June. Roots tuberous, with spreading rhizomes. Leaves 50–60cm long, 1–1.4cm wide. Flowers scented, 7–8cm long, or larger in 'Major'; tube about ¼ the length of the flower. Capsule large, broadly elliptic. For any good, moist soil in sun or partial shade. Hardy to −25°C or less.

Hemerocallis forrestii Diels   Native of SW China, especially in the Lijiang range at *c*.3000m growing in grassy places, flowering in June–July. Roots cylindrical, swollen towards

Hemerocallis fulva var. *littorea*

Hemerocallis fulva 'Kwanso'

the ends. Leaves rather lush and broad to 1.5cm wide. Inflorescence about equalling the leaves, or shorter. Flowers *c*.7cm long, with the tube less than ¼ the length. Anthers blackish. For moist soil in sun or partial shade.

Hemerocallis fulva L.   Probably native of China and Japan but not known in the wild state (all plants are sterile triploids); widely naturalized in Europe and North America by spread of pieces of rhizome. Plant forming large clumps of bright, pale leaves. Stems to 120cm. Flowers 7–10cm, the tube about 2.5cm long, brownish orange with darker markings inside. 'Kwanso' has double flowers, very strongly marked inside. For any position in rich soil or near water. Hardy to −20°C or less.

Hemerocallis fulva L. var. **littorea** Mak. Native of Japan, in W Honshu and Kyushu, growing in grassy places near the sea, flowering in August–October. Plant similar to *H. fulva*, but smaller with leaves dark green, and narrower, up to 15mm wide. Flowers 10–12cm long, the tube 1.5–2cm long. Inner petals subacute, about 2cm wide. Seeds fertile. For any good soil in full sun. Hardy to −15°C perhaps. This may be one of the diploid parents of *H. fulva* itself.

Hemerocallis middendorfii Trautv. & Mey. Native of Japan, in Hokkaido and of E Siberia, N China and Korea, growing in mountain meadows, flowering in June–July, later than *H. dumortieri*. Plant forming large clumps. Flowering stems to 70cm or more, longer than the leaves. Flowers 8–10cm long, orange-yellow, the inner petals 2–2.5cm wide, obtuse.

Hemerocallis minor Mill.   Native of N China, growing in scrub on rocky hillsides, flowering in May–June. Recorded by Roy Lancaster growing along the Great Wall north of Beijing. Roots not tuberous, slender, cylindrical and fibrous. Rhizomes not spreading. Leaves narrow, 30–45cm long, 5–9mm wide. Flowers 5–7cm with a long tube, more than ¼ the length of the flower. Capsule narrowly elliptic. For moist, sandy soil in full sun. Hardy to −25°C or less.

Hemerocallis yezoensis Hara   Native of Japan in Hokkaido, growing in grassy places and marshy meadows near the sea, flowering in May–June. Roots slender, not swollen. Leaves broad, pale green to 1.5cm wide. Inflorescence to 50–80cm. Flowers opening in the day, 7–8cm long, with a rather short tube. For moist soil in full sun. Hardy to −25°C or less.

Hemerocallis fulva

Hemerocallis altissima

Hemerocallis citrina

Hemerocallis exaltata

Hemerocallis 'Hyperion'

Hemerocallis 'Golden Chimes'

Hemerocallis 'Burford'

Hemerocallis 'Stella d'Oro'

Hemerocallis 'Marion Vaughan'

Hemerocallis 'Astolat'

***Hemerocallis* 'Astolat'** Introduced by V. L. Peck in 1974. Height 71cm. Flowers 16cm across, near-white self with a green throat. Parents: 'Tetra Catherine Woodbery' × seedling. Tetraploid. Mid- to late season.

'Burford' Details not known.

'Cherry Ripe' Introduced by L. W. Brummitt in 1959. Height 90cm. Flowers orangey red with a yellow stripe. Parents: 'Royal Ruby' × 'Pink Prelude'. Mid-season.

'Golden Chimes' Introduced by H. A. Fischer in 1954. Height tall, 115cm. Flowers chrome, yellow self. Parents: 'Bijou' × 'Kraus'. Early to mid-season.

'Hope Diamond' Introduced by M. McMillan in 1968. Height 36cm. Flowers 10cm across, nearly pure-white self. Parents: 'President Giles' × seedling. Remontant. Early to mid-season.

'Hyperion' Raised in 1925 by Franklin B. Mead. Rigid stems to 100cm. Flowers pale yellow. Scented. Early to mid-season. Deciduous.

'Luminous Jewel' Introduced by F. Childs in 1974. Height 71cm. Flowers 15cm across, near-white self with mint-green throat. Remontant. Mid-season.

'Marion Vaughan' Introduced by K. D. Smith in 1951. Height tall, 105cm. Flowers lemon-yellow with a white midrib on the petals. Mid-season.

'Pardon Me' Introduced by D. A. Apps in 1982. Height 60cm. Flowers bright-red, self with yellow-green throat. Parents: 'Little Grapette' × seedling. Remontant. Fragrant. Mid-season.

'Red Precious' syn. 'Red Diamond' Introduced by R. H. Coe in 1969. Height 55cm. Flowers 9cm, brilliant-red self. Evergreen. Mid- to late-season.

'Stafford' Introduced by H. J. Randall in 1959. Height 71cm. Flowers glowing crimson, with greenish yellow throat. Mid-season.

'Starling' Introduced by C. Klehm in 1979. Height 71cm. Flowers 15cm across, brown-purple blend. Tetraploid. Early to mid-season.

'Stella d'Oro' Introduced by W. Jablonski in 1975. Height to only 28cm. Flowers 5.6cm, gold self, with very small green throat. Deciduous, fragrant. Remontant. Mid-season.

Hemerocallis 'Cherry Ripe'

Hemerocallis 'Stafford'

Hemerocallis 'Red Precious'

Hemerocallis 'Pardon Me'

Hemerocallis 'Starling'

Hemerocallis 'Luminous Jewel'

Hemerocallis 'Hope Diamond'

'Perennial Pleasure'

'Wild Song'

'Joan Senior'

'Little Red Hen'

'Veiled Organdy'

'Berlin Red'

'Dancing Sheva'

'Elizabeth Ann Hudson'

'Fancy Folly'

'Ed Murray'

'Princess Lilli'

'Wally Nance'

Day lilies from Wisley, 20 July. Life size

Hemerocallis 'Banbury Cinnamon'
Introduced by L. W. Brummitt in 1965. Height tall 93cm. Flowers 12.5cm across, cinnamon, with yellow base and a green throat. Parents: 'St George' × 'Flat Top'. Mid- to late-season.

'Berlin Melon'   Introduced by Tomas Tamberg.

'Berlin Red'   Introduced by Tomas Tamberg in 1983. Height to 88cm. Flowers 15cm across, bright red with yellow throat. Parents; 'Dundee' × 'Prussia'. Tetraploid. Deciduous. Mid-season.

'Burning Daylight'   Introduced by H. A. Fischer in 1957. Height 71cm. Parents: 'Smiling thru' × seedling. Mid-season. Fragrant. Flowers, glowing orange self.

'Cynthia Mary'   Introduced by C. C. Pole in 1982. Height 73cm. Flowers 11cm, deep red with darker edges and yellow-orange throat. Early to mid-season.

'Dancing Shiva'   Introduced by S. C. Moldovan in 1974. Height 55cm. Flowers 12.5cm across, medium-pink blend with greeny yellow throat. Tetraploid. Remontant. Early season.

'Ed Murray'   Introduced by E. T. Grovatt 1971. Height 75cm. Flowers 10cm across, black-red self with a green throat. Parents: 'Tis Midnight' × seedling. Mid-season.

'Elizabeth Anne Hudson'   Introduced by R. W. Munson in 1975. Height 65cm. Parents: 'Bishop's Crest' × Tetra Sari'. Flowers to 14cm across, peach-rose edged purple with wine-coloured eye zone and gold throat. Tetraploid. Evergreen. Remontant. Early to mid-season.

'Fancy Folly' Details not known.

'Frans Hals'   Introduced by W. B. Flory in 1955. Height 60cm. Flowers bright-rust and orange bicolor with a creamy orange midrib on the petals. Parents: 'Baggette' × 'Correll'. Mid- to late-season.

'Jake Russell'   Introduced by H. M. Russell in 1956. Height 90cm. Flowers golden, self with a velvety sheen. Remontant. Early to late-season.

'Joan Senior'   Introduced by K. G. Durio in 1977. Height 63cm. Flowers 15cm across, nearly white self with a lime-green throat. Parents: 'Loving Memory' × 'Little Infant'. Remontant. Early to mid-season.

Hemerocallis 'Wild Song'

Hemerocallis 'Ed Murray'

'Little Red Hen' Introduced by D. A. Apps in 1979. Height 75cm. Flowers 9cm across, red self with a yellow throat. Parents: 'Golden Chimes' × 'Rebel Thunder'. Mid-season.

'Mighty Mogul' Introduced by S. C. Moldovan in 1973. Height 55cm. Flowers sultry, maroon self, with a green throat. Tetraploid. Mid- to late-season.

'Neyron Rose' Introduced by E. J. Kraus in 1950. Height 75cm. Flowers light red. Parents include 'Gypsy Amaryllis' and 'Dauntless'. Mid-season.

'Nova' Introduced by Mrs H. W. Lester in 1962. Height 55cm. Flowers lemon-yellow, self with a green throat. Parents: 'Jack Frost' × seedling. Early to mid-season.

'Penelope Vestey' Introduced by R. H. Coe in 1969. Height tall, 90cm. Flowers 11cm across, pink with a deeper eye zone and lemon throat. Semi-evergreen. Late-season.

'Perennial Pleasure' Introduced by Mrs W. T. Hardy in 1968. Height 65cm. Flowers 14cm across, light-yellow self with a green throat. Remontant. Mid-season.

'Pink Damask' Introduced by J. C. Stevens in 1951. Height 90cm. Flowers mid-red self. Remontant. Mid-season.

'Princess Lilli' Introduced by M. Kasha in 1978. Height 50cm. Flowers 12.5cm across, light lavender with a rich-purple eye zone and a pale-yellow throat. Parents: 'Heavenly Haviland' × 'Prairie Blue Eyes'. Mid-season.

'Stoke Poges' Introduced by M. J. Randall.

'Veiled Organdy' Introduced by Brother Charles Reckamp in 1972. Height 75cm. Flowers 16cm across, pinkish apricot overlaid gold, with a greeny yellow throat. Parents: ('Minted Gold' × 'Noah's Ark') × 'Heavenly Harp'. Tetraploid. Mid-season.

'Wally Nance' Introduced by Wild in 1976. Height to 62cm. Flowers 15cm across, bright ruby red with small green throat. Early to mid-season.

'Wild Song' Introduced by A. J. & H. Wild in 1965. Height 71cm. Flowers 14cm across, golden-peachy self. Mid-season.

Hemerocallis 'Frans Hals'

Hemerocallis 'Joan Senior'

'Banbury Cinnamon'

'Cynthia Mary'

'Jake Russell'

'Frans Hals'

'Stoke Poges'

'Berlin Melon'

'Penelope Vestey'

'Neyron Rose'

'Pink Damask'

'Burning Daylight'

'Nova'

Hemerocallis 'Mighty Mogul'

Day lilies from Wisley, 20 July. Life size

Hemerocallis 'Cherry Cheeks'

Hemerocallis 'Pink Sensation'

Hemerocallis 'Siloam Purple Plum'

Hemerocallis 'Blushing Belle'

Hemerocallis 'Chicago Two Bits'

Hemerocallis 'La Pêche'

Hemerocallis 'May Colven'

Hemerocallis 'Chicago Petticoats'

Hemerocallis 'Chicago Royal Robe'

Hemerocallis 'Elizabeth Yancey'

Hemerocallis 'Nob Hill'

Massed day lilies in mid-summer at Wisley

Hemerocallis 'Catherine Woodberry'

Hemerocallis 'Come Hither'

Hemerocallis 'Luxury Lace'

Hemerocallis **'Blushing Belle'** Introduced by
D. F. Hall in 1962. Height 71cm. Flowers
melon-blushed rose. Early to mid-season.

'Catherine Woodberry' Introduced by F. W.
Childs in 1967. Height 75cm. Flowers 15cm
across, orchid self with green throat. Very
fragrant. Mid- to late season.

'Cherry Cheeks' Introduced by Mrs R. C.
Peck in 1968. Height 71cm. Flowers 15cm
across, rose-pink blend with a greeny-yellow
throat. Tetraploid. Mid- to late-season.

'Chicago Petticoats' Introduced by J. E.
Marsh and C. Klehm in 1980. Height 60cm.
Flowers 13cm across, pink blend. The parents
were seedlings. Tetraploid. Deciduous. Early to
mid-season.

'Chicago Royal Robe' Introduced by G. E.
Lenington in 1978. Height 63cm. Flowers 14cm
across, plum-purple self with a green throat.

Parents: 'Chicago Pansy' × seedling.
Tetraploid. Semi-evergreen. Early season.

'Chicago Two Bits' Introduced by J. E.
Marsh in 1972. Height 65cm. Flowers 15.5cm
across, violet-purple with a deeper eye zone and
a green throat. Semi-evergreen. Tetraploid.
Mid-season.

'Come Hither' Introduced by D. F. Hall in
1960. Height 71cm. Flowers pink, with wine-
purple eye zone. Early to mid-season.

'Elisabeth Yancey' Introduced by Yancey
Harrison in 1973. Height 71cm. Flowers 14cm
across, very light-pink self with a green throat.
Remontant. Semi-evergreen. Early season.

'La Pêche' Introduced by R. W. Munson in
1976. Height to 60cm. Flowers 13cm across,
peach-yellow self with yellow throat, fragrant.
Tetraploid. Semi-evergreen. Early to mid-
season. Remontant.

'Luxury Lace' Introduced by Miss E.
Spalding in 1959. Height 80cm. Flowers
mauve, orange self with a green throat.
Remontant. Mid-season.

'May Colven' Introduced by Mrs R. C. Peck.
Height 73cm. Flowers 15cm across, rose-pink
blend with green throat. Parents: 'Mary Gray'
× seedling. Tetraploid. Mid- to late-season.

'Nob Hill' Introduced by Mrs H. W. Lester in
1962. Height 90cm. Flowers pale pink bi-tone.
Early to mid-season.

'Pink Sensation' Introduced by J. W. Terry
in 1953. Height 75cm. Flowers light pinky-red
self. Mid-season.

'Siloam Purple Plum' Introduced by Mrs R.
Henry in 1970. Height 43cm. Flowers 7cm
across, dark-red-purple self with a green throat.
Early to mid-season.

ALSTROEMERIA

'Marie-Louise'

'Sarah'

'Margaret'

'Frederika'

'Bianca'

'Sophia'

'Diana'

'Victoria'

'Beatrix'

Alstroemeria specimens from Chanctonbury Nursery, Ashington, Sussex, July 20th. ½ life size

Alstroemeria aurea

Alstroemeria psittacina

Alstroemeria aurea Graham syn. *A. aurantiaca* D. Don (*Liliaceae-Alstroemeriaceae*)   Native of S Chile, including Chiloe, growing in moist woodland, flowering in December–March. Plant far-spreading by thin, fleshy roots. Stems to 1m or more. Leaves lanceolate. Flowers 3–4cm long, the outer petals tipped with green. For moist soil in sun or partial shade. The hardiest species, to −15°C or less with protection for the roots, which tend to be very invasive.

Alstroemeria haemantha Ruiz & Pavon Native of Chile, especially around Valparaiso, growing on well-drained, rocky hillsides, flowering in December–January. Plant spreading by fleshy roots to form large patches. Stems to *c*.1m. Leaves glaucous beneath. Flowers *c*.5cm long, red to orange. The outer petals oblong to obovate. Hardy to −10°C, perhaps less.

Alstroemeria ligtu L.   Native of Chile, growing in dry scrub in rocky, sandy soil, flowering in November–January. Plant wide spreading by underground fleshy roots. Stems 60–100cm. Leaves narrowly linear or linear-lanceolate. Flowers variable in colour, usually pinkish lilac, reddish or whitish, *c*.3.75cm long. *A. ligtu* is said to be usually pink-flowered in the wild, and the 'ligtu hybrids' that are usually sold are hybrids between *A. ligtu* and *A. haemantha*, raised by Clarence Elliott in around 1927 when he and Balfour Gourlay introduced the parents from Chile. For well-drained soil in full sun. Hardy to −15°C.

Alstroemeria pelegrina L.   Native of Chile and Peru, growing on sand dunes along the coast, flowering in December–January. Plant spreading by fleshy roots; stems 30–50cm. Leaves lanceolate. Flowers purplish or reddish, *c*.5cm long. For well-drained soil, moist in summer. Hardy to −10°C perhaps.

Alstroemeria psittacina Lehm. syn. *A. pulchella* L. fil.   Native of Mexico and N Brazil, flowering in November–February. Plant forming clumps of stems to *c*.1m, from shortly spreading fleshy roots. Leaves oblong to oblong-spathulate. Flowers *c*.3.75cm long. For sun or partial shade in good, well-drained soil, moist in summer. Hardy to −10°C.

Alstroemeria hybrids   Most of the large-flowered cultivars shown here have been raised for the cut-flower trade in Holland by Van Straaveren B. V. of Aalsmeer. They make, however, excellent garden plants, with a long flowering season, requiring rich, well-drained soil in full sun. They will probably survive temperatures of at least −10°C, if the fleshy roots are protected with a good mulch of dry peat in winter. They are hybrids between *A. aurea* and other species originally raised by J. Goemans, and are mainly triploid, so that they do not set seed and are not easily used for breeding by other growers! They have stems 50–75cm. Shown here are:
'Beatrix' (syn. 'Stradoran');
'Bianca' (syn. 'Zelblanca');
'Diana' (syns. 'Stablaco', 'Mona Lisa');
'Frederika' (syn. 'Straronza');
'Margaret';
'Marie-Louise';
'Sarah' (syn. 'Stalicamp');
'Sophia' (syns. 'Stajello', 'Yellow King');
'Victoria' (syn. 'Regina') all raised by Van Straaveren.
'Rosy Wings'   An older cultivar of unknown origin. Height to 30cm.

Alstroemeria 'Diana'

Alstroemeria pelegrina

Alstroemeria 'Rosy Wings'

Bomarea × *cantabrigiensis* at Great Dixter

Alstroemeria ligtu hybrids at Cobblers, Sussex

Bomarea × **cantabrigiensis** Lynch (*Liliaceae-Alstroemeriaceae*)   A hybrid between *B. hirtella* and *B. caldasiana* Herb., raised at the University Botanic Garden, Cambridge before 1920. This has grown outside in a bay between the glasshouses at Cambridge since 1922 and so should be quite hardy if the rootstock is covered. The twining leafy stems grow to 2m or more and the flower clusters are *c*.20cm across.

Bomarea hirtella Herb. syn. *B. edulis* (Tussac) Herb.   Native of Cuba, Mexico and Belize south to Peru, growing on the edge of forests at 1400–3000m, flowering in July–October in S England. Roots tuberous and edible, with slender stems scrambling and twining to 2m or more. Leaves lanceolate. Flower clusters *c*.15cm across, the flowers 2.5–3.7cm long. For any good soil in sun or partial shade. Hardy to −10°C or less.

Bomarea hirtella at Kew

Alstroemeria haemantha

Libertia formosa

Libertia formosa

Phaiophleps nigricans 'Aunt May'

Fascicularia pitcairniifolia

Diplarrena moraea

Sisyrinchium bellum

Phaiophleps nigricans formerly *Sisyrinchium striatum*

Aristea grandis

Phaiophleps biflora

Belamcanda chinensis

Aristea grandis Weim. (*Iridaceae*)   Native of South Africa, in the Drakensberg mountains of S Natal, growing in moist grassland by rock outcrops and by streams at up to 2250m, flowering in January–February. Plant with solitary or few upright stems 60–80cm tall from a tufted rootstock. Flowers in stemless clusters of 3–8, blue, *c*.20mm across, each lasting only one day. For a sunny position, moist in summer, dryish in winter. Hardy to −10°C, perhaps less. *A. major* Andrews (syn. *A. thyrsiflora*), from the Cape, is a tall plant, to 2m, with a solid, spike-like inflorescence of hundreds of flowers. It is a beautiful waterside plant for a warm climate. Hardy to −5°C perhaps.

Belamcanda chinensis (L.) DC. (*Iridaceae*) Native of E Siberia, China, S Japan and the Himalayas to N India, and naturalized in Malaysia and in North America, from Connecticut south to Georgia, Indiana and Kansas, growing in scrub, open woods and grassy places, flowering in June–August. Plant with branched stems to 1m from a fan of *Iris*-like leaves. Flowers *c*.5cm across. Capsule 4cm long, splitting to reveal shining black seeds. For any soil in a warm position, moist in summer. Hardy to −15°C.

Diplarrena moraea Labill. (*Iridaceae*)   Native of Tasmania and SE Australia, in New South Wales and Victoria, growing in moist, grassy places in the mountains, flowering in October–December, or May–June in the north. Plant tufted. Stems 45–65cm. Leaves 8–12mm wide. Flowers 2 or 3 per bract, 4–6cm across, scented. For well-drained, sandy and peaty soil, moist in

summer. Hardy to −10°C for short periods. *D. latifolia* Benth. has wider leaves to 2.5cm and larger flowers 6–15cm across, 5 or 6 per bract.

Fascicularia pitcairniifolia (Verlot) Mez (*Bromeliaceae*)   Native of Chile, and naturalized in the Scilly Islands and off NW France, growing on rocks by the sea, flowering in June–August. Plant forming crowded rosettes of narrow leaves to 35cm long, glaucous, especially beneath. Leaves around the inflorescence becoming bright red at flowering time, then reverting to green. Flowers small, pale blue in a head *c*.5cm in diameter. *F. bicolor* Mez is said to be similar, but has purple flowers and shorter leaves, brownish beneath. For a position among rocks or on a wall. Hardy to −5°C.

Libertia formosa Graham (*Iridaceae*)   Native of Chile, flowering in spring. Plant forming large clumps. Leaves 15–45cm, to 1.2cm wide. Stems 50–120cm. Flowers in small umbels; longer petals 12–18mm. For well-drained soil and a sunny position. Hardy to −15°C. *L. ixioides* (Forster) Spreng. is a native of New Zealand and the Chatham Islands, and is later flowering, with the individual flowers on stalks longer than the minute bracts, and petals only 6–9mm long.

Phaiophleps biflora (Thunb.) R. C. Foster syns. *Symphostemon narcissoides* (Cav.) Miers ex Klatt, *Sisyrinchium odoratissimum* Lindl. (*Iridaceae*)   Native of W Argentina north to 46°S and Chile north to 50° 40′S, and common in Tierra del Fuego, growing in grassland and open scrub to 150m, flowering in November–

January, or May–June in the north. Plant with a short rhizome and 1–5 narrow, solid leaves to 22cm. Flowering stems 10–70cm, with 2–7 flowers each with a tube 7–20mm long, and reflexing petals to 18mm long, scented. Subsp. *lyckholmi* (Owen) D. M. Moore has purplish- or brownish-red to orange flowers, and is found at higher altitudes. For well-drained, sandy soil in full sun, moist in summer. Hardy to −15°C.

Phaiophleps nigricans (Phil.) R. C. Foster syn. *Sisyrinchium striatum* Smith   Native of Argentina and Chile, growing in woods and scrub, and becoming especially prolific after forest fires, flowering in summer. Plant with few to several fans of leaves to 40cm from a short rhizome. Leaves to 18mm across, striped in 'Aunt May' syn. 'Variegatum'. Stems to 45cm. Easily grown in any good garden soil, preferably rather moist. Short-lived but self-seeds freely. The leaves are killed by −15°C or so, and are often blackened by slighter frosts.

Sisyrinchium bellum S. Wats. (*Iridaceae*) **Blue-eyed Grass**   Native of California, from Humboldt Co. south to Ventura Co., growing in often-damp, grassy places below 1000m, in the coast ranges, flowering in February–May. Other forms of this species are found inland. Plant with several flattened and branched stems 40cm. Leaves greenish or glaucous, to 4mm wide. Flowers around 30mm across, usually deep blue. For moist, sandy soil, in full sun. Hardy to −15°C, though some plants from coastal areas may be tenderer. *S. idahoense* Bickn., from California to Washington and Idaho, differs in its leafless, unbranched stem.

'Hadspen Abundante'

'Prinz Heinrich'

Anemone tomentosa

Anemone vitifolia

'Honorine Jobert'

Specimens from Beth Chatto, Unusual Plants, 15 September. ⅙ life size

Anemone × *lesseri*

Anemone 'September Charm'

Anemone 'Honorine Jobert' at Cockermouth Castle

Anemone hupehensis (Brickell & Leslie 12470)
from Yunnan

Anemone 'Koenigin Charlotte' at Trewidden, Cornwall

Anemone × *hybrida* 'Hybrida'

Anemone vitifolia from Nepal

Anemone 'Luise Uhink'

Anemone hupehensis (Lémoine) Lémoine (*Ranunculaceae*)   Native of C & W China, from Hubei to Sichuan and Yunnan, growing in gorges on cliffs, among shady rocks in scrub and in open, stony places at 600–2500m, flowering in August–October, to November in the wild. Plant with a tufted rootstock, spreading by stolons. Leaves with 3 stalked leaflets, sparsely hairy, often purplish beneath, more or less evergreen. Stems 60–130cm, branched, with umbels of white, pale-pink or purplish-pink flowers; petals 5–6, rounded, crimson outside. For any good soil in sun or partial shade. Hardy to −15°C, possibly less. Var. *japonica* (Thunb.) Bowles & Stearn has numerous (20–30 or more) narrow petals, and is widely grown in E China and Japan. It was introduced by Robert Fortune who collected it among the graves of the natives around the ramparts of Shanghai. 'September Charm' is a good selection, raised by Bristol Nurseries in 1932, with stems *c*.75cm.

Anemone × hybrida Paxton **'Hybrida'**   This is the old garden Japanese anemone, so valuable for its late flowering. It is a hybrid between *A. vitifolia* and *A. hupehensis* var. *japonica* and is generally sterile and often triploid. It has tall, 1.2–1.8m or more, stems, and tough, wiry roots, spreading to form large colonies. The pale-pink form, with 6–11 petals, is the original 'Hybrida'. Other cultivars shown here are:
'Hadspen Abundance'   Introduced by Eric Smith of The Plantsmen, deep purplish pink; petals 6–9. Stems *c*.60cm.
'Honorine Jobert'   Raised in 1858; the commonest white, single; petals 6–9.
'Luise Uhink'   Flowers large, white; petals 6–10. Stems to 120cm.
'Prinz Heinrich' syn. 'Prince Henry'   Raised in 1902; deep rose-pink; 10–13 narrow petals.
'Koenigin Charlotte' syn. 'Queen Charlotte' Raised in 1898; the best large-flowered, mid-pink, with 6–8 petals; stems *c*.80cm.

Anemone × lesseri Wehrh.   A hybrid between the American *A. multifida* Poir, which may have red flowers (or green or yellowish), and *A. sylvestris* L., from Europe, which has white flowers. Stems to 45cm. Flowers 2–4cm across, in May–September. For deep, well-drained soil in sun or partial shade. Hardy to −25°C or less.

Anemone tomentosa (Maxim.) P'ei syn. *A. vitifolia* 'Robustissima'   Native of NE China, growing in scrub, open woods and among shady rocks, flowering in August–October. Plant forming a compact clump of much-branched stems to 1m or more, spreading by stolons. Leaves with 3 separate leaflets, lobed and toothed, densely white-hairy beneath. Flowers in umbels, 5–8cm across with 5–6 petals. For any good soil. Hardy to −25°C or less.

Anemone vitifolia Buch.-Ham. ex DC. Native of the Himalayas, from Afghanistan to N Burma and W China in NW Sichuan, growing in scrub and abandoned fields at 2000–3000m, flowering in August–September. Plant with a tufted rootstock, far spreading by underground stolons. Basal leaves 5–9-lobed and toothed, long, silky and woolly beneath, deciduous. Stems to 150cm, usually *c*.75cm, branched with umbels of few flowers, 3.5–5cm across; petals 5–6, usually white, though pink-flowered forms were recorded by Wilson in NW Sichuan. Hardy to −20°C or less.

Cimicifuga rubifolia at Wisley

Cimicifuga simplex 'Elstead Variety'

Cimicifuga simplex 'Brunette'

Cimicifuga rubifolia with *Veratrum nigrum*

Impatiens tinctoria subsp. *tinctoria* at Logan Botanic Garden

Cimicifuga japonica near Kyoto

Melianthus villosus at Kew

Melianthus major at Edington, Wiltshire

Cimicifuga japonica (Thunb.) Spreng.
(*Ranunculaceae*)   Native of Japan, in C & W
Honshu, growing in woods, often among ferns
in deep shade, flowering in August–October.
Plant with few, upright stems 60–80cm tall.
Leaflets broadly ovate to orbicular, 6–10cm long
and wide. Flowering stems usually leafless.
Flowers sessile, usually crowded; stamens
c.8mm long. For leafy soil in shade or partial
shade. Hardy to −15°C, perhaps less.

Cimicifuga rubifolia Kearney   Native of E
North America, in Tennessee and parts of
Illinois, growing in rocky woods, flowering in
June–July. Stems to 200cm. Leaves 2-ternate,
with large leaflets 12–20cm long, ovate to
suborbicular, irregularly lobed. Follicles 1 or 2,
8–10mm long, glabrous, prominently veined.
For moist rich soil in shade or partial shade.
Hardy to −20°C or less.

   This species has commonly been called *C.
racemosa* var *cordifolia* (Pursh) Gray in gardens,
and in the first printing of this book, and we are
indebted to James Compton for discovering
Kearney's monograph and naming the
cultivated plants of this confusing genus. He has
also pointed out that the name *Cimicifuga
ramosa* Nutt. should be rejected; all the plants
grown under that name are forms of *C. simplex*.

   C. racemosa (L.) Nutt. Black Cohosh or Black
Snakeroot, the common North American
species, has small leaflets, 3–10cm long, and a
single follicle. It is found in damp woods from
Massachusetts and S Ontario south to Georgia
and Missouri.

Cimicifuga simplex Wormsk. **'Elstead
Variety'**   Native of Japan, in all the the islands,
and of Sakhalin, the Kurile Is. and
Kamschatka, growing in subalpine and alpine
meadows, flowering in August–October, usually
in October in gardens. Plant with shortly
creeping rhizomes and upright stems c.100cm,
forming patches. Leaflets ovate or narrowly
ovate, 3–10cm long. Flowering stems arching,
black, little branched. Flowers on stalks
5–10mm long. Petals shallowly 2–lobed, styles
2–7. For moist, leafy soil in partial shade.
Hardy to −25°C or less. 'Elstead variety' has
brownish-purple stems and buds; 'White Pearl'
has pure-white flowers from green buds;
'Atropurpurea' has purplish leaves and buds;
'Brunette' has even darker leaves of a rich
purplish black, and pinkish-white flowers on
stems to 180cm. It was introduced by Blooms
from Denmark. *C. foetida* L. from Europe, W
Asia and the Himalayas to W China, has
greenish-yellow flowers in a long, nodding
spike, with shorter branches around its base.

Impatiens tinctoria A. Rich. subsp. *tinctoria*
(*Balsaminaceae*)   Native of C Africa, in E
Zaire, S Sudan, Ethiopia and N Uganda,
growing in damp mountain forests, shrub-filled
gullies, by streams and on shady banks at 750–
3000m, flowering in January, and in April–
November; in August–October in gardens in
Britain. Plant with large tuberous rootstock,
and thick, fleshy stems to 2m. Leaves with
blade 10–20cm long, narrowly ovate, elliptical
or lanceolate. Flowers with lower petals

3.5–5cm long. Spur very long, 8–12cm in
subsp. *tinctoria*, 3.8–6.5cm long in subsp.
elegantissima from Mount Elgon and the
mountains of C & S Kenya, which also appears
to be in cultivation. For rich, leafy soil, moist in
summer in a sheltered position. Hardy to −10°C
and long-lived; a plant has been growing
between the glasshouses at Wisley for over 12
years.

Melianthus major L. (*Melianthaceae*)   Native
of South Africa, in the S Cape Province,
flowering in August–September, i.e. in Spring.
In the wild and in mild climates a shrub to 3m,
but herbaceous in colder climates, growing to
1.2m in one season. Leaves glaucous, smooth,
to 30cm or more long. Flowers deep blood-red;
fruits inflated. One of the most handsome
foliage plants for exotic effect. Hardy to −15°C
with protection for the rootstock; to −10°C
perhaps, for short periods for the aerial parts.

Melianthus villosus Bol.   Native of South
Africa in the Drakensberg in Lesotho and
Natal, growing by streams, among rocks in
scrub and on the margins of forests at up to
c.1950m, flowering in December–January. In
the wild a shrub up to 2m, but herbaceous in
colder climates, and usually up to 1.5m. Plant
hairy, aromatic. Leaves c.15cm long. Flowers
greenish; fruits inflated, triangular. For any
good soil in full sun, moist in summer, but in a
warm position. Hardy to −10°C perhaps, for
short periods.

Aconitum henryi
'Spark's Variety'

Aconitum × *cammarum*
'Bicolor'

Aconitum compactum
'Carneum'

*Aconitum
leucostomum*

Aconitum lamarkii

Specimens from Wisley, 20 July. ½ life size

Aconitum × cammarum L. syn. *A. bicolor*
Schult. (*Ranunculaceae*) A group of hybrids
between *A. napellus* L. and *A. variegatum* L.,
with rather short spikes of large flowers and a
helmet as high as wide. Flower colour basically
blue. 'Bicolor' is the original form: stems to
1.2m, much branched; spikes rather short.
'Grandiflorum Album' is a beautiful pure white,
with longer spikes and well-spaced flowers.

Aconitum compactum Rchb. **'Carneum'**
Native of the Pyrenees and W Alps in France
and possibly Portugal to Switzerland, growing
in woods and damp meadows, especially along
streams, flowering in July–September. Plant
with upright stems to 1.5m. Basal leaves divided
to the base, with narrow, linear lobes; stem-
leaves crowded below the unbranched
inflorescence. Graham Thomas records that this
form provides flowers of a better pink in cool
climates. *A. compactum* is one of the *A. napellus*
group.

Aconitum henryi E. Pritz. ex Diels **'Spark's
Variety'** Native of China, in Hubei and
Sichuan, growing in scrub, flowering in July–
September. Plant with tuberous roots and stems
to 1.5m which begin upright but then twine or
scramble, though in 'Spark's Variety', shown
here, they are merely flexuous above. Leaves
mainly 3-lobed, the middle lobe short-stalked.
Flowers with a short, broad helmet. For any
good soil in partial shade. Hardy to −20°C.

Aconitum japonicum Thunb. Native of
Japan, in SW Hokkaido, Honshu, Shikoku and
Kyushu, growing in hills and mountains,
flowering in September–November. Plant
forming large clumps of stems to 100cm, rarely
climbing towards the top. Leaves 3–5 lobed,
coarsely toothed, with broad lobes.
Inflorescence much branched, with few-
flowered, short spikes. Hardy to −20°C
perhaps. Valuable for its handsome leaves and
very late flowering.

Aconitum laeve Royle Native of the
Himalayas, from Pakistan to W Nepal, growing
in open forest and scrub at 2000–3300m,
flowering in June–August. Plant forming
clumps of tall stems to 2m. Basal leaves to 30cm
across with broad lobes. Flowers to 2.5cm high,
with a tall, narrow, curved helmet; variable in
colour from white to pale yellow, or pinkish
purple. Hardy to −20°C, perhaps less.

Aconitum lamarkii Rchb. syn. *A. lycoctonum*
subsp. *neapolitanum* (Ten.) Nyman Native of
S Europe, from France and Spain and Morocco,
east to Bulgaria, N Greece and Romania,
growing in mountain woods and meadows,
often by streams, flowering in July–August.
Plant with few or several upright stems to *c*.1m,
from a tufted rootstock. Basal leaves 7–8-lobed,
the lobes deeply cut to beyond the middle.
Helmet 18–25mm. For moist, peaty soil in
partial shade or sun. Hardy to −20°C.

Aconitum leucostomum Vorosch. Native of
C Asia in the Saur Tarbagatau, Dzungarian Ala
Tau and Tien Shan, both in Soviet Kirgizia and
NW China (Sinjiang), growing in forest and
juniper scrub in the mountains, flowering in
June–July, and August in gardens. Plant with
few stems to 1.5m. Basal leaves pale green, with
3–7 lobes, the lobes cut to above the middle.
Flowers pinkish, the helmet *c*.15mm tall. For
any good soil in sun or partial shade. Hardy to
−25°C or less. *A. orientalis* Mill., from NE
Turkey and the Caucasus, is similar in its leaves
and flowers which are smoky lilac or pinkish, an

altogether interesting colour. It grows in
clearings in coniferous forest.

Aconitum septentrionale Koelle **'Ivorine'** syn.
A. lycoctonum L. subsp. *lycoctonum* in *European
Garden Flora* Native of N Europe from
Norway to Russia, growing on forest margins
and in rich meadows, flowering in June–July, or
even late May in gardens. Plant forming clumps
of upright stems to 90cm. Basal leaves deeply
4–6 lobed to ⅔, the lobes coarsely toothed.
Inflorescence glandular, narrow; flower usually
dark violet, but white in 'Ivorine', the helmet
18–25mm, tapering from a wide base. For any
good, cool soil in sun or partial shade. This is
the earliest Monkshood to flower and is very
distinct in its dense narrow spikes of white
flowers. Hardy to −25°C or less.

Aconitum japonicum at the Royal Botanic Garden, Edinburgh

Aconitum laeve in Kashmir

A. × cammarum 'Grandiflorum Album'

Aconitum septentrionale 'Ivorine'

Zauschneria californica subsp. *latifolia*

Zauschneria californica

Zauschneria cana at Wisley

Gaura lindheimeri Englemann & A. Gray
(*Onagraceae*) Native of Louisiana and Texas,
growing in prairies and pinelands, flowering in
April–October. Plant with a tufted rootstock
and numerous, rather stiff upright stems
forming a low bush to 1m high and wide.
Leaves oblanceolate or spathulate, to 7.5cm
long. Flowers *c*.2.5cm across. For a warm
sunny position in well-drained soil, tolerant of
both heat and drought. Hardy to −20°C
perhaps. *G. coccinea* (Nutt.) Pursh, widespread
in North America, has stems to 50cm, and
flowers to 16mm across, which may be deep
pink on opening, becoming red. For an even
drier, hotter position.

Lespedeza thunbergii (DC.) Nakai
(*Leguminosae*) Native of Japan, Korea and
China, growing on dry, grassy hills and scrub,
flowering in June–September, and to November
in gardens. Plant with a woody rootstock and
arching stems to 180cm, sometimes woody at
the base. Leaves with 3 narrowly oblong, ovate
or elliptic leaflets, 3–5cm long. Flowers 18–
25mm long, in spikes longer than the leaves.
Calyx-teeth acuminate, 1-nerved, the lowest
longer than the tube. *L. bicolor* Turcz., with
short racemes of flowers and shorter calyx teeth,
is shown in *Shrubs*, p. 169. For good soil in
warm position in full sun. Valuable for its late
flowering when pruned to the ground in spring.
Hardy to −20°C.

Lychnis cognata Maxim. (*Caryophyllaceae*)
Native of NE China (Heilongjiang) and Korea,
growing in open woods and grassy places in the
mountains, flowering in July–August. Stems
few, bristly-hairy or nearly glabrous, 40–100cm
tall, with ovate or elliptic leaves 5–8cm long.
Bracts broadly lanceolate, ciliate, 10–15mm
long, appressed to the calyx. Calyx 2.5–3cm
long. Flowers 3 or more in a head, 5–6cm
across, with a long tooth on the side of each
petal and deep notch on the apex. Hardy to
−20°C or less.

Lychnis miqueliana Rohrb. Native of Japan
in S Honshu, Shikoku and Kyushu, growing in

Gaura lindheimeri

Gaura lindheimeri

Lespedeza thunbergii at Kew

damp woods in the mountains, flowering in July–October. Plant with stems 50–80cm, sparingly branched. Flowers 5–6cm across with smooth, rounded petals. For moist soil in partial shade. Hardy to −10°C, perhaps less.

Zauschneria californica Presl. (*Onagraceae*) Native of California from Sonoma and Lake Cos. south to Baja California, growing in dry, open places, in cliffs and gravelly soil, flowering in August–October, with the occasional flower earlier. Plant usually with numerous stems to 90cm long, from a woody rootstock. Leaves green to greyish, ovate to linear. Flowers with a long tube 2–3cm long and petals 8–15mm long, usually scarlet, rarely pink or white in, for example, 'Albiflora'. For a warm position in dry, well-drained soil. Hardy to −15°C perhaps. A very variable species, divided into 3 subspecies, as follows. Subsp. *californica* has stems slightly woody at the base; leaves linear to lanceolate, 3–5mm wide, hairy but not white. Subsp. *angustifolia* Keck is woody at the base, has narrower linear leaves 2.5–3.5mm wide and flowers 30–40mm long. Both these are found below 1200m, mostly in the Coast Ranges. Subsp. *latifolia* (Hook.) Keck is entirely herbaceous, with leaves ovate to ovate-lanceolate, mostly opposite, green or silky, 7–17mm wide and often glandular. It is a mountain plant, found from Tulare Co. to SW Oregon, below 3000m. It is probably hardier than the coastal subspecies.

Zauschneria cana Greene   Native of California, from Monterey to Los Angeles Co., growing on dry slopes and roadside cliffs, in chaparral and coastal scrub below 600m, flowering in August–October. Plant with several stems, somewhat woody at the base, to 60cm. Leaves white-hairy, linear-filiform, up to 2mm wide, clustered. Flowers with the tube 2–3cm long, and petals 8–10mm long. For dry, hot, sunny position in well-drained soil. Hardy to −10°C, perhaps less. All *Zauschneria* may now be found under the name *Epilobium canum*!

Zauschneria californica 'Albiflora'

Lychnis miqueliana near Kyoto

Lychnis cognata

Polygonum cuspidatum

Aralia cordata near Kyoto, Japan

Polygonum amplexicaule

Fagopyrum dibotrys

Polygonum cuspidatum var. compactum

Polygonum campanulatum

Polygonum runcinatum

Polygonum molle

Specimens from Braken Hill, Platt, 28 July. ½ life size

Polygonum molle var. *rude*

Aralia cordata Thunb. syn. *A. edulis* Sieb. &
Zucc. (*Araliaceae*)   Native of Japan, in all the
islands, of Sakhalin, Korea and China, growing
in scrub and open forest in ravines in the
mountains, flowering in August–October. Plant
with a large, fleshy rootstock and arching stems
to 1.5m. Leaves to 1m long, twice pinnate, the
leaflets ovate to oblong 5–30cm long,
acuminate. Flowers pale green. Fruits black,
fleshy *c*.2mm long. For moist, leafy soil in shade
and shelter. Hardy to −25°C or less.

Fagopyrum dibotrys (D. Don) Hara syn. *F.
cymosum* (Trev.) Meissn. (*Polygonaceae*)
Native of the Himalayas from Pakistan to SW
China, growing in open forest and near
cultivation at 1300–3400m, flowering in June–
October. Plant with upright, unbranched stems
to 2m or more, from a stout rootstock. Leaf
blades 6–15cm long, the lowest long-stalked,
the upper sessile. Flowers *c*.5mm across; seed to
8mm long, used for food in the Himalayas,
along with the cultivated annual buckwheats *F.
esculentum* Moench and *F. tartaricum* (L.)
Gaertn. For good soil in partial shade. Hardy to
−20°C, perhaps less.

Polygonum amplexicaule D. Don syns. *Bistorta
amplexicaulis* (D. Don) Greene, *Persicaria
amplexicaulis* (D. Don) Decne. (*Polygonaceae*)
Native of Afghanistan to SW China, growing in
scrub and mountain meadows by streams at
2100–4800m, flowering in July–September.
Stems to 1m or more. Leaves clasping. Flowers
white, pink, red, or purple. Spikes 5–15cm
long, usually erect, but nodding in var. *pendula*
Hara from C & E Nepal and Bhutan. 'Arun
Gem', introduced from Nepal in 1971, belongs

Polygonum amplexicaule by a stream at Leeds Castle, Kent

Polygonum species amongst Hostas

Polygonum sachalinense

Polygonum vaccinifolium

to this var. A robust plant forming large clumps in moist ground. Hardy to −20°C.

Polygonum campanulatum Hook. fil. syns. *Aconogonum campanulatum* (Hook. fil.) Hara, *Persicaria campanulata* (Hook. fil.) R. D. Native of N India, Nepal, Sikkim, Bhutan, N Burma and SW China, growing in damp places in *Abies* or *Tsuga* forest, and scrub at 2100–4100m, flowering in June–September. Plant forming large clumps with shortly creeping rooting stems and erect flowering stems, 60–120cm. Leaves elliptic-ovate, 5–12cm long, white or pale salmon beneath with parallel side ribs. Flowers bell-shaped, *c*.5mm long, pink or nearly white. A pretty plant for a very damp position. Tolerant of shade but not tolerant of drought in summer. Hardy to −15°C.

Polygonum cuspidatum Sieb. & Zucc. var. **compactum** (Hook. fil.) Bailey syn. *Fallopia japonica* var. *compacta* (Hook. fil.) Trehane Native of Japan, Korea, Taiwan and China, growing in mountain scrub and meadows, flowering in July–October. Plant with creeping underground rhizomes and upright stems to 90cm. Leaves *c*.10cm long, broadly ovate to ovate-elliptic, truncate at the base. Flowers 2.5–3mm long, male and female on different plants, white when fresh, turning pink; the clone of var. *compactum* in cultivation is female.

Var. *cuspidatum* is a rampant, large plant with stems to 2m, still a little smaller than *P. sachalinense*. There is a slightly weaker variegated clone 'Spectabile'. For moist soil in partial shade. Hardy to −25°C.

Polygonum molle D. Don var. **rude** (Meissn.) Hara syns. *Polygonum rude* Meissn., *Persicaria molle* var. *rude* (Meissn.) Trehane Native of the Himalayas from N India to SW China, growing in forests, scrub and damp ground at 900–4250m, flowering in May–November. Plant shrubby at the base, with stem to 2.5m. Var. *rude* is distinguished from the other vars. by having appressed deflexed hairs on the stem, especially at the nodes (var. *molle* has ascending hairs). Leaves elliptic 10–18cm × 3–6.5cm, usually pubescent. Flowers yellowish white; fruits black, fleshy. Easily grown in sun or partial shade and moist soil. Valuable for its late flowering in gardens.

Polygonum runcinatum D. Don syn. *Persicaria runcinata* (D. Don) H. Gross Native of Bhutan and Sikkim, growing on cliffs and roadside banks, at 1000–3800m, flowering in May–October. Plant with soft, fleshy creeping and rooting stems to 30cm or more. Leaves *c*.7.5cm long. Flower-head *c*.1cm across. For moist, leafy soil in partial shade. Hardy to −10°C perhaps.

Polygonum sachalinense F. Schmidt syns. *Reynoutria sachalinensis* (F. Schmidt) Nakai, *Fallopia sachalinensis* (F. Schmidt) R. D. Native of Japan in Hokkaido and Honshu, Sakhalin and the S Kurile islands, growing in gorges, along shady streams and in damp clearings in woods in the mountains, flowering in August–September. Stems to 3m. Leaves 15–30cm × 10–20cm, glaucous and glabrous beneath, cordate. Inflorescence pubescent. A fine plant for a huge garden, especially where it can be viewed from above. Hardy to −25°C.

Polygonum vaccinifolium Wall. ex Meissn. syn. *Bistorta vaccinifolia* (Wall. ex Meissn.) Greene Native of Kashmir to SE Xizang, growing on rocks and open mountains, at 3000–4500m, especially common in the wetter areas of the C Himalayas, flowering in August–September. Flowering stems up to 15cm. Leaves 1–2cm × 0.6–1cm. Flower spikes 3–8cm; flowers 6mm. Requires peaty soil, cool and moist in summer, but well-drained, and best trailing over rocks.

Polygonum species Plant with trailing stems to 30cm long. Leaves cut to the midrib, *c*.5cm long. Flower spikes 1.5cm in August–September. For moist, leafy soil in partial shade; pretty, as shown here, for its unique leaf shape.

Gentiana asclepiadea at Wallington, Northumberland

Gentiana asclepiadea (Turkish form)

Gentiana cruciata in NW Turkey

Gentiana septemfida on the peat banks at Wisley

Gentiana affinis Griseb. (*Gentianaceae*) Native of North America, from the Rockies eastwards to W Minnesota and South Dakota, growing in damp grassland and marshy places, flowering in July–August. Plant with few upright stems to 45cm. Leaves 7–13 pairs below the flowers, 1.5–3cm long, linear-lanceolate. Flowers with calyx tube 5–7mm; corolla 2–3cm long, blue. For peaty soil in full sun. Close to the European *G. pneumonanthe*. Hardy to −20°C or less.

Gentiana asclepiadea L. Native of the mountains of Europe, from the Jura and W Alps eastwards to the Caucasus, N & S Turkey and northern Iran, growing in mountain meadows and open woods at up to 2000m, flowering in July–September. Plant with several arching stems to 1m from a tufted rootstock. Leaves ovate-lanceolate to lanceolate. Flowers with corolla 30–50mm long, mid- or deep blue, commonly with a white throat in Turkey or Cambridge blue in Corsica, rarely pure white in 'Alba'. 'Knightshayes' has a pale throat similar to the Turkish form. For light shade or sun, in a cool position and leafy soil which does not dry out in summer. Hardy to −20°C or less.

Gentiana cruciata L. Native of the Alps east to the Caucasus, N Iran, W Siberia and Turkey, growing in alpine meadows and scrub, flowering in July–September. Plant with few or several stems from a central rosette of leaves. Stem leaves to 10cm long, 3cm wide. Flowers with a 4-lobed corolla, 15–30mm long. A rather coarse, leafy plant, but easy to grow in any good soil. Hardy to −20°C or less. Photographed in NW Turkey by James Compton.

Gentiana septemfida Pallas syns. *G. freyniana* Bornm., *G. lagodechiana* (Kuzn.) Grossh. Native of the Crimea, the Caucasus, N Turkey and N Iran, growing in alpine meadows and grassy scrub, and open birch or fir forest, at up to 3200m in Turkey, flowering in July–August. Plant with several decumbent or creeping stems to 30cm. Leaves ovate, narrower towards the flowers. Corolla 30–40mm long, with hairs between the main lobes, blue or purplish. For any moist, peaty soil in sun or light shade. Hardy to −20°C perhaps. Very variable. *G. freyniana* from N Turkey was described as having 3-veined leaves and no hairs between the main corolla lobes. *G. lagodechiana*, described from the S Caucasus, has flowers mostly solitary on short leafy side branches. *G. gelida* M. Bieb., from dry meadows in N Turkey and the Caucasus, has yellow flowers and is often larger than *G. septemfida*.

Gentiana tianshanica Rupr. Native of the Tien Shan in Soviet C Asia, and NW China south to Tibet (Xizang), growing in mountain meadows, flowering in August. Plant with several stems to 30cm from a basal rosette of leaves. Stem leaves sheathing at the base. Flowers with corolla *c*.2.5cm long, blue or purplish. An attractive plant for any good soil in a warm position. Hardy to −20°C or less.

Gentiana triflora Pall. Native of E Siberia, NE China, Sakhalin, Korea and Japan (var. *japonica* (Kusn.) Hara), in N Honshu and Hokkaido, growing in grassy places, especially on roadsides, from sea level to the mountains, flowering in August–September. Plant with few or several upright stems to 80cm from a thick

Gentiana tianshanica

Swertia iberica on the Zigana Pass

Gentiana affinis

Tripterospermum japonicum

rootstock. Leaves lanceolate. Flowers with corolla 4–5cm long, not opening wide, even in sun. For peaty, moist, but well-drained soil in sun or partial shade. Hardy to −20°C or less.

Swertia iberica Fisch. ex C. A. Meyer (*Gentianaceae*)   Native of the Caucasus and NE Turkey, growing in alpine meadows, by streams and in damp places in scrub and forest at 1600–2700m in Turkey, flowering in July–September. Plant with few upright stems 6.5–9cm tall, from a rosette of broad leaves. Stem leaves alternate. Flowers with bluish or reddish-purple petals, 11–15mm long. For moist, peaty soil in a cool position. Hardy to −20°C. Other species are found on mountains across the northern hemisphere.

Tripterospermum japonicum (Sieb. & Zucc.) Maxim. syn. *Crawfurdia japonica* Sieb. & Zucc. (*Gentianaceae*)   Native of E China, Taiwan, Korea, Sakhalin and Japan, in all the islands, growing in woods and grassy places, flowering in August–October. Stems very slender, twining, to 80cm, from slender, creeping rhizomes. Leaves broadly ovate to lanceolate, 4–8cm long. Flowers with corolla *c*.3cm long, rather pale blue. Fruits red-purple, fleshy. A delicate plant. For moist, peaty soil in partial shade with a low shrub to creep through. Hardy to −20°C perhaps. Shown here in Yakusima.

Gentiana triflora var. *japonica* near Shari, Hokkaido

Calamintha grandiflora (L.) Moench.
(*Labiatae*)   Native of Europe, from NE Spain
east to NW Iran and the Caucasus, growing in
damp woods and scrub, often on limestone,
flowering in June–October. Plant pleasantly
fragrant when bruised, with shortly creeping
stolons and stems to 60cm. Leaves pale green,
ovate, toothed. Calyx 12mm long, with a ciliate
margin; corolla 25–40mm long, bright pink.
C. sylvatica Bromf., from Ireland to North
Africa east to the Caucasus, is similar, but with
smaller, pink or lilac flowers, with purple spots
on the lower lip, *c*.15mm long. For any good
soil in sun or partial shade.

Calamintha nepeta (L.) Savi   Native of
Europe, from S England east to S Russia and N
Iran and south to Spain and North Africa,
growing in scrub and on dry banks, usually on
limestone, flowering in June–September. Plant
aromatic, with ascending pubescent branched
stems to 60cm. Leaves broadly ovate, 10–20mm
long. Flowers white or lilac, sometimes purple
spotted, 10–15mm long, much loved by bees.
For a warm, sunny place. Hardy to −15°C.

Dracocephalum nutans L. (*Labiatae*)   Native
of Siberia and NW China in Sinjiang, growing
in dry, rocky places and scrub, flowering in
May–July. Plant with a shortly creeping
rhizome and stems to 70cm, though usually less.
Leaves often reddish. Flowers nodding, 17–
22mm long. For a sunny, well-drained position.
Hardy to −25°C.

Dracocephalum ruyschiana L.   Native of
Europe, from Norway and the Pyrenees
eastwards to N Turkey, Siberia, C Asia and
China, growing in steppes, dry meadows and
rocky hills, flowering in June–July. Plant with
upright stems to 60cm, but usually forming
clumps 30cm high and wide. Leaves linear-
lanceolate, 2–7cm long. Flowers in short spikes,
in whorls of 2–6; corolla 2–2.8cm, blue to violet,
rarely pink or white. For well-drained but good
soil in full sun. Hardy to −25°C.

Lallemantia canescens (L.) Fisch. & Mey.
syn. *Dracocephalum canescens* L. (*Labiatae*)
Native of E Turkey, the S Caucasus and Iran,
growing in rough ground, abandoned fields,
rocky slopes and screes, often on limestone at
1300–3250m, flowering in June–August. Plant
with spreading, then upright stems to 50cm tall.
Lower leaves toothed, 2–6cm long, greyish.
Flowers purple or bluish, 28–40mm long. For
well-drained, dry soil in full sun. Hardy to
−25°C.

Meehania fargesii (Léveillé) Wu (*Labiatae*)
Native of W China in Yunnan and Sichuan,
growing in woods, scrub and wet, shady
ravines, at *c*.1500m, flowering in April–June.
Plant usually not forming stolons, unlike *M.*
urticifolia (see vol. 1, p. 75). Stems to 40cm,
slightly hairy above. Leaves and lower bracts
stalked, the blade *c*.6cm wide and long, cordate.
Upper bracts not leafy. Flowers *c*.4.5cm long,
in loose terminal spikes. Calyx teeth acute. For
a moist position, in some shade. Hardy to
−10°C, perhaps less.

Melittis melissophyllum L. (*Labiatae*) **Bastard**
Balm   Native of Europe, from England south
to Spain and Portugal, and east to Russia,
Greece and just reaching NW Turkey, growing
in hedges, scrub and mountain woods,
flowering in May–June. Plant with a clump of
upright stems 20–70cm tall. Leaves to 7cm in W
Europe. Flowers 25–40mm, usually purple or
pink in W Europe, white with a purplish lip in

Nepeta clarkei by a lake in Kashmir

Nepeta clarkei

Nepeta connata

Calamintha nepeta

Nepeta subsessilis var. *yesoensis*

Dracocephalum nutans

Micromeria thymifolia

Calamintha grandiflora

Meehania fargesii in Sichuan

Dracocephalum ruyschiana

Melittis melissophyllum

E Europe, and in subsp. *carpatica* and subsp. *albida*, which have larger leaves, to 15cm long. For any good soil in partial shade; the most attractive form in cultivation has white flowers with a pink lower lip. Hardy to −20°C.

Micromeria thymifolia (Scop.) Fritsch (*Labiatae*) **Thyme-leaved Savory**   Native of SE Europe, from Hungary and N Italy to Yugoslavia and Albania, growing in rock crevices, flowering in June–August. Stems to 50cm, branched. Leaves 5–20mm long. Flowers 5–9mm long, white and violet, with a 13–veined calyx. Hardy to −15°C, but dislikes wet soil in winter.

Nepeta clarkei Hook. fil. (*Labiatae*)   Native of the Himalayas from Pakistan to Kashmir, growing, often in great quantity, in rather dry valleys by streams and lakes at 2700–3300m, flowering in July–September. Plant forming large upright clumps to 80cm. Leaves ovate-lanceolate to lanceolate, 2.5–6cm long. Flowers pure blue (not purplish), with a white patch on the lower lip. Hardy to −25°C or less, but eaten by slugs in winter if not protected.

Nepeta connata Royle ex Benth.   Native of the Himalayas, from Pakistan to N India, growing in scrub and grassy places at 2100–3600m, flowering in July-September. Stems few, unbranched, to 60cm. Leaves 8–20cm, heart-shaped at the base. Flowers *c*.2cm long, purplish. For any good soil in full sun. Hardy to −25°C. *N. nervosa* Royle ex Benth. is similar, but has a spike of pale blue or, more rarely, purple flowers, 1.5cm long, and shorter linear–lanceolate leaves. It is common in Kashmir.

Nepeta subsessilis Maxim. var. **yesoensis** Fr. & Sav.   Native of Japan, in Hokkaido and C & N Honshu, growing on shady rocks by streams in the mountains, and on sheltered coastal cliffs, flowering in July–September. Stems several, to 100cm, but nearer 30cm in gardens, from a tufted rootstock. Leaves ovate, 6–10cm long, short-stalked. Flowers *c*.3cm long, usually bluish, rarely white. For moist, rich soil in partial shade. Hardy to −20°C perhaps.

Lallemantia canescens at Harry Hay's, Surrey

Wild Marjoram *Origanum vulgare* on chalk downs near Wye, Kent

Origanum calcaratum Juss. syn. *O. tournefortii* Ait. (*Labiatae*) Native of Crete, Amorgos, Ikaria and other C Aegean islands, growing on limestone rocks, flowering in April–October. Plant with many stems to 30cm from a woody rootstock. Leaves broadly ovate to orbicular, glaucous, pubescent. Bracts 8–13mm long, 4–10mm wide, acute. Calyx with a large entire or almost undivided upper lip, and lower lip either absent or of 2 very small teeth. Corolla 10–17mm long. Easy to grow in well-drained, dry soil in full sun, possibly planted in a wall. Hardy to −10°C, or less if dry.

Origanum laevigatum Boiss. Native of S Turkey and Cyprus, growing in grassland, maquis, scrub and open woods at up to 2000m, flowering in April–October. Plant with upright stems to 70cm from a woody and suckering rootstock. Inflorescence very diffuse. Leaves ovate to elliptical, glaucous, glabrous. Bracts 3–6mm, lanceolate, acute, purple. Calyx with 5 equal teeth, 3–6mm long. Corolla 8–16mm long, purple. Stamens not exserted. For well-drained soil in full sun. Hardy to −15°C, probably less.

Origanum rotundifolium Boiss. Native of NE Turkey, in the Çoruh gorge and near Erzurum and of Soviet Georgia, growing in walls, rocks and rocky slopes at up to 1300m, flowering in June–September. Plant with a woody base and creeping underground stolons. Flowering stems hairy, to 30cm long. Leaves roundish, with conspicuous veins. Bracts 8–25mm × 7–27mm, yellowish green. Calyx 5–9mm, 2-lipped, with 5 teeth. For well-drained soil in sun or partial shade, best growing out of a wall. Hardy to −10°C, perhaps less. *O. acutidens* (Hand.-Mazz.) Ietswaart is similar, but has longer glabrous stems and much branched to 50cm. The leaves are ovate, with inconspicuous veins,

and the calyx teeth are acuminate. It is found in E Turkey at up to 3000m, on rocky slopes and screes, but proved short-lived in cultivation in S England, probably killed by damp rather than cold.

Origanum scabrum Boiss. & Held. Native of Greece, growing in rocky places in the Taygetos mountains of the Peloponnese (with subsp. *pulchrum* (Boiss. & Held.) P. H. Davis in Euboea), flowering in June–September. Plant with creeping underground rhizomes and flowering stems to 45cm. Leaves cordate at the base, glabrous. Bracts 7–8mm wide, ovate, purple. Upper lip of calyx with 3 teeth. In subsp. *pulchrum* the leaf margins are smooth, not scabrid, the calyx is more deeply divided and the bracts are ovate-elliptic. For well-drained, stony soil in full sun. Hardy to −15°C or less.

Origanum vulgare L. **Wild Marjoram** Native of most of Europe, Turkey and C Asia eastwards to Taiwan, growing in dry grassy places or, in the south, in open woods, flowering in May–October. A very variable species, both in its wide natural distribution and in cultivation. Stems to 100cm or more from a woody base, but also with suckers. Leaves and stems variably hairy. Inflorescence compact or diffuse. Bracts 4–5mm purple. Calyx with 5 equal teeth, 2–4mm long. Corolla 3–10mm long, purple, pink or white. For well-drained soil in full sun. Hardy to −20°C or less. Some of the commoner cultivars are 'Aureum', with golden leaves; 'Compactum', with numerous short stems to 15cm, a very free-flowering and valuable plant; 'Prismaticum', with spicules 12–20mm long, often grown for cooking, as 'Oregano'; and 'Roseum' (shown here) which has pink flowers.

Origanum hybrids Origanum species hybridize very readily both in the wild and in gardens. The following have been named and propagated, and others are likely to appear, between any of the species cultivated.

Origanum 'Barbara Tingay' A hybrid between *O. calcaratum* and *O. rotundifolium*, raised in around 1980.

Origanum 'Emma Stanley' A form or hybrid of *O. scabrum*, possibly with *O. amanum*, which appeared in the garden of Roger Poulett at North Mundham in Sussex in around 1985. A very striking plant with smooth, glaucous leaves and neat, particularly well-coloured spicules. Hardy to −15°C perhaps.

Origanum 'Hopleys' Introduced by David Barker of Hopleys Nurseries in *c*.1980. This is probably a form of *O. vulgare*, close to subsp. *gracile* (syn. *O. tytthanthum* Gontsch.). It is native of Turkey and Iran east to Pakistan. It may, however, be a hybrid between *O. vulgare* and *O. laevigatum*, under which it has usually been listed. Stems to 70cm. Spicules slender, compact. Corolla *c*.6mm long. For well-drained soil in full sun. Hardy to −15°C perhaps.

Origanum 'Kent Beauty' A hybrid between *O. scabrum* and *O. rotundifolium*, raised at Washfield Nurseries, Hawkhurst, Kent in around 1978. 'Kent Beauty' was selected from among a number of seedlings which appeared near where the parents were growing. It has much branched, semi-prostrate stems to 35cm from a woody and suckering rootstock. Stem leaves glaucous and glabrous. Bracts 1.6cm × 1.5cm, rounded. Corolla 13mm long. For well-drained soil in full sun, preferably on a raised bed. Hardy to −10°C.

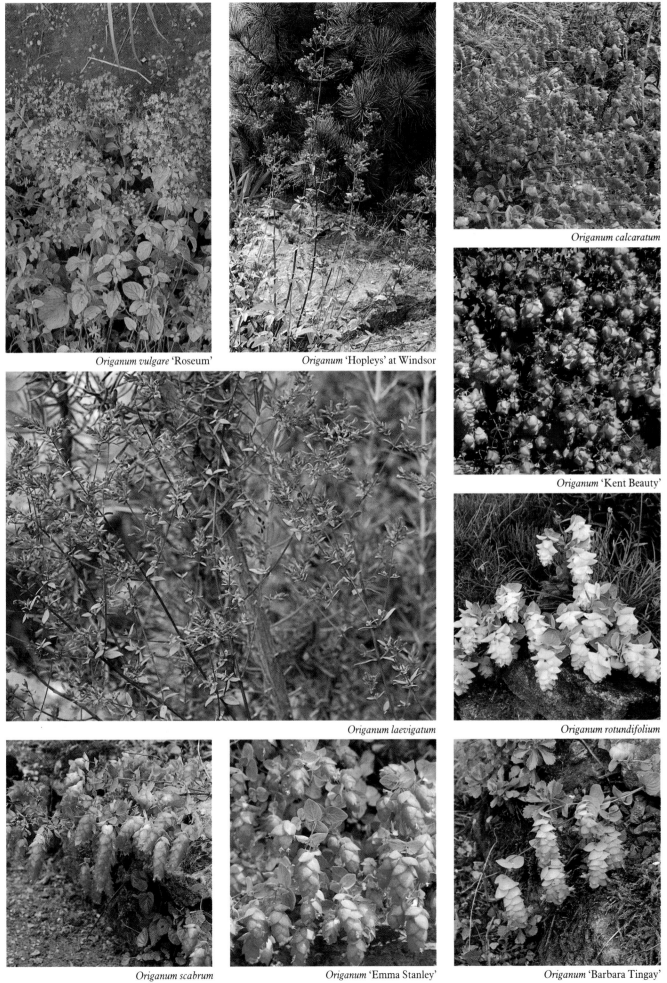

Origanum vulgare 'Roseum'

Origanum 'Hopleys' at Windsor

Origanum calcaratum

Origanum 'Kent Beauty'

Origanum laevigatum

Origanum rotundifolium

Origanum scabrum

Origanum 'Emma Stanley'

Origanum 'Barbara Tingay'

Leonotis dysophylla (pale form)

Leonotis dysophylla near Cathedral Peak, Natal

Leonotis leonurus at Sissinghurst

Chelonopsis moschata at Sellindge, Kent

Agastache foeniculum

Agastache cana (Hook.) Woot. & Standl. (*Labiatae*)   Native of W Texas and S New Mexico, growing on dry slopes in the mountains, flowering in July–August. Plant aromatic, to 60cm. Stems branching; leaves ovate-lanceolate, serrate, to 4cm long. Flowers pink, 25mm long. For a hot, dry position in full sun. Hardy to −20°C.

Agastache foeniculum (Pursh) O. Kuntze syn. *A. anethiodora* Britt.   Native of North America, from Ontario west to Washington, south to Colorado, and naturalized in the east in New England, growing in fields, dry scrub and hills, flowering in June–September. Plant smelling of aniseed; stems to 1.5m, glabrous. Leaves ovate, whitish beneath. Bracts often tinged violet; flowers blue. For dry soil in full sun. Hardy to −25°C.

Chelonopsis moschata Miq. (*Labiatae*)   Native of Japan, in Hokkaido, Honshu and Shikoku, growing in wet places along streams, flowering in August–September. Plant with numerous slender stems, 50–100cm, from a woody rootstock. Leaves narrowly ovate to broadly oblanceolate, 10–20cm long. Flowers 1–3 in the leaf axils, 4–4.5cm long. Nutlets 7–8mm long. For a moist, cool position in light shade. Hardy to −20°C.

Leonotis dysophylla Benth. syn. *L. ocymifolia* (Burm. fil.) Iwarsson var. *raineriana* (Visiani) Iwarsson   Native of South Africa, in the E Cape Province and into Natal and Transvaal, growing in grassland in the mountains, to 2000m in the Drakensberg, flowering in November–February. Plant 1–5m, sometimes woody at the base, and suckering underground. Leaves broadly ovate, 5–17cm long, the margins crenate. Calyx 15–30cm long, 2-lipped. Flowers 24–45mm long, velvety-hairy outside, orange or rarely very pale pink. Hardier than *L. leonurus*, but needing a hot, dry position. The albinistic form of this species is more cream-buff than white, with brownish-red pollen. Hardy to −15°C, perhaps.

Leonotis leonurus (L.) R. Br. **Wild Dagga**   Native of South Africa from Cape Province to Natal and Transvaal, growing in grassy places, on the edge of scrub and on roadsides below 1800m, flowering in November–July. Plant with upright stems to 2m or more. Leaves linear, 5–10cm long. Calyx shorter than 15mm, teeth equal. Flowers 40–50mm long, rarely white in var. *albiflora* Benth., usually grown as the cultivar 'Harrismith White'. For a warm, dry, sunny position. Hardy to −10°C, perhaps less with frost protection for the root.

Perovskia atriplicifolia Benth. (*Labiatae*)   Native of Afghanistan to S Xizang, growing in open, rocky places, flowering in July–September. Plant to 1m, with numerous stems from ground level. Leaves entire, ovate-oblong, to 4cm. Flowers with a blue-hairy calyx. For any dry soil in full sun. Hardy to −10°C, or less. (Not illustrated.)

Perovskia 'Blue Spire'   Probably a hybrid between the entire-leaved *P. atriplicifolia* and the bipinnate-leaved *P. abrotanoides* Kar., raised by Notcutts. Plant spreading below ground and becoming woody at the base. Leaves deeply laciniate, nearer to *P. abrotanoides*. Flowers with very woolly calyces. For dry soil in full sun. Hardy to −25°C.

Perovskia 'Blue Spire' at the Royal Botanic Garden, Edinburgh

Perovskia 'Blue Spire'

Agastache cana

Helenium hoopesii in the Yellowstone National Park, Wyoming

Silphium perfoliatum

Helenium 'Wyndley'

Heliopsis 'Light of Loddon'

Heliopsis 'Ballerina'

Helenium autumnale L. (*Compositae*) Native of North America, from Quebec south to Florida, and west to Manitoba, Oregon, Nevada and Arizona, growing in wet meadows and marshes, flowering in August–October. Plant forming large clumps of stems to 1.8m. Leaves elliptic oblong or lanceolate. Flowers 5–7cm across, with a yellow centre in wild *H. autumnale*, a brown centre in the closely related *H. nudiflorum*, from the Midwest. Most cultivars are probably hybrids between these and *H. bigelovii* from California, which also has a yellow centre. Typical cultivars are: 'Moerheim Beauty', flowers brownish-red; stems to 80cm; raised by Ruys in 1930. 'Riverton Beauty', flowers yellow; stems to 1.5m. 'Wyndley', flowers yellow marked with red; stems to 60cm.

Helenium hoopesii Gray Native of California, in the Sierra Nevada, from Tulare Co. north to S Oregon, and east to Wyoming and New Mexico, growing in meadows along streams and on marshy hillsides at 2000–3000m, flowering in July–September. Plant with a handsome rosette of large oblanceolate leaves to 30cm long, from a thick aromatic rootstock. Poisonous to sheep and generally a sign of overgrazing in the parts of the Rockies where it is common. For any good soil. Hardy to −25°C or less.

Helianthus decapetalus L. (*Compositae*) **Wild Sunflower** Native of NE North America, from SW Quebec to Minnesota and Nebraska, south to Georgia, Kentucky and Missouri, growing in open woods, clearings and scrub, flowering in August–October. Plant with a creeping rhizome, forming large patches of stems to 1.5m tall. Leaves ovate, acute, thin in texture, to 20cm long. Flower-heads 5–6.5cm across with 8–12 or more 'petals'. A large garden variety, 'Multiflorus', is sometimes considered a hybrid with *H. annuus*. 'Corona Dorica' is a form with enlarged central florets.

Helianthus salicifolius A. Dietrich syn. *H. orgyralis* DC. Native of Nebraska to E Colorado south to W Missouri, Oklahoma and Texas, growing in meadows, clearings in forest and prairies, usually on limestone, flowering in August–October. Plant with long rhizomes, forming clumps of tall stems to 2m or more. Leaves linear to linear-lanceolate, recurved, usually 1–3mm across. Flower-heads *c*.5cm across. 'Lemon Queen' sounds more beautiful.

Heliopsis helianthoides (L.) Sweet (*Compositae*) Native of New York and S Ontario west to Minnesota and south to North Carolina and Illinois, growing in open woods, scrub and dry hillsides, flowering in July–September. Plant forming clumps of stems to 1.5m. Leaves ovate-lanceolate to oblong-ovate. Flowers with 'petals' that remain attached when dead. 'Light of Loddon' has single flowers; 'Ballerina' semi-double; and 'Golden Plume' (syn. 'Goldgefieder') and 'Incomparabilis' have double zinnia-like flowers of brash orange-yellow. For any good soil in full sun. Hardy to −25°C or less.

Silphium perfoliatum L. (*Compositae*) Native of E North America, from Ontario to South Dakota, south to Georgia, Missouri and Oklahoma, growing in damp woods on river banks, in scrub and moist meadows, flowering in July–September. Stems to 2.5m, forming a large clump. Lower leaves coarsely toothed, with winged petioles; upper leaves joined at their bases to form a cup. Flower-heads 5–7.5cm across. For rich, moist soil in sun or shade. Hardy to −25°C or less.

Helianthus salicifolius at Bressingham

Helenium autumnale

Helianthus decapetalus in New York State, near Purchase

Helianthus decapetalus

'Orlando'

'September Ruby'

'Lye End Beauty'

'Herbstschnee'
syn. 'Autumn Snow'

'Jenny'

'Andenken an
Alma Potschke'

'Harrington's
Pink'

'White Swan'

'Pink Zenith'

'Coombe Margaret'

'Carnival'

'Barr's Pink'

'September Glow'

'Mrs S. T. Wright'

'Ada Ballard'

'Lady-in-Blue'

'Chequers'

'Little Pink Beauty'

'Chatterbox'

Michaelmas daisy specimens from Wisley, 1 October. ²⁄₃ life size

Wild asters in Wyoming

Aster thomsonii

Aster amellus L. (*Compositae*)   Native of
Europe, from NC France and Poland
southwards to N Italy and Bulgaria, eastwards
to Russia and C Asia, Turkey (subsp. *ibericus*)
and the Caucasus, growing in scrub and on the
edges of woods, flowering in June–August.
Plant with erect stems to 70cm. Leaves oblong
to lanceolate. Flower-heads large, solitary;
petals blue, white or occasionally red. Hardy to
−25°C.

Aster × dumosus hort.   This is a group of
dwarf Michaelmas daisies which form rounded,
bushy plants to *c*.40cm high. They are probably
hybrids between *A. dumosus* L., a species from
North America, and *A. novi-belgii*. Leaves
linear or linear-lanceolate, entire, to 8cm long.
Flower-heads up to 2cm across, white or pink,
to lavender-blue, produced in August–October.
Hardy to −25°C or less.

Aster × frikartii '**Mönch**'   This is a very good
selection of *A. × frikartii*, which is a hybrid
between *A. amellus* and *A. thomsonii* (q.v.).
Raised by Frikart in Switzerland in *c*.1920, the
name 'Mönch' refers to a famous Swiss
mountain. This particular form is highly
regarded for its long flowering season. Plant to
120cm high. Flowers lavender-blue, *c*.6cm
across, freely produced in a loose panicle from
July–October. Hardy to −20°C.

Aster novae-angliae L.   Native of North
America, from Quebec to Alberta, south to
North Carolina, Kentucky, Arkansas, Kansas
and Colorado, growing in damp scrub,
meadows and on shores, flowering from
August–October. Also commonly cultivated
and seen as an escape elsewhere in North
America and Europe. Stems stout, up to 2m
high. Leaves lanceolate, to 12cm long, entire.
Flower-heads numerous, violet-purple or pink,
to 5cm across. Involucral bracts recurving,
sticky. There are several varieties available.
Hardy to −25°C.

Aster novi-belgii L.   Native of E North
America, from Newfoundland to Quebec and
Nova Scotia, south to Georgia, growing in damp
scrub, meadows, and on shores, usually within
100 miles of the sea, flowering from late July–
October. The name '*novi-belgii*' comes from
'New Belgium', the early name for New York.
Plant to 1.2m high. Leaves lanceolate to linear-
lanceolate, to 12cm long. Flowers blue-violet.
Involucral bracts spreading. There are many
garden varieties, with flowers ranging in colour
from white and pink through to light and dark
blue and purple; they need to be divided every
few years, preferably in the spring. Hardy to
−25°C or less.

Michaelmas daisy cultivars   (In brackets is
the species group to which the cultivar belongs.)

'**Ada Ballard**' (*novi-belgii*)   1m. Large flowers
in September.
'**Andenken an Alma Potschke**' (*novae-
angliae*)   105cm. September–October.
'**Barr's Pink**' (*novae-angliae*)   1.3m. Large
semi-double flowers in September.
'**Carnival**' (*novi-belgii*)   60cm.
'**Chatterbox**' (× *dumosus*)
'**Chequers**' (*novi-belgii*)   1m. Raised by R. A.
Lidsey. Flowers *c*.5cm across.
'**Coombe Margaret**' (*novi-belgii*)
'**Harrington's Pink**' (*novae-angliae*)   120cm.
Leafy growth. Clear-pink flowers in
September–October. Good for cutting.
'**Herbstschnee**' syn. 'Autumn Snow' (*novae-
angliae*)   130cm. Recently introduced from
Germany, large flowers in bushy heads from
August–September.
'**Jenny**' (× *dumosus*)   30cm. August–
September.
'**King George**' (*amellus*)   60cm. An old
cultivar, easy to grow. August–October.
'**Lady-in-Blue**' (× *dumosus*)   25cm. Compact
bush, with numerous semi-double flowers from
August–October.
'**Little Pink Beauty**' (× *dumosus*)   40cm. Good
semi-double. September–October.
'**Lye End Beauty**' (*novae-angliae*)   130cm.
This occurred in a garden in the late 1950s. Rich
cerise-lilac flowers in August–September.
'**Mrs S. T. Wright**' (*novae-angliae*)   (Named
after the wife of the first Superintendent of the
RHS gardens at Wisley.)
'**Orlando**' (*novi-belgii*)   1.5m. Raised by Mr
Percy Picton. Flowers *c*.5cm across in
September–October.
'**Pink Zenith**' (*amellus*)   60cm. Upright habit.
August–October.
'**September Glow**' (*amellus*)
'**September Ruby**' (*novae-angliae*)   120cm.
September–October.
'**White Swan**' (*novi-belgii*)

Aster thomsonii C. B. Clarke   A native of the
W Himalaya, from Pakistan to Uttar Pradesh,
growing in forests and shrubberies, at 2100–
3000m, flowering in July–September. Stems
erect, branched, to 1m. Leaves ovate to elliptic,
toothed, to 10cm long. Flower-heads usually
solitary, pale lilac, 3.5–5cm across. Best
increased by seeds or cuttings. Hardy to −20°C.

Aster 'King George'

Aster × frikartii 'Mönch'

Aster novae-angliae

Aster ericoides
'Golden Spray'

Aster cordifolius
'Silver Spray'

Aster ericoides
'Pink Cloud'

Aster sedifolius

Aster macrophyllus

Aster ericoides
'Delight'

Aster pilosus
var. *demotus*

Aster lateriflorus
'Horizontalis'

Aster ericoides
'White Heather'

Specimens from Perryhill Nursery, 30 September. ½ life size

Aster species with *Artemisia*, in Idaho

Aster ericoides 'Hon. Vicary Gibbs'

Aster cordifolius L. (*Compositae*)   Native of North America, from Nova Scotia and Quebec south to Wisconsin, Georgia, Alabama and Missouri, growing in open woods, thickets and clearings, flowering from August–October. Plant erect, much branched, with glabrous stems to 2m, arising from a creeping rhizome. Leaves broadly ovate, cordate, sharply toothed, to 12cm long. Flowers numerous, small, star-like, ranging in colour from violet or blue to nearly white, to 2cm across, borne in loose graceful sprays. Hardy to −25°C and less. *A. cordifolius* 'Silver Spray' grows to 1.5m and bears very pale lilac flowers in long arching sprays.

Aster divaricatus L. syn. *A. corymbosus* Ait. Native of North America, from S Maine west to Oregon, south to Georgia, Alabama and Tennessee, growing in dry woods and clearings, flowering in July–October. Very variable and easily confused with other species. Stems dark purple, to 1m high, from creeping rhizomes. Leaves cordate, lobed at the base, to 7cm long, coarsely toothed. Flowers white, with a pale-yellow disc. Flower-heads *c.*3cm across, in corymbs. Hardy to −25°C and less.

Aster ericoides L.   Native of North America, from Maine west to British Columbia, south to New England, Georgia, Texas and Arizona, growing in dry open soil or thickets, flowering in July–October. Plant to 1m high, bushy. Stems slender, erect, much-branched above, arising from a short rhizome. Leaves almost rigid, linear, entire, to 7cm long. Flower-heads numerous, white or tinged rose, to 1cm across. Hardy to −25°C and less. *Aster ericoides* cultivars include: **'Delight'**, **'Golden Spray'** (80cm), **'Hon. Vicary Gibbs'**, **'Pink Cloud'** (80cm), **'White Heather'** (1m).

Aster hemisphericus E. J. Alex.   Native of North America, from Alabama west to Texas, north to Missouri and Kansas, growing in prairies, dry woods and rocky slopes, flowering in late August–October. Plant with slender stems, to 1m high, arising from a stoloniferous rhizome. Leaves linear to linear-oblanceolate, hard and thick. Inflorescence with 3–12 erect flower-heads 3–6cm wide. Hardy to −25°C.

Aster lateriflorus (L.) Britt. **'Horizontalis'** *A. lateriflorus* is native of North America, from Quebec, Nova Scotia, Ontario and Minnesota south to Georgia, Tennessee and Arkansas, growing in dry to moist fields, clearings, thickets and on shorelines, flowering from August–October. Plant with slender, purplish or green stems, to 1.5m, with spreading branches. Leaves linear-lanceolate to broadly lanceolate, toothed, to 12cm long. Flower-heads numerous, white or pale purple, to 1.5cm across. 'Horizontalis' is a common cultivar, with very wide-spreading branches.

Aster macrophyllus L.   Native of North America, from Quebec west to Minnesota, south to North Carolina, Tennessee, West Virginia, Ohio, Indiana and Illinois, growing in dry to moist, open woods, thickets and clearings, flowering from August–September. A rather coarse plant, with reddish stems, to 1.5m high, from a thick rootstock. Basal leaves large, cordate, toothed; upper leaves variable, often smaller and narrower. Flowers lavender to violet, *c.*2.5cm across, borne in a broad corymb. A very variable plant, with many different forms. Hardy to −25°C.

Aster pilosus Willd. var. **demotus** Blake syn. *A. tradescantii* hort.   This is the commonest variety of *A. pilosus* and is native from Maine west to Minnesota, and southwards throughout the USA, growing in dry thickets, clearings, fields and by roadsides, flowering from August–October. Plant to 1.5m high. Leaves linear-lanceolate. Numerous small flower-heads (white or tinged rose) to 1.5cm across. Hardy to −25°C.

Aster sedifolius L. syn. *A. acris* L.   Native of S Europe, from France, Spain and Portugal, eastwards to Russia and the Caucasus, growing on dry hills and waste places, flowering in August–September. Plant with branching stems, forming a rounded bush to 120cm, but usually *c.*50cm. Leaves very narrow, white-hairy in subsp. *canus* from E and SE Europe. Flowers blue to lilac, rather small, and spidery, with 5–10 'petals'. For dry soil in full sun. Hardy to −20°C or less. The cultivar 'Nanus' is said to be more compact, to 45cm, and so less likely to flop to one side.

Aster sedifolius

Aster divaricatus

Boltonia asteroides

Chrysanthemum serotinum at Kew

Chrysanthemum yezoense

Aster albescens (DC.) Hand.-Mazz.
(*Compositae*)   Native of the Himalayas, from
Kashmir to SW China and Burma, growing in
light forests, shrubberies and on open slopes, at
2100–3600m, flowering in June–September. A
rambling subshrub, to 2m, with large leaves to
12cm. Flower-heads *c*.8mm across, lilac, purple
or rarely white. Hardy to −10°C, perhaps.

Aster tartaricus L. fil.   Native of Japan, N
China and Siberia, from Lake Baikal eastwards,
growing in subalpine meadows and wet places,
flowering in August–October. Plant with erect
stems, up to 2m. Leaves lanceolate or oval-
lanceolate, narrowed to the base, entire, the
lower ones up to 30cm long. 2.5–3.3cm across.

Aster albescens

Aster tartaricus

Aster turbellinus

Chrysanthemum rubellum 'Clara Curtis'

Chrysanthemum rubellum 'Mary Stoker'

Aster turbellinus Lindl. Native of North America, from Illinois to Nebraska, south to Louisiana, Arkansas and Kansas, growing in dry prairies, open woods and on rocky outcrops, flowering in September–October. Plant to 1m. Leaves lanceolate or oblong-lanceolate, entire, to 8cm long. Flower-heads *c*.2cm across, violet, usually solitary at ends of branches.

Boltonia asteroides (L.) L'Her. (*Compositae*) Native of North America, from New York and New Jersey to Ohio south to Maryland and the mountains of North Carolina, growing on gravelly shores and sandy thickets, flowering in mid-July–September. Plant to 2m. Leaves linear to oblanceolate, entire, to 12cm long. Hardy to −25°C.

Chrysanthemum rubellum Sealy, now strictly

Dendranthema zawadskii (Herbich) Tzveler var. *latilobum* (Maxim.) Kitam. (*Compositae*) Native of parts of Russia, in the Carpathians and the Urals, Czechoslovakia and Poland, and east across Siberia to Japan, Korea and N China, growing on stony slopes, somewhat calcicole, flowering in August–October. Plant woody at base, to 60cm. Leaves broadly triangular-ovate, much divided, to 5cm long, coarsely toothed or lobed. Flower-heads terminal, solitary, or rather few in a loose corymb, to 8cm across, fragrant. Petals pale pink, or white; disc yellow. Hardy to −20°C. There are a number of extremely free-flowering clones or hybrids of this plant, with stems *c*.60cm e.g.: 'Clara Curtis' and 'Mary Stoker'.

Chrysanthemum serotinum L. now strictly *Leucanthemella serotina* (L.) Tzveler, syn. *C.*

uliginosum Pers. Native of E Europe, from SE Czechoslovakia and EC Yugoslavia eastwards to N Ukraine and NE Bulgaria, growing in wet places, flowering in September–November. A bushy, erect plant, with stems to 2m. Leaves lanceolate to oblong-lanceolate, deeply divided. Flowers with green centres, to 7cm across, turning to the sun. Good for cutting.

Chrysanthemum yezoense Maek. now strictly *Dendranthema yezoense* (Maek.) D. J. H. Hind Native of Japan, in Hokkaido and Honshu, growing on rocks near seashores, flowering from September–December. Plant to 40cm, stoloniferous, from long-creeping rhizomes. Leaves wedge-shaped, to 4cm long and wide, tapered at base. Flowers white, daisy-like in branching sprays. A good plant for well-drained soil in full sun. Hardy to −15°C.

221

Eupatorium perfoliatum

Eupatorium purpureum near New York

Solidago 'Goldengate'

Eupatorium cannabinum by the Stour in Dorset

Vernonia novaboracensis

Vernonia crinita

Eupatorium rugosum

Solidaster × luteus

Solidago 'Crown of Rays'

Eupatorium maculatum

Eupatorium cannabinum L. (*Compositae*)
Hemp Agrimony   Native of Europe, from
Scotland to North Africa and Spain, and east to
Turkey and C Asia, growing in moist places,
fens, on river banks and by streams, flowering
in July–September. Plant forming large clumps
of stems to 120cm with rather soft leaves, deeply
3–5 lobed. Flower-heads 2–5mm across in a
large, flat-topped inflorescence, usually mauve-
pink but a white form is listed in Trehane's
Index Hortensis. Like the American *Eupatoria*,
this is much visited by butterflies. For any rich,
moist soil in sun or partial shade. Hardy to
−25°C or less.

Eupatorium maculatum L. 'Atropurpureum'
Joe Pye Weed   Native of North America, from
Newfoundland west to British Columbia, and
south to New York and in the mountains of
North Carolina, New Mexico and Washington,
growing in damp places in open woods,
meadows and river and lake shores usually on
base-rich soils, flowering in July–September.
Plant forming large clumps of tall, purple stems
to 2m or more. Leaves simple, oblong-
lanceolate to narrowly ovate-lanceolate, in
whorls of 4–5. Flower-heads 8–20 flowered in a
large flat-topped inflorescence. Hardy to −25°C
or less. 'Atropurpureum' has rich-reddish-
purple flowers.

Eupatorium perfoliatum L. **Thoroughwort**,
Boneset   Native of E North America, from
Quebec to Manitoba, south to Florida,
Louisiana and Texas, growing in wet woods,
scrub, fens and damp grassland, flowering in
July–October. Whole plant roughly hairy with
rather few stems to 1.5m. Leaves opposite, the

lower often joined at the base round the stem,
usually long acuminate. Flower-heads 10–40
flowered, in a rather flat-topped inflorescence,
whitish or purplish. Hardy to −25°C.

Eupatorium purpureum L. **Green-stemmed
Joe Pye Weed**   Native of E North America,
from New Hampshire west to Minnesota and
Nebraska, and south to N Florida and
Oklahoma, growing in damp places in woods,
usually on basic soils, flowering in July–
September. Plant forming large clumps of
glaucous stems to 2m or more, purple only at the
nodes. Leaves lanceolate to ovate, in whorls of
2–5. Flower-heads 3–7 flowered, in a large
pyramidal inflorescence, pale pinkish, mauve or
creamy white. For any rich, moist soil in sun or
partial shade. Hardy to −25°C or less. A fine
sight when covered with butterflies.

Eupatorium rugosum Houtt. syn. *E. urticifolium*
Reich. **White Snakeroot**   Native of E North
America from Quebec to S Saskatchewan and
south, in the mountains, to Georgia and Texas,
growing in woods and especially scrub, flowering
in July–October. Stems to 1.5m from a tough,
knobbly rhizome, forming large clumps to 1.5m.
Leaves ovate, stalked, coarsely toothed, to 18cm
long. Flower-heads 15–30 flowered, pure white.
For any good soil in sun or partial shade. Hardy
to −25°C.

Solidago 'Crown of Rays' (*Compositae*)   A short
plant to 50cm with small flowers on radiating rays.
Several wild species from North America have an
inflorescence of this shape, e.g. *S. juncea*. For
any soil in full sun. Hardy to −25°C or less.

Solidago 'Goldengate'   Raised by Burleydam
in 1948. Stems to 30cm in a slowly spreading
clump. For any soil in full sun. Hardy to −25°C
or less.

× *Solidaster luteus* (Everett) M. L. Green ex
Dress syn. *Aster* 'Hybridus luteus'   A supposed
hybrid between *Aster ptarmicoides* and *Solidago
canadensis*, known since before 1910. Stems to
60cm; flowers *c*.5mm across, pale yellow
produced in July–September. 'Lemore' raised
by Thos. Carlisle Ltd in 1948 is probably the
plant shown here. For any good soil in full sun.
Hardy to −25°C or less.

Vernonia crinita Raf. (*Compositae*) **Ironweed**
Native of Missouri, Kansas, Arkansas and
Oklahoma, growing in wet meadows, marshes
and open woods, flowering in July–September.
Plant forming clumps of stout stems to 3m tall.
Leaves linear or linear-lanceolate, to 2cm wide.
Flower-heads 55–90 flowered, 1.2–2cm across,
with numerous curling threads on the bracts.
For any good, moist soil in sun or partial shade.
Hardy to −20°C or less.

Vernonia novaboracensis (L.) Michx.   Native
of Massachusetts and S New York south to
West Virginia, Ohio, Georgia and Mississippi,
growing in marshy meadows and clearings in
woods, flowering in August–October. Plant
with branching stems to 2m. Leaves lanceolate
to oblong-lanceolate, to 4.7cm wide. Flower-
heads 30–50 flowered, around 10mm across,
red-purple or white, with threads on the bracts.
For any good, moist soil in sun or partial shade.
Hardy to −25°C or less.

Tricyrtis 'White Towers'

Tricyrtis 'White Towers' at Washfield Nurseries, Kent

Tricyrtis latifolia

Tricyrtis affinis

Tricyrtis hirta in Kagoshima, Kyushu

Tricyrtis hirta

Tricyrtis affinis Mak. (*Liliaceae*) Native of
Japan, in Hokkaido, Honshu, Shikoku and
Kyushu, growing in woods and on mossy banks
in the mountains, flowering in August–October.
Stems few or several, spreading, from a tufted
rootstock. Leaves hairy, acuminate, 8–18cm
long, the upper clasping the stem. Flowers 1 to
several in the leaf axils and terminal, *c.*2cm,
long-stalked; petals spreading, not reflexed. For
leafy or peaty soil in partial shade. Hardy to
−20°C perhaps.

Tricyrtis formosana Baker syn. *T. stolonifera*
Matsum. Native of Taiwan, growing in forest
and wet shady scrub, at up to 3000m, flowering
in August–September. Plant often spreading by
stolons, forming wide colonies of stems to
80cm. Leaves rather shining, deep green with
darker spots, the upper clasping the stem.
Flowers 2.5–3cm. For moist, loose, leafy soil in
partial shade and shelter. Hardy to −15°C.
Probably the most easily grown species.

Tricyrtis hirta (Thunb.) Hook. Native of
Honshu, Shikoku and Kyushu, growing on
shady rocks, flowering in August–October.
Stems 40–80cm, from a tufted rootstock,
sometimes pendulous, hairy. Leaves narrowly
ovate-oblong to broadly lanceolate, 8–15cm
long. Flowers 2–3 in the leaf axils, and tufted
and terminal, on stalks shorter than the 2.5–
3cm-long flowers. For moist, leafy soil in partial
shade and shelter. Hardy to −15°C.

Tricyrtis latifolia Maxim. syn. *T. bakeri*
Koidz. Native of Japan, in all the large
islands, and of China, growing in woods in the
mountains, flowering in July–September. Stems
few, hairy, upright or arching, to 80cm. Leaves
obovate, 8–15cm long, 4–9cm wide.
Inflorescence cymose. Flowers 2–2.5cm long.
For leafy soil in partial shade. Hardy to −15°C.

Tricyrtis 'Lilac Towers' and **'White Towers'**
These are very similar except for the flower
colour and are perhaps hybrids between *T. hirta*
and possibly *T. affinis*, having hairy stems and
leaves, always stiffly upright, with several
flowers on short stalks in the leaf axils. 'Lilac
Towers' is often sold as *T. hirta*. Both are easily
grown in leafy soil in partial shade. Hardy to
−15°C.

Tricyrtis formosana at the Savill Gardens, Windsor

Tricyrtis formosana

Tricyrtis 'Lilac Towers'

Tricyrtis 'Lilac Towers'

Liriope muscari

Ophiopogon planiscapus 'Nigrescens'

Ruscus aculeatus

Disporum smithii

Disporum smithii (Hook.) Piper (*Liliaceae*)
Native of W North America, from C California
to British Columbia, growing in moist,
evergreen woods and redwood forest in the
Coast Ranges, flowering in March–May,
fruiting in August–October. Plant with much-
branched stems to 20cm, usually *c*.30cm from a
tufted rootstock. Leaves ovate to ovate-
lanceolate, 5–12cm long. Flowers whitish, in
clusters of 1–5, 1.5–2.5cm long. Berries 12–
15mm long. For a leafy soil in a shady, sheltered
position. Hardy to −15°C, perhaps less.

Liriope muscari (Decne.) Bailey (*Liliaceae*)
Native of China, Japan, from C Honshu
southwards, Taiwan, Korea and Vietnam,
growing in woods, flowering in August–

October. Plant tufted with grassy leaves 4–7
(–12)mm wide, up to 60cm long. Flower spikes
often flattened, usually exceeding the leaves.
Flowers 5–8mm across. Seeds exposed, black.
For leafy soil in shade or partial shade. Hardy to
−10°C perhaps.

Ophiopogon planiscapus Nakai (*Liliaceae*)
Native of Japan, in Honshu, Shikoku and
Kyushu, growing in woods and scrub at low
altitudes, flowering in July–August. Plant with
thickened tuberous roots, spreading by stolons
to form loose patches. Leaves 15–50cm long,
usually around 20cm, and 4–6mm wide.
Flowering stems 15–30cm, 3-angled, flattened.
Flowers 6–7mm long. Seeds blue. For leafy or
peaty soil in sun or shade. Hardy to −15°C,

perhaps less for short periods. 'Nigrescens' syn.
'Arabicus' is an unusual form with blackish
leaves. *O. japonicus* (L. fil.) Ker-Gawl. is
smaller with narrower, 2–3mm-wide leaves. It is
commonly planted as ground cover or as low-
maintenance grass substitute. Hardy to −15°C.

Ruscus aculeatus L. (*Liliaceae-
Asparagaceae*) Native of Europe, from the
Azores, North Africa and S England eastwards
to the Caucasus, with var.
angustifolius Boiss. commoner in SE Europe and
the Mediterranean area to the Caucasus,
growing in oak woods, scrub and on rocky
limestone slopes, flowering in February–May
and September–October. Plant with stiff
evergreen stems to 80cm from a slowly

Tricyrtis flava subsp. *ohsumiensis*

Ophiopogon planiscapus

creeping, tough rootstock, forming dense
thickets. Leaves (strictly flattened stems, called
cladodes) stiff, spiny, *c*.2.5cm long, 2–3 times as
long as wide in var. *aculeatus*, 3 times as long as
wide in var. *angustifolius*. Plants usually male or
female, but hermaphrodite and self-fertile
clones are valued in gardens for their free-
fruiting habit. Berries *c*.1cm across, long lasting
through the winter. For any dryish soil. Hardy
to −25°C or less.

Tricyrtis flava Maxim. subsp. **ohsumiensis**
(Masam.) Kitam. (*Liliaceae*)   Native of
Kyushu, growing in woods in the mountains,
flowering in September–October. Plant with a
dense clump of stout stems to 50cm. Upper
leaves elliptic to oblong, 5–20cm long, glabrous.
Flowers 2.5–3.5cm long with minute spots. For
moist, peaty soil in partial shade. Hardy to
−15°C.

Tricyrtis macrantha Maxim.   Native of
Shikoku, with subsp. *macranthopsis* (Masam.)
Kitam. in C Honshu, growing on smooth, wet
rocks and cliffs in humid gorges where there is
permanently running water at least in summer,
flowering in August–October. Stems few with
pale-brown, coarse hairs, from a tufted
rootstock, with orchid-like fleshy roots running
across the rocks. Leaves cordate at the base,
7–17cm long. Flowers 3–4cm long, pendulous,
very fleshy. Subsp. *macranthopsis* has more
deeply cordate leaves and glabrous stems. For
careful cultivation in very well-drained, leafy
soil in shade and shelter, with ample water in
summer. Hardy to −15°C, perhaps less. *T.
ishiiana* (Kitag. & T. Koyama) Ohwi, from
Honshu, is very similar, but has 3–5 flowers in a
terminal corymb.

Tricyrtis perfoliata Masam.   Native of
Kyushu, growing on shady rock ledges,
flowering in September–October. Stems usually
pendulous, to 70cm, not branched, glabrous.
Leaves very shiny, the upper broadly lanceolate
to narrowly ovate-oblong, 7–18cm long,
perfoliate, long acuminate. Flowers upright,
solitary, 2.5–3cm long. For moist, leafy, well-
drained soil and shelter. Hardy to −15°C perhaps.

Tricyrtis macrantha at Washfield Nurseries, Kent

Tricyrtis perfoliata at Washfield Nurseries, Kent

Miscanthus sinensis by suphur springs in Hokkaido

Cortaderia selloana 'Rendatleri'

Cortaderia selloana 'Aureo-lineata'

Pennisetum orientale

Cortaderia richardii (Endl.) Zotov (*Gramineae*)
Toetoe   Native of New Zealand, growing in swampy places and along rivers in the lowlands, flowering in November–March. Plant forming huge clumps with arching stems to 6m. For moist, sandy soil in full sun. Hardy to −15°C, perhaps. *C. fulvida* (Buchanan) Zotov, from upland habitats, has more upright stems to 2m, with a nodding head of flowers, pinkish when young, and is possibly hardier.

Cortaderia selloana (Schult. & Schult. fil.) Asch. & Graebn.   Native of South America, growing in moist, sandy soils, flowering in late summer, August–October in gardens. Plant dioecious, forming huge clumps of lax leaves to 3m long, with very sharply toothed cutting edges. Inflorescence to 3m; rather erect in the

Cortaderia richardii at Harry Hay's

Molinia caerulea 'Variegata'

Cortaderia selloana 'Pumila'

Cortaderia selloana 'Sunningdale Silver'

male, with spreading branches in the female. Spikelets c.15mm long, white or pinkish, shining. For deep, good soil in full sun. Hardy to −20°C. Several named clones are cultivated: **'Aureo-lineata'** syn. 'Gold Band' has yellow-striped leaves and stems to 2.5m. **'Pumila'** is a small form with erect plumes to 1.5m. **'Rendatleri'** has pinkish, spreading and drooping plumes to 3m tall. **'Sunningdale Silver'** has upright plumes around 2.2m.

Miscanthus sinensis Anderss. (*Gramineae*) Native of Japan, in all the islands, Taiwan and China, growing on hillsides and in sunny places in the mountains, flowering in August–October. Plant forming clumps of upright stems to 2.5m. Leaves with flat blades, 1–2cm wide. Inflorescence of numerous narrow racemes 15–

30cm long forming a corymb. Spikelets 5–7mm long, with a tuft of white or purplish hairs. For any soil in sun or partial shade. Hardy to −20°C. Numerous cultivars are grown in gardens. 'Zebrinus' has white patches across the leaves and stems at regular intervals. 'Silberfeder' ('Silver Feather'), has stems to 2.2m and white hairs on the spikelets. It is the most free-flowering form in cool climates. Some others do not get enough summer heat in England to flower freely. Var. *purpurascens* (Anders.) Rendle has reddish-purple leaves.

Molinia caerulea (L.) Moench (*Gramineae*) Native of N Europe eastwards to Siberia, south to N Turkey and the Caucasus and naturalized in North America, growing in bogs, heaths and on wet, peaty mountainsides, often covering

many square miles and colouring golden in winter, flowering in June–August. Plant forming large dense clumps. Leaves flat. Flowering stems to 130cm. Spikelets 6–9mm long. For acid, sandy, soil in full sun. 'Variegata', shown here, has white-striped leaves. Hardy to −25°C or less.

Pennisetum orientale (Willd.) Rich. (*Gramineae*) Native of North Africa and Turkey east to the Kopet Dağ, south to Arabia, growing on dry, rocky hillsides, flowering in May–July. Plant forming tufts of narrow leaves with flowering stems to 100cm, forming a mound. Spikelets bristly hairy, purplish when young, later greyish brown. For a warm, sheltered position in full sun. Hardy to −15°C, perhaps less in dry areas.

Polystichum
aculeatum

Polystichum
polyblepharum

Polystichum
munitum

Polystichum setiferum
'Bevis'

Polystichum
rigens

Polystichum setiferum
Divisilobum 'Densum Erectum'

Specimens from Wisley, 28 July. ⅓ life size

Onoclea sensibilis

Asplenium scolopendrium L. (*Aspleniaceae*)
Hart's-Tongue Fern   Native of Europe,
including the British Isles, Asia and North
America, growing in various habitats but most
luxuriantly on banks in cool woodland, often on
lime-rich soils and in high-rainfall areas, also
occasionally in crevices in mortared walls.
Fronds evergreen, to 60cm but much smaller in
dry situations. Easily grown in a soil rich in
leaf-mould, in shade. As well as spores and
division, this may be propagated by inducing
the base of the leaf-stalk to form plantlets. Very
variable indeed and many varieties have been
named. Most fall into broad groups. Crispum
group: with strongly undulate and often rather
broad fronds. Muricatum group: frond surface
roughened. Cristatum group: fronds variously
forked at apex.

Matteuccia struthiopteris (L.) Todaro
(*Woodsiaceae*)   Native of Europe, W Asia, E
United States, Canada, China and throughout
Japan. The typical habitat is light shade on
rocky stream-banks, where it may form
extensive colonies. Rhizome short but
producing long stolons by which it spreads quite
rapidly once established. Fronds deciduous,
very erect, forming characteristic pale-green,
'shuttlecock', 60–120cm tall. Fertile fronds
shorter, from the centre of the crown. Hardy
and quick to establish, given light shade and a
moist but well-drained, leafy soil.

Onoclea sensibilis L. (*Woodsiaceae*)   Native of
much of North America east of the Rocky
Mountains, from Newfoundland south to
Florida and Texas, and to NE Asia from E
Siberia to Japan and Korea, growing in wet,
grassy places, open, damp woodland and
occasionally on open hillsides. Rhizome fairly
slender, far-creeping, throwing up fronds
singly. Fronds deciduous, rather long-stalked,
up to 1m tall but more often 45–70cm. Fertile
fronds erect, rather shorter than the sterile ones,
with the pinnae-lobes contracted to bead-like
structures. An easily grown fern, spreading
quite vigorously when well established in a
moist, light soil in light shade. The fronds die
quickly with the first frosts, providing attractive
autumn colour.

Polystichum aculeatum (L.) Roth
(*Dryopteridaceae*)   Native of Europe (including
the British Isles) and much of Asia, growing in
deciduous woodland, often on limy soil, and
sometimes on shaded limestone outcrops. Fronds
thick, leathery, evergreen, more or less bipinnate;
pinnules wedge-shaped at base, often rather
convex. Fronds forming a fairly upright
shuttlecock to 80cm tall. Very hardy and easily
grown in light shade in any reasonable soil. Similar
variation to *P. setiferum*, but fewer cultivars.

Polystichum munitum (Kaulf.) Presl   Native
of W North America, often forming extensive
colonies in cool mountain forests. Rhizome
short; fronds to 1m or more, evergreen, fairly
erect, pinnate with finely serrate pinnae, each of
which has an enlarged basal lobe on the side
facing the frond tip. A robust clump-forming
species easily grown in light shade and a peaty
or leafy soil.

Asplenium scolopendrium 'Crispum'

Polystichum setiferum Divisilobum group

Polystichum polyblepharum (Roem.) Presl.
Native to C & S Japan and S Korea, growing on
the woodland floor in deciduous and mixed
forest at low altitudes. Fronds erect, tufted, to
1m tall, very glossy on the upper side,
bipinnate, with rather square pinnules.
Apparently hardy and a very beautiful fern,
easily grown in woodland conditions and a cool,
leafy soil – probably dislikes limy soils.

Polystichum rigens Tagawa   Native of Japan
in S Honshu, growing in woods. Fronds
evergreen, leathery, shining, 30–45cm long,
bipinnate, narrowly ovate-oblong; pinnules 10–
12mm long. Scales on the stalk black-brown,
lanceolate, 1–1.5mm wide, ciliate. For moist,
acid soil in shade and shelter. Hardy to −10°C
perhaps.

Polystichum setiferum (Forssk.) Woynar
Native of Britain and N Europe with similar
species in both Asia and North America,
growing in deciduous woodland, most often in
limy soils. Fronds thin-textured, bipinnate,
evergreen to 1m long, arching to form an open
shuttlecock. Pinnules distinctly stalked. Hardy
and easily grown in light shade in cool, leafy,
acid or alkaline soil. Young unfurling croziers
have dense, often silvery scales. Propagated by
division or spores. Many variations in frond
shape have been found, most falling into
distinct groups of similar cultivars. For
example, Cristatum group: frond tip is
repeatedly forked to produce a flat crest.
Grandiceps group: a large crest in 3 dimensions,
broader than rest of frond. Cruciatum group:
each pinna is forked from the base to give a
criss-cross or lattice effect. Acutilobum group:
pinnules lanceolate-ovate, long pointed; fronds
tending to lie flat; often proliferous.
Divisilobum group: each pinna is bipinnate;
sometimes proliferous. Plumosum group:
pinnules are extra-finely divided and more leafy;
usually sterile. Bevis is an exceptionally fine
clone of this group. Cultivars within these
groups do not breed true from spores and so are
treated as clones, propagated by division or by
bulbils where present.

Matteuccia struthiopteris in the S Caucasus near Telavi, with *Veratrum* and *Alchemilla*

231

Athyrium nipponicum in China

Athyrium nipponicum
'Pictum'

Athyrium filix-femina
(crested form)

*Hypolepsis
millefolium*

Athyrium filix-femina
(heavily crested form)

Specimens from Wisley, 1 August. ⅓ life size

Onychium japonicum at Washfield Nurseries, Hawkhurst, Kent

Adiantum pedatum L. (*Adiantaceae*)   Native
of North America, from Quebec to Alaska,
south to California and Georgia, and of E Asia,
from Japan and Kamchatka to Sikkim and N
India, growing in cool deciduous or coniferous
forest, or on rocks by waterfalls. Fronds
deciduous, on stalks 15–50cm high, usually
about 25cm. Leaflets (pinnules) 2–4cm wide.
Hardy and easily grown in a cool, moist and
shady position. Lime-tolerant in that it grows
on tufa. Slow to establish from divisions of
mature plants but easy from young plants. The
rhizomes need to be covered by a layer of loose
leaf mould or decaying leaves. Var. *aleuticum*
Rupr. is found on the west coast of the USA,
Utah and in Quebec. Forma *imbricatum* has
overlapping pinnules. Var. *subpumilum* W. H.
Wagner is a compact variety from Vancouver.

Adiantum venustum D. Don   Native of the
Himalayas and W China, growing on mossy
banks and boulders, in light shade, at up to
3500m. Rhizome slender, spreading quite
widely but not so rapidly as to be troublesome.
Fronds usually deciduous, 20–30cm tall, on a
polished deep-brown stalk 10–15cm long. Blade
broadly triangular and much divided into many
triangular-obovate segments 6–10mm long.
Sterile segments finely toothed along the apical
margin, fertile ones with the sporangia under
infolded flaps on the margin. Very hardy and
quick to establish on peat banks or in rock
crevices in light shade or, if not too dry, under
trees. Readily propagated by division.

Athyrium filix-femina (L.) Roth.
(*Woodsiaceae*)   This species has one of the
widest distributions found among ferns,
occurring in Europe, Asia, North Africa, C
North America. It is a characteristic species of
deciduous woods on various, usually acidic
soils, but may also be found in drier and more
open habitats. Rhizome short; fronds
deciduous, generally 60–100cm tall, pale green,
bipinnate, with bluntly toothed pinnules. The
rachis may be green or reddish – the latter forms
are perhaps the more attractive. Innumerable
aberrant forms were brought into cultivation
and named in the 19th century and the species
remains remarkably prolific of crested, plumose
and other variants.

Athyrium nipponicum (Mett.) Hance.   Native
of woodland habitats in NE Asia where it occurs
in two colour forms. The commoner type has
green fronds, but in 'Pictum' they are a light
grey-green with a paler central band and
purplish-pink midrib. The latter is the more
popular garden plant and breeds largely true

Athyrium otophorum

Oreopteris limbosperma

Adiantum venustum at Wisley

from spores. Rhizomes shortly creeping and slender; fronds 30–50cm tall, loosely clustered, rather thick-textured but deciduous. Among plants raised from spores, individuals occur with somewhat crested fronds, but most gain little in attractiveness from this aberration.

Athyrium otophorum (Miq.) Koidz.   Native of Japan and China, growing in deciduous woodland. Rhizome short, erect; fronds 60–80cm tall, thick textured but deciduous, bipinnate with toothed pinnules. Plants in cultivation mostly have greyish-green fronds with wine-red midribs to the frond and the pinnae. Hardy to −10°C perhaps and requiring a moist, shaded site to develop to its full luxuriance, forming a very handsome and decorative fern. Propagation is easy from spores, sown fresh, or by division of established clumps in early spring or in autumn.

Hypolepsis millefolium Hook.
(*Dennstaedtiaceae*)   Native of New Zealand, generally growing in fairly open situations on hills to over 1000m. Rhizome slender, long, forming extensive colonies. Fronds deciduous, 20–50cm tall, triangular and very finely divided, arising singly from the rhizome. Hardy to −15°C and easily grown in light shade and a leafy, acid soil. Propagated by division, but small pieces may fail to establish.

Onychium japonicum (Thunb.) Kunze. Widespread in E Asia, from the Himalayas to China, Japan, Taiwan and south to Malaysia. Rhizome creeping. Fronds more or less evergreen, to 60cm tall, very finely divided, with the ultimate segments linear-lanceolate. Hardiness varies depending on origin but plants from higher altitudes in China and Korea appear to be quite hardy, forming colonies of lacy fronds. For acid soil with plenty of humus and a situation in partial shade. Alternatively, it makes a fine specimen in a cold greenhouse.

Oreopteris limbosperma (All.) Holub. syn. *Thelypteris limbosperma* (All.) H. P. Fuchs Native of much of Europe and North America, with an allied species in NE Asia, growing on wet stream-banks on acid soils, in both lowland and upland areas and a characteristic species of acid 'flushes' on moorland. Rhizome fairly short, usually decumbent. Fronds erect, 30–90cm tall, deciduous; when young, bearing conspicuous silvery scales. The under-surface is covered with minute yellowish glands which release a lemony scent when the frond is brushed. Easily cultivated in cool, moist, acid soil but not tolerant of drought or lime.

Adiantum pedatum in Virginia

Athyrium filix-femina wild in Perthshire

Polypodium australe

Osmunda regalis

Polypodium vulgare
'Bifidograndiceps'

Polypodium australe
'Cornubiense'

*Blechnum
penna-marina*

Polypodium vulgare
'Longicaudatum'

Specimens from Wisley, 5 August. ⅓ life size

Osmunda cinnamomea in New Hampshire

Osmunda regalis (young fronds) at Wisley

Woodwardia fimbriata

Blechnum magellanicum at Logan

Osmunda regalis in Connemara

Blechnum magellanicum (Desv.) Mett.
(*Blechnaceae*)   Native of S South America,
growing in light forest and in more open
situations up to *c*.500m. A robust evergreen fern
with a slowly creeping rhizome, forming
colonies of erect, very leathery pinnate fronds to
80cm tall; fertile fronds similar but with much
narrower pinnae. The bristle-like scales at the
base of the stalk differ from the ovate scales
found on other similar species with which it has
been confused. Hardy to −10°C. This species is
commonly cultivated as *B. tabulare*, which,
however, is a distinct and somewhat more
tender species.

Blechnum penna-marina (Poir.) Kuhn
Native of South America, north to S Brazil,
New Zealand and many subantarctic islands,
growing in woods, on rocky slopes and in scrub.
Rhizome creeping, with fronds at intervals, in
clusters, to 17cm. Pinnae up to 8.5mm long.
Fertile leaves usually longer than the sterile
ones, taller with narrower pinnules with rolled
margins. Hardy to −10°C, perhaps less.

Osmunda cinnamomea L. (*Osmundaceae*)
Native of North, Central and South America
and also in NE Asia (the latter sometimes
distinguished as var. *fokiensis* Copeland),
growing in a variety of habitats at low altitudes,
including moist woods, bogs and stream-banks.
Rhizome large, slowly creeping. Fronds
deciduous, 40–60cm or taller, of two sorts;

sterile fronds loosely erect, bipinnatifid, with a
conspicuous tuft of woolly reddish-brown scales
at the base of each pinna. Fertile fronds stiffly
erect, usually shorter than the sterile ones and
confined to the centre of the crown, bipinnate,
but with very contracted pinnules – normal
green pinnules are usually absent. Hardy and
easy to grow in damp woodland or by the
margins of pools or streams.

Osmunda regalis L.   Very widely distributed
in Europe, North and South America, Africa
and Asia, generally growing in swampy areas,
fens and other damp woodland. Rhizome erect
and becoming massive with age. Fronds erect,
deciduous, 60–150cm tall, bipinnate, with the
fertile pinnules confined to the contracted apex
of the fronds. One of the better ferns for
autumn colour, the fronds becoming a warm
russet-orange. Easily cultivated, preferably
from spores but, unlike most ferns, those of
Osmunda remain viable for only a few days, so
must be sown as soon as possible. A crested
form 'Cristata' is grown, as is 'Purpurascens',
with attractive 'stems' and young foliage.

Polypodium australe Fee (*Polypodiaceae*)
Native of the British Isles, W Europe, Madeira
and the Azores, growing in similar habitats to
P. vulgare. Fronds to 30cm, broadly ovate:
pinnae somewhat toothed, the lower ones
inflexed. Fertile fronds appear in late summer.
Easily cultivated and quite hardy, this species

has given rise to numerous cultivars (often
attributed to *P. vulgare*). These include some
very attractive foliose and plumose forms with
much expanded, pinnately lobed pinnae.
Examples include the Cambricum and
Pulcherrimum groups.

Polypodium vulgare L.   Native (as an
aggregate of similar species) to Europe, Asia,
North America and South Africa, growing in
various habitats, including rocks, walls and
trees as well as on the ground. Rhizome fairly
thick, creeping and branching usually on or
near the surface. Fronds evergreen, to 30cm
long. Outline oblong, with the pinnae similar in
length to the base of the frond. Hardy and easy
to grow in most light soils but the rhizome
should be scarcely buried. Crested cultivars and
other types of variation occur.

Woodwardia fimbriata Rees syn. *W. radicans*
var. *americana* Hook. (*Blechnaceae*)   Native to
W North America, from W British Columbia to
California and east to Arizona and Nevada,
growing in moist, shady places and on stream-
banks at up to 2500m. Rhizome short and stout.
Fronds to 1.5m, more or less evergreen,
leathery in texture and fairly short-stalked.
Segments finely but sharply toothed. Plants
from the northern part of the range should be
hardy to −10°C. In western USA it is said to be
easily grown and handsome, being well suited to
a moist site in light shade.

Arachniodes aristata from Japan

Arachniodes standishii in a wood near Kyoto, Japan

Gymnocarpium dryopteris with *Endymion non-scriptus*

Dryopteris filix-mas 'Cristata'

Dryopteris affinis 'The King'

Dryopteris marginalis

Dryopteris erythrosora

Specimens from Wisley, 5 October. ⅓ life size

Arachniodes aristata (Forst.) Tindale (*Dryopteridaceae*)   Widely distributed from India and E Asia to Australia, the more hardy forms are probably those from S Japan and China, growing as isolated plants on the woodland floor, generally in areas with a fairly high rainfall. Rhizome long-creeping; fronds evergreen, 30–60cm tall, including the long stalk, somewhat leathery and rather satiny in texture on the upper side, bi- to tripinnate with oblong, whiskery-toothed pinnules. Depending greatly on provenance it may be quite hardy and is a very handsome fern. *Arachniodes pseudoaristata* (Tagawa) Ohwi and *A. simplicior* (Makino) Ohwi are closely allied. A cultivar of the latter, 'Variegata', has yellowish bands down the centre of each frond and its pinnae. It is perhaps not very hardy and is grown as a house plant.

Arachniodes standishii (Moore) Ohwi   Native almost throughout Japan and also in Korea, where it is often the dominant fern, forming extensive colonies in woodland in low mountains. Rhizome short; fronds 60–90cm tall, rather thin-textured but evergreen, bi- to tri-pinnate with coarsely toothed pinnules. Plants originating in N Honshu and Hokkaido will be very hardy but those in cultivation are probably from further south and require a sheltered site.

Dryopteris affinis (Lowe) Fraser-Jenkins syn. *D. borreri* Newman (*Dryopteridaceae*)   Native of much of Europe, including the British Isles, growing in woods and on shady banks, usually

Dryopteris affinis in Scotland

Dryopteris wallichiana in Kashmir

Dryopteris shiroumensis at Kew

on acid soils and most luxuriantly in areas of high rainfall. Rhizome short and erect. Fronds to 120cm tall, semi-evergreen, the midrib and stalk densely clothed with golden-brown scales which are particularly conspicuous on the unfurling fronds in spring. Rather similar to *D. filix-mas*, but differing in the almost untoothed, square-tipped pinnules and more abundant scales. Vigorous, easily cultivated and much more handsome than *D. filix-mas*. The cultivar 'The King' (Cristata group) is symmetrically crested and is common in gardens. Unlike many fern cultivars, it breeds 'true' from spores.

Dryopteris erythrosora (Eaton) O. Kuntze Widely distributed in NE Asia, from China to the Philippines and Taiwan and very common in C & S Japan, growing in woods and on banks at low altitudes and frequently self-sowing in gardens there. Rhizome short; fronds to 70cm tall, leathery and evergreen. The young fronds are often attractively tinged pink or bronze and the developing sori are frequently bright red. Hardy and easily grown but requiring constant moisture in the growing season. Best in light shade as the mature fronds may become a sickly yellow in a more exposed situation.

Dryopteris filix-mas (L.) Schott Native in many parts of the temperate northern hemisphere, including the British Isles, where it is one of the most common ferns. Found in a wide range of habitats but most luxuriant in damp woodland at low altitudes. Rhizome short and stout; fronds to 120cm or more, deciduous,

bipinnatifid; pinnules oblong, crenate or serrate, rounded at the tip but not narrowed at the base. The species is hardy and vigorous and will grow almost anywhere. In its wild form it is much less attractive than *D. affinis*, but it has given rise to many cultivars, some of which are highly garden-worthy. There are many types of variation, including the 'Cristata', 'Linearis', 'Plumosa' and 'Foliosa' groups.

Dryopteris marginalis (L.) A. Gray Native of North America, from Georgia to Canada westwards to the Rockies, growing in damp woods and swamps. Rhizome short; fronds to 60cm or more, bipinnate, deciduous. Pinnules deeply crenate-toothed; sori conspicuously near the margins as the specific epithet suggests. This, together with the rather erect bluish fronds, makes it quite distinctive. In the wild, this species has hybridized with numerous others and it is possible that some of the plants in cultivation are also hybrids.

Dryopteris shiroumensis Kurata & Nakamura Native of Japan, in C Hokkaido, growing in woods. Plants forming compact clumps. Rhizome stout. Fronds to 60cm or more. The pinnules overlap and are deeply divided to the midrib, and symmetrically curved. For shade and shelter. Hardy to −10°C, perhaps less.

Dryopteris wallichiana (Spreng.) Hylander Native of much of Asia, parts of Africa and of South America, although numerous names have

been applied to the different provenances. The usual habitat is woodland, generally at fairly low altitudes, but it also occurs on open stream-banks at higher altitudes, up to about 4000m in the Himalayas. Resembles *D. affinis* in size, vigour and frond shape, but the abundant scales are almost black, occasionally deep reddish brown. They are particularly conspicuous on the unfurling fronds in spring. The fronds are evergreen, usually collapsing at the base of the stalk during the winter but not turning brown. Hardy and easily cultivated in cool shade and leafy acid or neutral soil. Propagated by spores; even established plants are slow to produce offsets allowing division.

Gymnocarpium dryopteris (L.) Newman (*Dryopteridaceae*) **Oak Fern** Widespread in the temperate regions of North America, Europe and Asia, usually forming carpets in deciduous or mixed forests in cool areas and generally on acid soils. Rhizome very slender, black, far-creeping. Fronds deciduous, pale green and thin-textured, on stalks up to 30cm tall but usually less. Blade 10–25cm long, broadly triangular and held almost horizontally. Hardy and easily grown where the natural habitat can be emulated – it requires shade and a cool root-run in soil containing plenty of acid leaf mould in which the rhizomes should be just covered. The cultivar 'Plumosum' has broader pinnules, giving the fronds a more solid appearance.

Some Gardens to visit, with good collections of Herbaceous Perennials

England

The times and dates of opening may change, especially of those gardens which are privately owned. An asterisk denotes a garden open only occasionally. Many are open under The National Gardens Scheme, which publishes yearly a 'yellow book' of Gardens of England and Wales Open, giving opening dates, times, and directions for finding each garden. Details of other gardens open may be found in *The Good Gardens Guide*, edited by Graham Rose and Peter King and published yearly by Barrie & Jenkins, London.

(Those gardens marked with an asterisk are open on only a few days in the summer.)

Arley Hall, near Knutsford, Cheshire
Beth Chatto Gardens, Elmstead Market, Suffolk
Bodnant Garden, near Colwyn Bay, North Wales (The National Trust)
Bressingham Gardens, Diss, Norfolk
Cambridge University Botanic Garden, Brookside
Chelsea Physic Garden, Royal Hospital Road, London SW3
Cobblers, Crowborough, Sussex*
Coldham, Little Chart, Ashford, Kent*
Garden House, Buckland Monachorum, Devon
Great Dixter, Northiam, Sussex
Harewood House Gardens, near Leeds, West Yorkshire
Hatfield House, Hertfordshire
Hidcote Manor, Chipping Camden, Gloucestershire (The National Trust)
The High Beeches, Handcross, Sussex
Highdown, Goring-by-Sea, near Worthing, Sussex
Jenkyn Place, Bentley, Hampshire
Kew, The Royal Botanic Gardens, near Richmond, Surrey
Knightshayes Court, Tiverton, Devon (The National Trust)
Leeds Castle, near Maidstone, Kent
Liverpool University Botanic Garden, Ness, Neston, South Wirral
Longstock Park Gardens, near Stockbridge, Hampshire*
Marwood Hill, Barnstaple, Devon
Myddelton House, Bulls Cross, Enfield, Middlesex
Old Rectory Cottage, Tidmarsh, Berkshire*
The Old Vicarage, Edington, Wiltshire*
Oxford University Botanic Garden, Oxford
Powis Castle, near Welshpool, Powys, Mid-Wales (The National Trust)
Sandling Park, near Hythe, Kent*
Savill Gardens, Windsor Great Park, Berkshire
Sissinghurst Castle, Cranbrook, Kent (The National Trust)
Stancombe Park, Dursley, Gloucestershire*
Wakehurst Place, Haywards Heath, Sussex (The National Trust)
Wallington, Morpeth, Northumberland (The National Trust)
Washfield Nurseries, Hawkhurst, Kent
Wisley, The Royal Horticultural Society's Garden

Scotland

Aberdeen, Cruickshank Botanic Garden of the University, St Machar Drive, Old Aberdeen
Branklyn Garden, Perth (The National Trust for Scotland)
Cluny, Aberfeldy, Perthshire
Crathes Castle, Aberdeenshire (The National Trust for Scotland)
Edinburgh, The Royal Botanic Garden, Inverleith Row
Inverewe, Poolewe, Wester Ross (The National Trust for Scotland)
Jack Drake, Inshriach Alpine Plant Nursery, Aviemore, Inverness-shire
Kildrummy Castle Garden, Strathdon, Aberdeenshire
Logan Botanic Garden, Port Logan, Dumfries and Galloway

Pitmedden Garden, Ellon, Aberdeenshire (The National Trust for Scotland)

Ireland

Beech Park, Clonsilla, Co. Dublin
Glenveagh Castle, Letterkenny, Co. Donegal
Mount Stewart, Newtownards, Co. Down (The National Trust)
Mount Usher, Ashford, Co. Wicklow
National Botanic Gardens, Glasnevin, Dublin

North America

Alabama
Birmingham Botanical Garden, 2612 Lane Park Rd., Birmingham, AL 35223, 205-879-1227

Arizona
Filoli Center, Canada Rd., Woodside, CA 94062, 415-364-2880

California
Huntington Botanical Gardens, 1151 Oxford Road, San Marino, CA 91108, 818-405-2100
Rancho Santa Ana Botanic Garden, 1500 North College Ave., Claremont, CA 91711, 714-625-8767
Regional Parks Botanic Garden, Tilden Regional Park, Berkeley, CA 94708, 415-841-8732
Santa Barbara Botanic Garden, 1212 Mission Canyon Rd., Santa Barbara, CA 93105, 805-682-4726
Strybing Arboretum & Botanical Gardens, Ninth Avenue at Lincoln Way, San Francisco, CA 94122, 415-559-3622
University of California Botanical Garden, Centennial Dr., Berkeley, CA 94720, 415-652-3343
University of California Botanic Gardens – Riverside, Dept. of Botany & Plant Science, Riverside, CA 92521, 718-787-4650
Western Hills Nursery, 16250 Coleman Valley Rd., Occidental, CA 95465, 707-874-3731

Colorado
Denver Botanic Gardens, 909 York Street, Denver, CO 80206, 303-575-2547

Connecticut
Hillside Gardens, Litchfield Rd., P.O. Box 614, Norfolk, CT 06058, 203-542-5345
White Flower Farm, Litchfield, CT 06759-0059, 203-496-9600

Delaware
Mt. Cuba Center, P.O. Box 3570, Greenville, DE 19807

District of Columbia
United States National Arboretum, Agricultural Research Service, U.S. Dept. of Agriculture, 3501 New York Ave., NE Washington, D.C. 20002, 202-472-9279

Idaho
University of Idaho, Plant Science Dept., Moscow, ID 83843

Illinois
Chicago Botanic Garden, Lake Cook Rd., Glencoe, IL 60022, 312-835-5440
Glen Oak Botanical Garden, Peoria Park District, 2218 N. Prospect Rd., Peoria, IL 61603, 309-685-4321

Maine
The Abby Aldrich Rockefeller Garden, Seal Harbor, ME. Open one day a week for a very short season only by reservation, if you know how to obtain the unlisted number.

Maryland
William Paca House & Garden, 1 Martin St., Annapolis, MD 21401, 301-269-0601/267-6656

Massachusetts
Berkshire Garden Center, Box 826, Rtes 102 & 183, Stockbridge, MA 10262, 413-298-3926
The Botanic Garden of Smith College, Lyman Plant House, Northampton, MA 01063, 413-584-2700, ext. 2748
Garden in the Woods of the New England Wild Flower Society, Hemenway Rd., Framingham, MA 01701, 617-888-3300

Michigan
Cranbrook House & Gardens, 380 Lone Pine Rd., P.O. Box 801, Bloomfield Hills, MI 48103, 313-645-3149
Matthaei Botanical Garden, University of Michigan, 1800 North Dixboro Rd., Ann Arbor, MI 48105, 313-764-1168

Missouri
Gilberg Perennial Farms, 2906 Ossenfort Rd., Glencoe, MO 63038
Missouri Botanical Garden, 4344 Shaw Rd., St. Louis, MO 63110, Mailing Address: P.O. Box 299, St. Louis, MO 63166, 314-577-5100
Woodland and Floral Garden, University of Missouri, Columbia, MO 62511

New York
Brooklyn Botanic Garden, 1000 Washington Ave., Brooklyn, NY 11225, 718-622-4433
The Cloisters, The Metropolitan Museum of Art, Fort Tryon Park, New York, NY 10040, 212-923-37700
Mary Flagler Cary Arboretum Institute of Ecosystem Studies, Box AB, Millbrook, NY 12545, 914-677-5358
The Conservatory Garden, Central Park, 105th St. & Fifth Ave., New York, NY 1003, 212-360-8236
Minn's Gardens, Dept. of Floriculture & Ornamental Hort., Cornell University, Ithaca, NY 14850
The New York Botanical Garden, Bronx, NY 10458, 212-220-8700
Old Westbury Gardens, 71 Old Westbury Rd., Old Westbury, NY 11568
Pepsico World Headquarters, Anderson Hill Rd., Purchase, NY 10577
Wave Hill, 675 W. 252 nd St., Bronx, NY 10471, 212-549-2055

North Carolina
The North Carolina Botanical Garden & Coker Arb., UNC-CH Totten Center, 457-A Laurel Hill Rd., Chapel Hill, NC 27514, 919-967-2246
North Carolina State University Arboretum, Raleigh, NC 27695

Ohio
Gardenview Horticultural Park, 16711 Pearl Rd., Strongsville, OH 44136, 216-238-6653
Sunnybrook Farms & Homestead Garden, 9448 Mayfield Rd., Chesterland, OH 44026, 216-729-7232

Pennsylvania
Bowman's Hill Wild Flower Preserve, Washington Crossing Historic Park, Washington Crossing, PA 18977, 215-862-2924
Longwood Gardens, P.O. Box 501, Kennett Square, PA 19348, 215-388-6741

Tennessee
Memphis Botanic Garden, 750 Cherry Rd., Memphis, TN 38117, 901-685-1566

Virginia
Andre Viette Farm & Nursery, Rte 1, Box 16 (Route 608), Fisherville, VA 22939, 703-943-2315

Wisconsin
Boerner Botanical Gardens in Whitnall Park, 5879 South 92nd St., Hales Corners, WI 53130, 414-425-1130/529-1870

How to obtain Herbaceous Plants

The Hardy Plant Society, which aims to promote the growing of hardy herbaceous plants, publishes annually *The Plantfinder*, which gives a list of the plants available in cultivation in the British Isles, and the nurseries by which they are offered. From this it is easy to find which nurseries specialize in particular genera. Many nurseries, however, have a few plants which do not appear in *The Plantfinder*, so are worth asking for, and some of the plants shown in this book, which are hard to find, may be available from some of the following which are known personally to the authors:

David Austin, Bowling Green Lane, Albrighton, Wolverhampton, WV7 3HB
Axletree Nursery, Starvecrow Lane, Peasmarsh, Rye, East Sussex TN31 6XL
The Botanic Nursery, Rookery Nurseries, Atworth, Melksham, Wilts SN12 8NU
Broadleigh Gardens, Bishops Hull, Taunton, Somerset TA4 1AE
Bullwood Nursery, 54 Woodlands Road, Hockley, Essex
Church Hill Cottage Gardens, Charing Heath, Ashford, Kent TN27 0BU
Jack Drake, Inshriach Alpine Nursery, Aviemore, Inverness, PH22 1QS
Edrom Nurseries, Coldingham, Eyemouth, Berwickshire TD14 5TZ
Green Farm Plants, Bentley, Nr Farnham, Surrey GU10 5JX
Hopleys Plants Ltd., High Street, Much Hadham, Herts SG10 6BU
Tim Ingram, Copton Ash, 105 Ashford Road, Faversham, Kent ME13 8XW
Longstock Park Nursery, Stockbridge,Hants SO20 6EH
Monksilver Nursery, Oakington Road, Cottenham, Cambridge CB4 4TW
The Old Manor Nursery, Twining,Glos GL20 6DB
Perry Hill Nurseries, Hartfield, East Sussex TN7 4JP
Spinners, Boldre, Lymington, Hants SO41 5QE
Unusual Plants, Beth Chatto Gardens, Elmstead Market, Colchester, Essex
Washfield Nursery, Horn's Road, Hawkhurst, Kent TN18 4QU

Australia
New South Wales, Overland Nursery, 6 Arrunga Road, Arcadia
New South Wales, Viburnum Gardens, 8 Sunnyridge Road, Arcadia
Queensland, Ferris Nursery, Old Gympio Road, Mooloolay
South Australia, Lassocks Garden Centre, 334 Henley Beach Road, Lockleys
South Australia, Love In A Mist Nursery, 15 Seaview Road, McLaren Vale
South Australia, Peter Engel's Garden Centre, 1700 Main North Road, Salisbury Plains
Victoria, Scotsburn Nurseries, 300 Perry Road, Keysborough
Victoria, Smith & Gordon Wholesale Nursery, 9 Glentilt Road, Glen Iris

North America
Andre Viette Farm and Nursery, Route 1, Box 16, Fisherville, VA 22939, 703-943-2315
Burpee Ornamental Gardens, 300 Park Ave., Warminster, PA 18991, 215-647-4915
Busse Gardens, Route 2, Box 238, Cokato, MN 55321, 612-286-2654
Canyon Creek Nurseries, 3527 Dry Creek Road, Oroville, CA 95965, 916-533-2166
Carroll Gardens, P.O. Box 310, Westminster, MD 21157, 800-638-6334
The Crownsville Nursery, 1241 Generals Highway, Crownsville, MD 21032, 310-923-2212

Clifford's Perennial and Vine, Route 2, Box 320, East Roy, WI 53120, 414-642-7156

Garden Place, 6780 Heisley Road, P.O. Box 83, Mentor, OH 44060, 216-255-3705

Gilbert H. Wild and Son, 1112 Joplin Street, Sarcoxie, MO 64862-0338, 417-548-3514

Gilson Gardens, Box 227, Perry, OH 44081

Hillside Gardens, Litchfield Road, P.O. Box 614, Norfolk, CT 06058

Holbrook Farm & Nursery, Rte 2, Box 223B, Fletcher, NC 28732, 704-891-7790

John Scheepers, Inc., 63 Wall Street, New York, NY 10005, 212-422-117

Judy's Perennials, 436 Buena Creek Rd., San Marcos 92069

Klehm Nursery, 197 Penny Road, South Barrington, IL 60010, 312-437-2880

Kurt Bluemei, 2740 Greene Lane, Baldwin, MD 21013, 301-577-7229

Lamb Nurseries, E. 101 Sharp Ave., Spokane, WA 99202, 509-328-7956

Lilypons Water Gardens, 6800 Lilypons Road, P.O. Box 10, Lilypons, MD 21717–0010, 310-874-5133

McClure and Zimmerman, 1422 W. Thorndale, Chicago, IL 60660, 312-989-0557

Mileager's Gardens, 4838 Douglas Avenue, Racine, WI 53402-2498, 414-639-2040

Montrose Nursery, Box 957, Hillsborough, NC 27278, 919-732-7787

Native Gardens, Route 1, Box 494, Greenback, TN 37742, 615-856-3350

Robin Parer Geraniaceae, 122 Hillcrest Ave., Kentfield, CA 94964

Russell Graham, 4040 Eagle Crest Road, N. W. Salem, OR 97304, 503-362-1135

Siskiyou Rare Plant Nursery, 2825 Cummings Road, Medford, OR 97501, 503-772-6846

Sunny Border Nurseries Inc., 1709 Kensington Road, Kensington, CT 06037, 203-828-0321. (Wholesale only.)

Van Ness Water Gardens, 2460 North Euclid Upland, CA 91786, 714-982-2425

Walters Gardens, P.O. Box 137, Zeeland, MI 49464, 616-772-4697

Wayside Gardens, Garden Lane, Hodges, SC 29653, 800-845-1124

We-Du Nurseries, Route 5, Box 724, Marion, NC 28752, 704-738-8300

Western Hills Nursery, 16250 Coleman Valley Road, Occidental, CA 95465, 707-874-3731

White Flower Farm, Route 63, Litchfield, CT 06759, 203-567-0801

Woodlanders Inc., 1128 Collection Ave., Aiken, SC 29801, 803-648-7522 (Does not ship.)

Note

Many nurseries require payment for their catalogs. Most carry a wide range of perennials; some have specialities.

A similar book to *The Plantfinder* is published in Germany, called *Der Pflanzeneinkaufsführer*, by Anne and Walter Erhardt. It lists species, not cultivars, and gives suppliers in Germany and the Netherlands.

In North America, a similar book to *The Plantfinder* is published by the Andersen Horticultural Library, Minnesota, entitled *Andersen Horticultural Library's Source List of Plants and Seeds* published August 1989. It is available from Andersen Horticultural Library, Minnesota Landscape Arboretum, 3675 Arboretum Drive, Box 39, Chanhassen, MN 55317, at $29.95.
A similar guide is also published in Canada.

The NCCPG, the National Council for the Conservation of Plants and Gardens, exists to preserve plants which are rare in cultivation, and to protect valuable gardens. One of its achievements has been to draw attention to these rare plants by publishing their names on 'Pink Sheets', and to set up a scheme of National Collections of useful genera of garden plants, both species and cultivars. Collections of the following genera of herbaceous plants have been formed.

The addresses of National Collection Holders and further information may be obtained from the NCCPG, c/o The Royal Horticultural Society's Garden, Wisley, Woking, Surrey GU23 6QB.

Acanthus, Achilles, Aconitum, Agapanthus, Ajuga, Alchemilla, Anemone, Anthericum, Aquilegia, Arabis, Artemisia, Asphodelus, Aster, Astilbe, Astrantia, Athyrium, Bellis, Bergenia, Calamintha, Caltha, Campanula, Cimicifuga, Clematis, Convallaria, Cortaderia, Crocosmia, Delphinium, Dianella, Dianthus, Dicentra, Digitalis, Doronicum, Dryopteris, Echinops, Epimedium, Erigeron, Erodium, Eryngium, Erysimum, Euphorbia, Ferns, Gentiana, Geranium, Geum, Helenium, Helianthemum, Helianthus, Helichrysum, Heliopsis, Helleborus, Hemerocallis, Hesperis, Heuchera, Hosta, Iris, Kniphofia, Lamium, Leucanthemum, Libertia, Ligularia, Linum, Liriope, Lobelia, Lupinus, Lychnis, Meconopsis, Mertensia, Monarda, Nepeta, Nymphaea, Oenothera, Omphalodes, Ophiopogon, Origanum, Ourisia, Paeonia, Papaver, Paradisea, Penstemon, Phlox, Phormium, Platycodon, Polygonatum, Polygonum, Polypodium, Polystichum, Potentilla, Primula, Pulmonaria, Pyrethrum, Ranunculus, Rheum, Rodgersia, Ruscus, Salvia, Sarracenia, Saxifraga, Scabiosa, Schizostylis, Sedum, Senecio, Sidalcea, Sisyrinchium, Symphytum, Thalictrum, Tricyrtis, Trillium, Trollius, Verbascum, Veratrum, Verbena, Veronica, Vinca, Viola, Watsonia, Yucca.

Bibliography

General

Beckett, Kenneth A., *Growing Hardy Perennials* Croom Helm and Timber Press 1981.

Clausen, R. R. and Ekstrom, N. H., *Perennials for American Gardens* Random House 1989.

McGourty, Frederick, *The Perennial Gardener* Houghton Mifflin, Boston 1989.

Thomas, Graham Stuart, *Perennial Garden Plants* 2nd ed. Dent 1982.

Trehane, Piers, *Index Hortensis volume 1: Perennials* (Obtainable by post from the publisher). Quarterjack Publishing, Wimborne, Dorset 1989.

Walters *et al.* eds., *European Garden Flora* Cambridge 1984.

Royal Horticultural Society Dictionary of Gardening, 2nd ed. revised, Oxford University Press 1977.

'Curtis's Botanical Magazine'; since 1974 'The Kew Magazine', London

'Journal of the Royal Horticultural Society', since June 1975 'The Garden', R.H.S. London

'The Plantsman', 1979 onwards, Royal Horticultural Society, London

BIBLIOGRAPHY

Regional Floras

Europe

Coste, H., *Flore de La France* Paris 1901.

Heywood *et al.*, eds., *Flora Europaea* Cambridge University Press 1964–1980.

Komarov, V. L. *et al.*, eds., *Flora of the USSR* Moscow and Leningrad, 1933–1964 (translated by the Israeli Program for Scientific Translations).

Polunin, Oleg, *Flowers of Greece and the Balkans* Oxford University Press 1980.

Polunin, Oleg, *Flowers of Southwest Europe* Oxford University Press 1973.

Polunin, Oleg and Walters, Martin, *A Guide to the Vegetation of Britain and Europe* Oxford University Press 1985.

Strid, Arne, *Mountain Flora of Greece* vol.1, Cambridge University Press 1986.

Thompson, H. S., *Subalpine Plants* G. Routledge 1912.

Vvedensky A. I., ed. *Conspectus Florae Asiae Mediae* Tashkent 1971 onwards.

Africa

Bond, Pauline and Goldblatt, Peter, *Plants of the Cape Flora. A Descriptive Catalogue* Journal of South African Botany, supplementary volume no. 13 Cape Town 1984.

Hilliard, O. M. and Burtt, B. L., *The Botany of the southern Natal Drakensberg* National Botanic Gardens, Kirstenbosch Cape Town 1987.

Asia

Davis, P. H. *et al.*, *Flora of Turkey* Edinburgh University Press 1965–1987.

Grierson, A. J. C. and Long, D. G., *Flora of Bhutan* Edinburgh University Press 1983 onwards.

Ohwi, J., *Flora of Japan* in English, Smithsonian, Washington 1965.

Polunin, Oleg and Stainton, Adam, *Flowers of the Himalaya* Oxford University Press 1984.

Rechinger, K. H., *Flora Iranica* Graz 1963 onwards.

Wilson, E. H., *A Naturalist in Western China* Methuen 1913.

Northern America

Britton, N. L. and Brown, A., *An Illustrated Flora of the Northern United States and Canada* New York 1913.

Fernald, M. L., *Gray's Manual of Botany*, 8th ed. 1950.

Kearney T. H. and Peebles R. H. *et al.*, *Arizona Flora* University of California Press 1951.

Munz, P. A. and Keck, D. D., *A Californian Flora* University of California Press 1968.

Niering, A., *The Audubon Society Field Guide to North American Wildflowers, eastern region* Knopf, New York 1979.

Spellenberg, R., *The Audubon Society Field Guide to Northern American Wildflowers, western region* Knopf, New York 1979.

South America

Moore, David M., *Flora of Tierra del Fuego* Nelson and Missouri Botanical Garden, 1983.

New Zealand

Allan, H. H., *Flora of New Zealand*, volume I Govrt. Printer Wellington 1961, 1982.

Moore, L. B. & Edgar, E., *Flora of New Zealand*, volume II Wellington 1970.

Salmon, J. T., *New Zealand Plants and Flowers in Colour* Reed 1963

Plant Monographs

Campanulas Lewis, Peter and Lynch, Margaret, Christopher Helm, 1989.

Diascia, A Revision of Series Racemosae Hilliard, O. M. and Burtt, B. L., Jl. S. Afr. Bot. 5(3):269–340(1984)

Gentians Wilkie, David, revised edition Country Life 1950.

Geraniums, Hardy Yeo, Peter, Croom Helm and Timber Press 1985.

Geranium, A Revision of Geranium in Africa south of the Limpopo Hilliard, O. M. and Burtt, B. L. Notes from the Royal Botanic Garden, Edinburgh vol. XLII no. 2 1985.

Hellebores Mathew, Brian, Alpine Garden Society 1989.

Iris, The Mathew, Brian, Batsford 1981.

Iris, A taxonomic review of Iris L. series Unguiculares, Davis Aaron P. and Jury S. L., Bot. Journ. Linn. Soc. (1990), 103:218–300.

Kniphofia, The South African Species of Codd, L. E. *Bothalia* vol. 9, parts 3 & 4 1968.

Meconopsis, The genus Taylor, George, New Flora and Silva 1934.

Meconopsis Cobb, James S. L., Christopher Helm 1989.

Paeonia, A Study of the Genus Stern, F. C., The Royal Horticultural Society 1946.

Peonies of Greece Stearn, William T. and Davis, Peter H. The Goulandris Natural History Museum 1984.

Phlox, The genus Wherry, Edgar T., Morris Arboretum Monographs, 111 Philadelphia 1955.

Primula, the Genus Wright Smith, W., Forrest, G. and Fletcher H. R. (reprints of several papers from Trans. Proc. Bot. Soc. Edinb. 1941–49) J. Cramer Vaduz 1977.

Saxifrages of Europe Webb, D. A. and Gornall, R. J. Christopher Helm, 1989.

Waterlilies Swindells, Philip; Croom Helm and Timber Press 1983.

Books and articles of general interest, including planting and design

Brown, Jane, *Lanning Roper and his Gardens* Weidenfeld and Nicholson 1987

Buchan, Ursula, *An Anthology of Garden Writing* Croom Helm 1986

Chatto, Beth, *The Dry Garden*

Fish, Margery, *We made a Garden* Collingridge and Transatlantic Arts London and New York 1956

Fish, Margery, *Cottage Garden plants* Collingridge and Transatlantic Arts London and New York 1961

Gorer, Richard, *The Development of Garden Flowers* Eyre and Spottiswood 1970

Hobhouse, Penelope, *Colour in your Garden* Collins 1985

Jekyll, Gertrude, *Colour Schemes for the Flower Garden* Country Life 1919

Page, Russell, *The Education of a Gardener* Collins 1962

Lloyd, Christopher, *Foliage Plants* revised edition Viking 1985

Robinson, William, *The Wild Garden* reprinted by The Scolar Press 1977, but see: Elliott, B., *Some Sceptical Thoughts about William Robinson*, The Garden vol. 110 part 5 214–217(1985)!

Thomas, Graham, *The Art of Planting* Dent 1984

Thomas, Graham, *Plants for Ground Cover* revised ed. Dent 1977

Verey, Rosemary, *Good Planting* Frances Lincoln 1990

Glossary

* indicates a cross-reference

Acuminate gradually tapering to an elongated point

Acute sharply pointed, with an angle less than 90°

Amplexicaul with the base of the leaf encircling the stem

Anther the part of the *stamen which contains the pollen

Anthesis the time of opening of the flowers

Axil the angle between the leaf stalk and the stem

Bract a modified leaf below a flower

Bracteole a small *bract

Bulbil a small bulb, sometimes produced by a plant instead of a seed

Calyx the outer parts of a flower, usually green

Canaliculate with the sides turned upwards, channelled

Capsule a dry fruit containing seeds

Carpel the part of the flower which produces the seeds

Ciliate with a fringe of hairs on the margin

Clavate shaped like a club, narrow at the base, swelling towards the apex

Clone the vegetatively propagated progeny of a single plant

Cordate heart-shaped, with rounded lobes at the base

Corolla the inner parts of the flower, comprising the petals, usually used when the petals are united into a tube

Crenate with shallow, rounded teeth

Cultivar a cultivated variety, denoted by a fancy name in inverted commas, e.g. 'Loddon Pink'

Decumbent trailing loosely onto the ground

Dentate with sharp, regular teeth

Diploid containing twice the basic number of chromosomes (the usual complement)

Exserted sticking out, usually of the *style or *stamens from the flower

Filament that part of the *stamen which supports the *anther

Flexuous wavy, usually of a stem

Forma a minor variant, less different from the basic species than a *variety. Abbreviated to **f.** or **ff.** if plural

Genus a grouping of *species, such as *Iris* or *Paeonia*

Glabrous without hairs or glands

Glandular with glands, which are usually stalked, like hairs with a sticky blob on the apex

Glaucous with a greyish bloom, especially on the leaves

Globose more or less spherical

Hastate with a broad but pointed apex, and two diverging lobes at the base

Hyaline transparent, often soft or papery

Hybrid the progeny of two different species

Incised with deep cuts in the margin

Inflorescence the flowers and flower stalks, especially when grouped

Laciniate deeply and irregularly toothed and divided into narrow lobes

Lanceolate shaped like a spearhead, widest below the middle, with a tapering point

Leaflets the parts of a compound leaf

Linear long and narrow, with parallel sides

Lyrate with a broad, but pointed apex and lobes becoming smaller towards the leaf base

Monocarpic usually dying after flowering and fruiting

Nectary the part of the flower which produces nectar

Oblanceolate shaped like a spearhead, but widest above the middle

Obtuse bluntly pointed, with an angle greater than 90°

Orbicular almost round

Ovate almost round, but with a pointed apex, broader than lanceolate

Palmate with lobes or leaflets, spreading like the fingers of a hand

Panicle a branched *raceme

Pedicel the stalk of a flower

Peduncle the stalk of an *inflorescence

Peltate shaped like a round shield, with the stalk in the centre

Petal generally the coloured part of the flower

Pinnae leaflets of a *pinnate leaf

Pinnate with leaflets on either side of a central axis

Pinnatifid with lobes on either side of a central axis

Pinnule a small *pinna

Puberulent with a fine but rather sparse covering of hairs

Pubescent with a fine coating of hairs, denser than *puberulent

Raceme an *inflorescence with the flowers on a central stem, oldest at the base

Rhizome an underground modified stem, often swollen and fleshy

Rootstock the part of the plant from which the roots and the stems arise

Rosette an encircling ring of leaves

Scarious dry and papery, usually also transparent

Sepal the outer, usually green parts of the flower vs. petal

Serrate sharply and finely toothed

Sessile without a stalk

Spathulate with a broad, rounded apex and tapering into a narrow stalk

Species group of individuals, having common characteristics, distinct from other groups; the basic unit of plant classification. Abbreviated to **sp.** or **spp.** if plural

Stamen the pollen-bearing part of the flower, usually made up of *anther and *filament

Staminode a sterile *stamen, often a flattened *filament

Stigma the sticky part of the flower which receives the pollen

Stolon a creeping and rooting, usually underground stem which produces new plants

Style that part of the flower which carries the *stigma

Subcordate weakly heart-shaped at the base

Suborbicular almost round, but usually slightly narrower

Subspecies a division of a species, with minor and not complete differences from other subspecies, usually distinct either ecologically or geographically. Abbreviated to **subsp.** or **subspp.** if plural

Tetraploid with four times the basic number of chromosomes

Triploid with three times the basic number of chromosomes: these plants are usually sterile, but robust growers and good garden plants

Truncate ending abruptly, as if cut off at right angles

Umbel an *inflorescence in which the branches arise from a single point, usually forming a flat or gently rounded top

Undulate wavy, usually of the edges of a leaf

Variety a group of plants within a *species, usually differing in one or two minor characters. Generally referring to natural variations, the term *cultivar is used for man-made or chosen varieties. Adjective varietal, abbreviated to **var.** or **vars.** if plural

Index

INDEX

INDEX

INDEX

INDEX

INDEX

INDEX

The Roger Phillips' series of indispensable reference guides.